D1798139

A SEEKER'S PATH TO ENLIGHTENMENT

AN OVERVIEW

DEVKUMAR JAYARAM

© Copyright (2020) by Devkumar
All rights reserved.

ISBN : 978-1-7353152-3-2
Color Hardcover

Illustration by
Niezaar Solomons, Diya Dev

Cover Design
Ira-Rebeca P

Editing and Layout
Tamlyn Hagerman, Diya Dev

New Layout
Self

This book is dedicated to everyone.

ACKNOWLEDGEMENT

I'm very grateful to the following Master's, Teacher's, Channeler's, and higher dimensional beings from Living Librarian who have been sharing wisdom and knowledge to humanity worldwide.

Adria Wind Horse Estribou, Audrey Colette, Billie Chainey, Brad Johnson (Adronis +), Camillo Loken, Daniel Scranton (Arcturians Council +), Dante Starshine (Pleiadian Council), Debbie Solaris, Dianne Robbins (Inner Earth Civilization +), Diya Dev, Dolores and Julia cannon, Esther and Jerry Hicks (Abraham) Mary and Gary O'Brien (DZAR) , Guy Steven Needler, Ishwar Puri, Ina Lukas (And the Alchemists), Jonathan C. Martin (The Pleiadians +), Jim Charles and Max Rempel (Hucolo.org,) Justin Furuta, Karen Neumann (Theos), Lee Carroll (Kroyn), Louise Kay (Aikon), Maria Chambers, Marina Jacobi, Meline Lafont (Saint Germain), Michael Newton, Natalie Glasson (Sacred School of Omna +), Natasha Bailey, Nicole Frolick, Nora Herold (Pleiadian Collective +), Patrick L. Hogan, Pooja Dhar Raina, Pravrajika Divyanandaprana Mataji, Pulkit Mathur, Rajan Thirumalai, Randall Monk, Rob Gauthier (Treb +), Sadhguru, Sara Landon (The Council), Seraphim, Shaun Swanson (Ishuwa +), Sheldan

Nidle (Sirian), Shivangi Bhatt, Shivani Yadav, Solara An-Ra (Councils of Light), Suzanne Lie (Arcturian +), Swami Sarvapriyananda, Swami Satchidananda, Taryn Crimi (Angelic Guides), Vera Ingeborg, and Wieteke Koolhof (Arjun).[1]

There are few souls who come into your life, even for a moment, and wake you up from ignorance, even though they don't even know that they have done such a great help by awakening your soul. The following are some of those who came in my life, and if I look back, I can see the gradual spiritual progress I have been making because of these people.

Gratitude

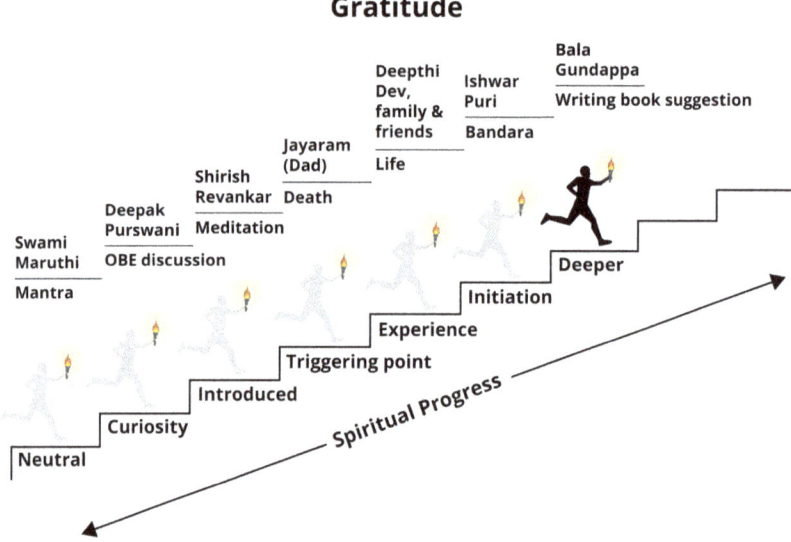

Also, I am thankful to the following members for supporting this book.

Gurukul kids and members classes

Lakshmi Yerra, Payal Kamat Vaidilingam, Rachna Patel, Anushka Kalkar, Diya Dev, Trayi Yerra, Ayan Ranadive, Yuvaan Iyer, Dhruv Dev, Rishi Gadkari, Saanika Kadam, Namita Parekh, Shreya Ranadive, Nirmala Tetala, Nagalakshmi Jayaram, Sunanda Kasette, Sanatan Kadakia and Niyati Kadakia.

Topic suggestions

Jyotsana Jayasimha

Life stories

Special thanks to Tamlyn Hagerman for sharing her life stories.

Images contributions

Vikas Kashyap, Arjun Kalkar, Kanak Yadav, Niezaar Solomons, Purvi Kashyap, Shahieda Williams, Faizel Wiliiams, Anwar Williams, and Pixabay.com.

Video Editor

John Miller

---

1. "+" indicates channeling additional higher dimensional beings.

CONTENTS

PART III
CLEANSING

INTRODUCTION

The name of the book "Path to Enlightenment" came to me intuitively one day while I was writing this book. The name changed the course of the direction of what I originally intended to write, but it turned out for the better. It allowed me to go much deeper into the understanding of who we are and the connection we have with the Ultimate Creator.

I've been on this spiritual path for more than 14 years now. My journey started after a wake-up call in 2007 that completely changed my life. Even though I was career-oriented, I started questioning everything about this reality. My quest to find answers led me to read hundreds of books on spirituality. I attended various spiritual sessions. I entered into an inner exploration to find insights within. During these periods, I made notes for myself for reference and never realized that one day it was going to be part of a book. So I'm just passing the information that I learned over a period that has completely changed my way of thinking and has allowed me to perceive reality in a new way.

I hope this book will help you in your quest to find answers as well one day.

The book covers some basic high-level understanding based on:

- Teachings provided by various masters, teachers, and light-workers.
- Messages from higher dimensional beings channeled through channelers.
- My intuitions and insights during meditation and life experience.

You may be wondering why you would need to read an enlightenment book? Some people would think that it is impractical to reach enlightenment for a commoner, especially for a person who never envisioned this path in their life.

To answer that, let me give you an analogy. In any business world, there are always long term and short term goals. All short term goals ultimately lead to the success of a long term goal. Similarly, this book is written to help you easily navigate life with experience and acquire wisdom. So, the foundation is built upon by adding practical tips and techniques to overcome some of the issues or problems that we all face in our daily lives (short term goal). These short term goals will eventually build a foundation for you to become more compassionate, blissful, and experience unconditional love leading you in the path to enlightenment (long term goal).

Currently, two critical changes are taking place on earth at this time. Firstly, human beings are in the process of a great shift, shifting from 3rd density to 4th density beings. Secondly, the earth is shifting to the next higher dimensional planet at the same time. It is similar to upgrading the software and the hardware of a computer. After a certain period, it becomes incompatible for any new version of software to be installed on existing hardware. Imagine the hardware is your body and the software is the higher frequency energy that is coming from this galaxy and the entire cosmos. (More details about this in the ascension chapter).

There are so many spiritual books available in the bookstores that you may be wondering what is so special about this book?

This book aims to provide you with some structures, guidelines, and tips based on my corporate world experience. I then elaborate on how I applied that skillset in my journey and the lessons I learned about spirituality while writing this book. So this book helps those who are new to spirituality or someone who needs some direction and structure in place to pursue their spiritual growth. The entire book is simple, easy to understand, straight to the point with numerous examples, analogies with illustrations, and some of my personal experiences/techniques.

Suppose, you've purchased a new self-assembling table for yourself. You start assembling it without even reading the instructions manual. Later, it turns out the table looks crooked and not perfectly aligned.

You start removing the entire table and reassemble it again after reading the manual. This time it turns out to be perfectly aligned.

Similarly, this book can be considered as a manual to provide you with wisdom and knowledge of both East and West culture that can bring clarity, helping you navigate the journey of life with ease and your path to enlightenment as a seeker.

There are few things to keep in mind while reading this book or any book.

Perspective is a point of view from one person or a group of people. There are many masters/teachers whose teachings may vary a little. Some of their teachings might be completely different. However, you need to understand the overall perspective of what everybody is saying/teaching. It will allow you to come up with a personal understanding rather than comparing the various teachings you have found/heard, word for word. Why? Because everybody has their own outlook and story to tell. Do not get attached to a particular perspective, including this book, and conclude that this is the only truth, ignoring all other perspectives. That mindset has created separation and fighting between people and even nations. Be open-minded and listen to all views presented to you. Each path you observe allows internal growth and the ability to make informed choices of your own, and those choices facilitate your growth.

Understanding: There is a saying, *"Change is the only constant, and the rest is always changing."* Similarly, even our grasp of the same information and knowledge keeps changing as we grow older and become wiser based on our life experience. The book is written based on an understanding at this particular moment. It can always change, so be open-minded.

Discernment: Use your discernment while reading this book; even the information in this book might appear distorted to a certain extent. One reader can see this as absolute truth, while another reader can see it as distorted information. So if the information doesn't resonate with you, move on to the next topic.

Incomprehensible topics: There are some topics in this book that are difficult to comprehend from a human mind perspective due to our limited conscious awareness. Such subjects are to be read with ease and not be overthinking, for example, topics regarding timelines, dimensions, etc.

We have been living in a box all these years, so it is time to wake up and start raising our consciousness, there is a whole new world out there with more knowledge and wisdom waiting to be discovered.

As we start raising our consciousness, the light within us will begin expanding to its full capacity.

xxi

The ultimate goal of this book is to **wake you up** from the amnesia state your Personal Self is in, reconnect with the Source, and grow to your full potential. I hope to provide you with information that can help you bring clarity while still living in an illusion and integrating your divine inner soul with your physical self, thus having a perfect balance of Body, Mind, and Soul.

MUST READ

God has been expressed as It / He / Her sometimes.

Some of the synonym used in this book

God: Source (most of the section), Creator, I AM, All THAT IS, Consciousness, Primordial, Absolute, Brahman, Universe (used in some section of part 3, new age terminology), Sachkhand and Totality of Consciousness.

Soul: Atman. True Self

Enlightenment: Moksha, Liberation, Self-Realization.

Earth: Gaia.

Definitions

Yogi: A yogi is a practitioner of yoga, including a sannyasin or practitioner of meditation.

Samsara: Saṃsara is the repeating cycle of birth, life, and death.

Vritti: Literally means "whirlpool", and is a technical term in yoga meant to indicate that the contents of mental awareness are disturbances in the medium of consciousness.

Maya: Maya is an illusion where things appear to be present but are not what they seem.

PART I

INQUIRY

The first steps that any person who wakes up will usually begin to start inquiring about everything, the reality, and who they are. They want to know more about the Source, or All That Is.

Analogy: Imagine that, there is polluted water in a jug. The water does not realize it is impure. This analogy relates to yourself. You are in a sleep-like state without realizing how much built-up emotions, limitations, and disconnection from the Source you really are in. But once you start waking up, you start inquiring about everything.

Similarly, the polluted water knows it's dirty and needs to clean itself up.

Polluted Water

Part one of this book deals with inquiry and answers basic questions. It aims to deal with the approach and process that you can take to reach a state of self-realization.

1

QUESTIONING

Have you ever been in deep thought with a burning question about your life? Or came across a situation and wondered why it is happening to you?

This was the case with me.

I was born and raised in India. Every once in a while, from about the age of fifteen years old, I found myself having a persistent thought. When I was doing something, like walking or being alone, the same persistent thought would occur over and over again.

Often, I found myself thinking, *"I am alive and see physically through my eyes everything, but once I die, what happens to me? Am I nothing? Is it just as simple as this, or does something happen to my entire being that I need to understand while I am still alive here on earth?"*

There was no one to answer my query at that time. There was no such thing as the internet, or Google, to find answers to my questions. Of course, there might have been a few books to read, and the possibility of finding the information from libraries, or ashrams. However, I never sought those avenues out.

Furthermore, India is greatly known for its spirituality. Scattered throughout the past and present, many great saints who were born there had become enlightened. Yet, I wasn't involved in or aware of spirituality at that time. At that age, I was more concerned with my daily subjects of mathematics, physics, and chemistry, than the concept of spirituality.

Fast forward to the future, I grew up, attained my degree, and moved to the United States. I started working and soon after got married. Being more occupied with my daily life, I didn't have much time to think about my deep burning questions within me until one fateful day.

In 2007, my parents decided to come to the United States from India to visit my family and I. That year was the first time I witnessed death right in front of my eyes. It was a personal experience for me; the passing of my own father. When he died of cardiac arrest, I was in complete shock and overwhelmed with fear. On the outside, I appeared calm, yet on the inside, I was going through a lot of turmoil.

Let me give you some perspective about my life before this incident happened. From childhood, my parents never took us, my siblings and I, to any of the funerals. As parents, they didn't want us exposed to any of these sad events.

Coming back to the incident, the death of my father raised various thoughts and questioning myself:

- How could he die so suddenly? My father was perfectly fine the day before when I saw him playing with my daughter.
- Was it my fault that I could not take him to the doctor? The previous day, my father had a little temperature. When I queried it, my father said, 'It is nothing, I have taken medication. I will be fine tomorrow. There is no need to go to the doctor.' I trusted my father's judgment about his body, so I ignored the signs. Would he have been okay if I had taken him to the doctor's office?

4

- Why did he drink and smoke so much? Surely those bad habits would affect his heart considerably?
- Why did he die at such a young age? My father was only 65 years old. There were older people than him who are healthier and still alive.
- The morning of his death, I was in a rush to get to the office. I remember catching a glimpse of him playing with my daughter on the way out the front door. I should have stayed a little longer, perhaps spent more time with him?
- Where is my father now? Could he be here? In front of us, yet in a form that we won't be able to see him?"

Internally I started blaming myself, determined to make it my fault because I neglected him. But after all these years of spiritual exploration, I now know for sure that this incident was meant to happen to facilitate a turning point in my life. The incident changed the direction of my life.

Otherwise, I wouldn't have been who I am today and wouldn't have been writing this book for you to read. They say, there is a written contract that we all agree to, that dictates, that we plan to support each other's souls' evolution before we are born in this world.

From that incident, everything started slowing down in a fast phase environment. What I thought, about the most important aspects of my life, such as my career, earnings, and survival became secondary.

The quest to find a deeper meaning of life started me on a new path. I started noticing my life from a different angle and was observing things happening around me that I never paid attention to before.

Some of my observations were:

Happiness

Most of us try to find happiness through external means rather than seeking it inside. Statements will look like this:

If I get a good position with a good salary, I will settle down and be happy.

If I buy a house, car, have gadgets, and wear the latest fashion clothes, then I will be the happiest person in the world

Although, once you get what you are looking for, you become happy only for a while. Then you begin looking again for something else to bring you happiness. The cycle continues forever without an end.

Comparison

You always try to compare yourself with others. It's in our nature. For example, if any of your friends bought something and spoked over the phone about it, and how good it was, you will often get influenced. You find yourself wanting the same thing because they have it. Your thoughts do not take into account whether it's a necessity or a simple wantedness.

Being Present

I've noticed that people most of the time will either dwell in their past or think about their future, but they never try to be in the present moment. I question myself, *why can't I be in the present moment?* I try to be in the present, but again my uncontrollable mind takes me into the past or makes me think about my future.

Complaining

People tend to complain about something or the other without realizing that their outside is a mere reflection of what's going on inside of them. For example, I noticed that most people complain about their jobs, their commute, how they hate what they are doing. Most people want to do something else which they love but don't take any initiatives to make those changes. Often they have a feeling within themselves that says *it's too risky to make changes*. They fear they may lose everything if it turns out to be a negative decision.

Influence

Everyone has been influenced in their life, including me, whether we realize it or not. From being peer pressured to hopping on the bandwagon. One time I heard from one of my friends that they got a security system because there was a break-in into someone's house in their neighborhood. My family overheard this, then forced me to buy a security system for our house, even though the event never happened to us but to someone else. Showing how much we get influenced by external events without knowing that everybody creates their reality, it was their reality and not ours.

The largest influence I've seen is in media, movies, and games. Have you noticed that most of the media always shows more negative things happening in the world than showing positive news? Also, most movies or games are about fighting, killing, creating fear, or showing more negativity in ways of dealing with issues or circumstances. You, as an audience watching movies, or playing games, will get influenced and carried away without realizing how it affects your vibration, as well as the mass consciousness on this planet.

You need to question yourself, what atmosphere do you want your kids to grow up in. How can they not be influenced by video games, shooting, and killing, if it is common in most games? Of course, there are positive impacts as well, but that percentage of the positive impact is small overall. If you look at the top sales figures for movies and games, most of them have a lot of violence and negative situations.

Beliefs

There were so many beliefs within me that I never questioned myself until that incident. Do any of those beliefs still hold any value or not? For example, I always believed that money would bring me stability and happiness in life. Yet now I realize it was not a belief that held any truth.

Similarly, there are so many disbeliefs that we hold. Have you ever tried to look into those beliefs? Have you ever checked whether it makes sense to have those beliefs?

Sickness

Whenever you get sick, you always tend to look for a cure externally by taking medication or going to the doctor. Yet, you have never questioned yourself, *what misalignment within me has caused the sickness?*

Attachment

You might get attached to many things like money, property, power, places, people, etc. They can be hard to let go of easily because you treat them as your property and start accumulating more of those things. The thought process behind it is that it's going to be with you forever, although you are fully aware that you die empty-handed. None of the treasures you accumulate in this physical life goes along with you when you finally depart this world. Then why do you still hold to it and value it so much?

Life

One day, I was watching a black and white documentary about life in New York City in 1870. People were walking by and riding horses as a tram passed by. They were showcasing their daily lives in the city. As I was watching the documentary, I realized that none of those people are alive today. I found myself wondering where they are now, and this situation will be the same for all of us who are here on this earth at this time as well. In another 100 years, we will become part of history, then what is our purpose of being here?

You may have a similar story, a thought, or a burning question that you have been searching the answer for.

Ultimately, all these thoughts lead to bigger questions. Namely:

- Who am I?
- Why am I here?

- What is my life purpose?
- Where is God? How did the entire creation happen?
- What am I supposed to do here?
- How can I be happy forever?
- Why am I not getting what I want?
- I want to be rich, so how do I manifest it?
- I don't like my job or my boss or my relationship. I need a change, but I don't know what to do.
- What career should I choose?
- I always dream, but I don't know the meaning of my dreams?
- Why am I attracted to people who always fight with me?
- How do I release my anger?
- What is Ascension?
- Is he the right person for me?
- How do I guide my children?
- Do I have a soul?
- Why I always feel Jealous of some one?
- How do I make a right decision?
- Is there the law of karma?
- Are there aliens or angels?
- Is there a universal law as such?
- What are the various path to enlightenment
- Where do I go after I die?
- Is there a heaven or hell?
- As human beings on this planet, where are we heading?
- I want to be spiritual, but I don't know where to begin.
- How do I raise my vibration?
- Why am I always sick?
- How do I heal myself?

These are some of the usual questions that everyone ponders about, including me, at the start of my journey. I will explain the process of growth and reflection, for some of those questions, in various sections within this book.

2

CLARITY

The chapter on clarity provides a foundation of simplicity for some of the questions that we ponder in life. However, the book does seek to expand on these questions by providing more profound details throughout the sections.

Some people relate this part of their journey to walking through the fog, and it slowly clears as their knowledge expands. You are aware of your surroundings but blinded by what is within you for some unknown reason. A person finds that they have this feeling of loss, or a desire to search for something they are unable to put in words.

Becoming inquisitive is one of the first characteristics of a new beginning. The questions we ask ourselves are often similar, even though we do not talk about it due to society's conditioning in some social circles. This does not mean it's wrong, only that they do not have tools to approach the topic, nor do they feel comfortable doing it. Everyone goes through their version of this path with similar questions, but they tend to find their answers at the end that leads them closer to the Source.

Purpose and direction are often great forces that you base your life on. Often a continuous set of goals cloud your judgment and lead you to never be happy with what you have. Remembering to be happy at that moment, with yourself as you are, is a necessary facet to growth and spiritual awareness.

People all have flaws within them, and you should be willing to accept them and love yourself. If you find yourself shaking your head, thinking, "No, I can't. I have done terrible things," or "I am not worth love." You should know that you are worth more than you could ever comprehend. You are part of a magnificent whole. The following chapters provide foundations for you to be more aware of your options and potential for growth.

If anything, why not make a promise to yourself to read this book until the end? You never know what little gems you could find. After all, what do you have to lose? Nothing. Yet, you have everything in the universe, the Source, and an untold amount of growth to gain.

Who Am I?

Throughout the millennia, human beings have been asking, "who am I?". You have a physical body, and you experience life through your five senses. In other words, you touch, see, taste, hear, and smell. So are you only this physical body?, Or are you something greater than what you think you are?

You are the consciousness functioning through the body-mind complex and having a human experience at the moment.

The body and mind are used as a vehicle to explore the physical dimensions. But over time, the awareness has started becoming so limited that you began considering this body and mind as your real identity. You forgot who you are and the connection you have with the Source energy.

In short, you are that expression of the Source and are here to express all that you are in human form.

What is God, and where is he?

When I was a child, I believed that God is an external being, that he or she resides on top of the hierarchy. I always thought you should pray and worship him by going to a temple, praying before an idol, or an image of God. In hindsight, after all these years of profound learning, it's clear that God is an endless and everlasting ocean of pure consciousness, knowledge, and bliss. God exists within you. You are that spark of a greater existence, and its presence is everywhere. There is no place where there isn't God. It is "All That is".

For example, imagine that you are the leaf of a beautiful tree. What if, you as that leaf, are in search of a tree. You are unable to see the roots of the tree or the top of the tree, but you can see the leaves next to you. Furthermore, the profound key to this analogy is that the tree is God or the Source. You, like a leaf, are part of this tree of life or consciousness.

There is no point searching outside of the tree when you are part of the tree, i.e. the Source. You could then conclude you are a part of God; there is always a connection. You might not see or remember your roots as yet.

You

God or
Source

What is the purpose of my life?

The purpose of life is to expand and find out who you are. This knowingness will ultimately lead you to self-realization and becoming one with the Source.

Why am I here?

You are here to have an experience of life and gain wisdom learned through experiences, which ultimately leads to spiritual growth.

Suppose a company is trying to release a new video game. The genre of this new game is an adventure. There are total of twelve levels, and each level has its own rules. The game always starts at twelve in this case and works down to level one, as the level goes deeper and deeper, the game becomes increasingly harder.

The purpose of this game is to explore each level if the players want to and come back to level twelve where they started. Although, at each level, it is necessary to accumulate points to win that level to get back to where they began.

Now imagine the programmers of the company who built this game wanted to try it out, so each of them becomes a character of the game. Some players started exploring four or five levels below, whereas some bold players started exploring down to level one, two, and three. Keep in mind that as they go deeper, they know it will be more difficult to play, and the risk of losing their memory of who they were if they crossed level three.

Initially, these bold players who are at level three and below, had their memory intact. They started exploring and accumulating points, but as time passed, they completely lost their memories. Forgot they were supposed to acquire points, win the level, and get back. Rather they fell into the trap, losing all their points, and are still playing the game at level three without a vision or a goal to achieve.

Only a few players were able to win and come out of that level. Now these players who succeeded in level three, join forces with players in the higher levels and are trying to help those players who are still stuck in level three and below. They try to remind them who they are and how to play the level.

Your life is exactly similar to this video game. The company is nothing but the Source or God. The programmers are human beings, (the players) who are currently playing the game of life. Initially, you came from the Source intending to have an experience based on the theme you choose in higher planes. As you stepped down your vibrations and frequency from higher subtle planes to lower denser planes (similar to level twelves to level three in the video game), you became more physical.

Subsequently, the connection to the Source slowly started fading as you engrossed yourself more physically and forgot your true nature of who you were. You started playing the game of duality, not realizing that the law of karma exists and governs all your deeds in this world, thus getting trapped into the cycle of birth and death. Life after life, you accumulated more karma without ever realizing how to exit from this cycle.

Now you are caught in this Maya Matrix. You find yourself doing the same action/mistake repeatedly due to the nature of forgetfulness encoded during your pre-birth. Therefore, you do not remember your previous lives and the mistakes you have made. Now is the time to re-correct your path in this life and hopefully come out of your reincarnation cycle.

There are beings from higher dimensions who have joined forces with souls on this earth. Their purpose is to awaken the rest of humanity who are still in a sleep-like state, but this is a free-will planet. It's up to the individual to make their own choice towards becoming an enlightened being, to see through all, Or carry on playing the same old 'game' in this current 3D reality.

What is happening on earth at this time? where are we heading?

We are in the midst of the ascension. Ascension is nothing but a shift in consciousness by becoming aware of your True Self, who you are, and integrating your human self with your Divine Self. You need to understand that everything evolves, nothing is still, including mother earth (Gaia), a conscious being.

Humanity and earth are shifting from 3rd density to 4th density (third dimension to the fifth dimension). Human beings are in a transition period, similar to the video game analogy that I mentioned earlier. The level three characters have to win and move to the next level four.

This graduation has happened many times in history. However, this ascension is the first time that the planet and inhabitants are shifting together simultaneously which has never happened in the entire cosmos and is happening here in our time period. That is why there are so many souls (around 7.5 billion), taking birth now.

In essence, everyone is aware at a deeper level, that they have come here to participate in this ascension graduation.

Earth is already moving in the direction of 5D and asking all the inhabitants to join along its journey. Although, now it's up to you whether you want to stay in 3D or move along with earth to 5D. It's your choice and decision to make based on the free will that we all have. Alternatively, those who still choose to play the same game of duality will have to inhabit a different 3D reality planet and not earth anymore.

Note: More details about ascension found in later chapters.

Why don't I remember anything about my past lives?

One of the reasons for forgetfulness is due to amnesia put in place after your birth. The amnesia is present so that you can start with a clean slate again. You can determine how you handle the same issues this time with a new perspective. Otherwise, imagine what it would have been like if you remember all the negative things that you did in your previous lives? You would then be focusing on the past and constantly blame yourself. There would be no opportunity for progress or growth.

Instead, you are now capable of moving on with your life lesson and continuing with a new perspective to resolve the unfinished issues you have set yourself.

In the next chapter, I will continue to explain enlightenment or self-realization.

3

ENLIGHTENMENT OR SELF REALIZATION

What is Enlightenment or Self Realization?

E nlightenment or Self Realization is the highest state of spiritual attainment with a clear understanding of who you are. It is also called Nirvana, Moksha, Liberation, Awakening, etc.

It is a journey where all fears, doubts, worries, anger, and questions cease to exist. You become aware of your True Self, which is infinite, eternal, pure knowledge, consciousness, and bliss God.

Self-realization is not trying to be someone else but becoming your True Self.

A Self Realized Person:

- Always connected to the Source.
- They have unconditional love, devotion, and compassion.

- Is in complete bliss and peace.
- Transcends desire, suffering, attachment, and ego.
- Is non-judgmental to all beings, life, and situations.
- Complete alignment with the body, mind, and soul.
- They continue to work as the person that they were before, with an awareness of oneness and see themselves in everyone and everything that exists.

Regarding realization, where do you stand as an individual human being?

In the path of realization, you can categorize each person in one of these states.

1. Sleep state
2. Awake state
3. Enlightenment state

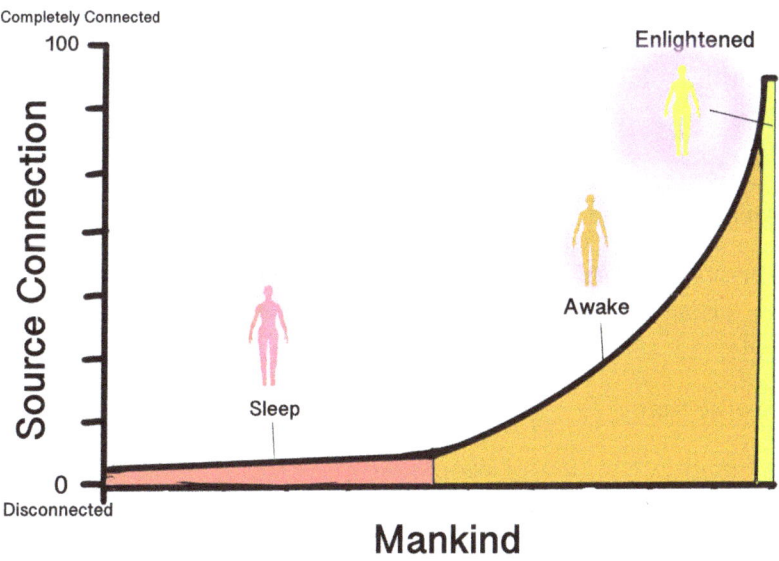

To give you an analogy, imagine the Source is an ocean, and you are a drop of water in that ocean.

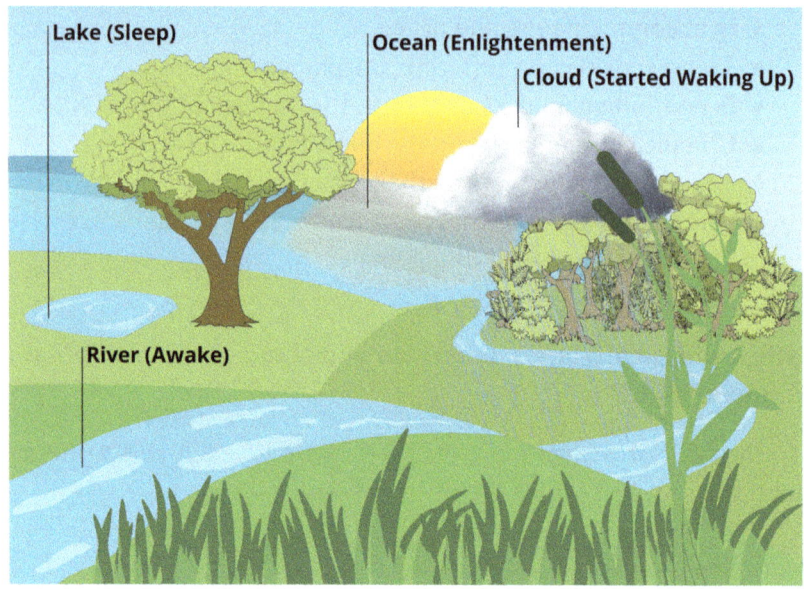

Sleep State

Most of humanity falls under this category with a range of complete disconnection (ignorance) from the Source, to a partial connection to the Source. In essence, living out of alignment with their authentic selves. They may or may not have clarity in their life, and are completely indulged in their physical activities.

Analogy / Lake

The drop of water in the lake is dormant and has no connection to the ocean. This is the situation for humans who are in a sleep state.

Awake State

A small percentage of people have started to wake up after realizing that some things are not working smoothly in their lives. Suddenly, they find out that they need to make drastic changes in their lives as they believe their present route is full of roadblocks and emotional turmoil.This may include trauma, stress, and negativity. With the need to improve themselves, their whole being begins to open up, and the truth slowly begins to unfold.

Analogy / River

Suppose the outside temperature is so high, the water present in the lake starts evaporating, and the overall water level drops. The water that evaporated travels through the clouds and becomes rain, eventually falling back to a river. This is the situation of a person who wakes up from sleep. After waking, the person starts making progress on the path of enlightenment similar to water flowing to the direction of the ocean (the Source).

Enlightened State

In this category, hardly a few people are in an enlightened state. In an enlightened state, a person is in total bliss and one with the Source. They have a complete understanding of this Maya/Matrix.

Analogy / Ocean

The person ultimately becomes enlightened similar to that drop of water in the river joining the ocean, they merge with the Source Energy and become one.

What should I do now?

The first thing you can do is *wake up* from the ignorance stage, knowing that you are that Absolute or Source. When you are reading this line, you have that capacity to *wake up* right now. It's just a matter of your willingness and surrendering to the Source. I'm sure one day you will reach that self-realization state if not this lifetime, maybe another or in thousands of other lifetimes. It is guaranteed that everyone will reach that level, and there is no exception whatsoever.

The question then lies, when do you want to start realizing your True Self? Of course, you have free will to make your own choices, and nobody is forcing you. This leads you to the conclusion that the only person who can enforce it, is you. So to explain in simple terms, you need to *go within yourself*, work it out, and clear all those suppressed negative emotions that are stacked up since childhood and from previous lifetimes. Start opening your heart and project unconditional love, compassion, joy, and peace to each other.

You can start initiating by seeking/spending some time and dedication to work on it. I've noticed that without dedication and commitment, it becomes just curiosity and things to know partially. When I discuss this with families and friends, they are keen to seek at the beginning, they start focusing, and then working on it. But as time passes by, their interest drops, and they are back to their daily routine.

I've also seen some people start seeking more information when there is trauma or an event that has happened in their life. They start looking for an answer, similar to what happened to me, but it does not have to be that way, that only through suffering, you find a need to wake up.

What is the difference between ascension and enlightenment?

They both ultimately lead to oneness with the Source, but there is a subtle difference. Imagine you are a kid who is studying in third grade. When you pass, you move to fourth grade. So by the time you grow up and become an adult, you would have achieved your degree. Look at moving from third grade to fourth grade as ascension and enlightenment; as a degree.

In business terms, consider short term goals as ascension and long term goal as enlightenment.

What is the path to reach enlightenment?

There are various paths to reach the enlightenment state. It's not one path that everybody has to follow. Therefore, you choose a pathway that aligns with your interests.

Imagine, there are various Amtrak trains in New York Penn station. Each train will ultimately reach the same final destination: San Francisco, California. But they will be taking different routes and journey times. You, as a passenger, have a choice to choose a train. Whether you want to take the express train, a slow train, or the longest train, that can take you via Georgia, Texas, Or via Yellowstone National Park Wyoming, before reaching San Francisco, it's your choice. The decision lies in your hands.

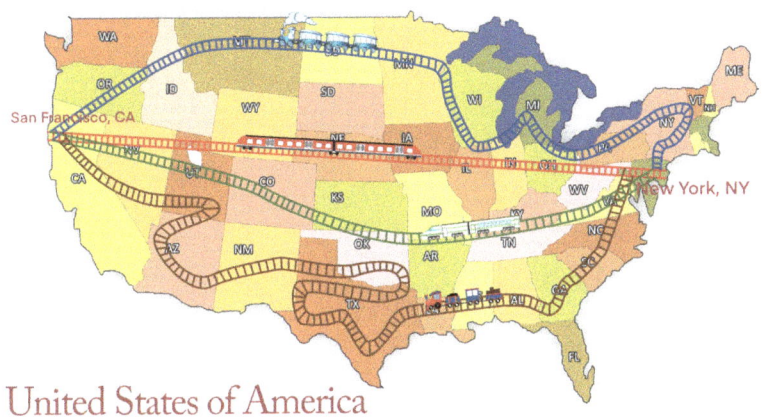

United States of America

So similarly, as a Being, you have various paths to choose from, but ultimately you are reaching the same final destination as everyone else to become one with the Source.

More details about the path specified in Chapter 10 : Path to Enlightenment.

In the next chapter, let's go through the approach that you can take.

4

APPROACH (R S S H T A M B S)

R S S H T A M B S

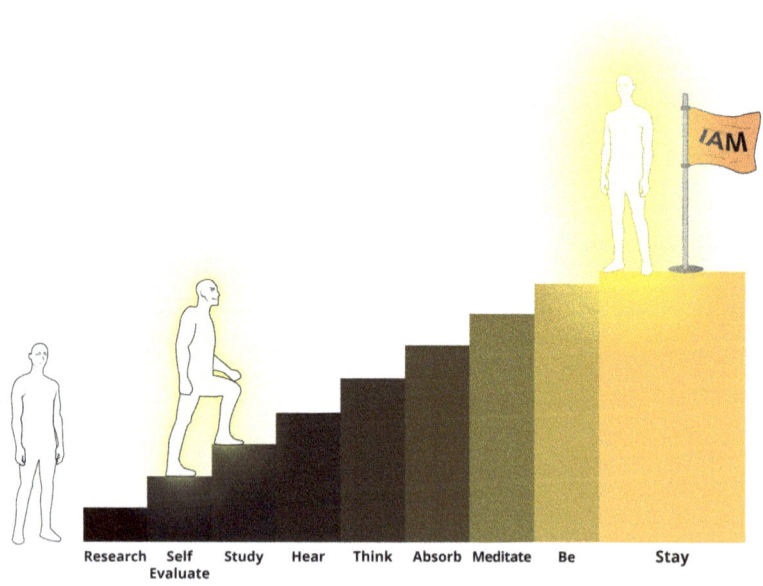

The practical way to wake up is to **Research, Self Evaluate, Study, Hear, Think, Absorb, Meditate, Be,** and **Stay** in Oneness.

Research

Our spiritual journey begins with researching the subject of You and the Source. There are so many ways to do the initial research.

- Use technology to right use, like Google, YouTube, spiritual websites, etc. There is a whole world of information related to the topic of spirituality.
- Find out your local meetup group who are on the same path, discuss spiritual topics.
- Look into spiritual seminars taking place in your area and attend to gain more knowledge.
- The research cannot end without finding a teacher or a guru / perfect living master. They say that whenever the seeker is ready, the master appears. You will find one whether it is a physical or non-physical being, be open to it.

Self Evaluate

From childhood, you were exposed to various cultures, religions, countries, education, families, and friends. You grow up, you assimilate all this information into your subconscious mind, and that turns into your behavior pattern and lifestyle. Now, it's time to think about those programmed behaviors/lifestyles that you have adopted. Check what is working and what isn't working. The goal is to become an enlightened person. So know the qualities of an enlightened being and use that as your guideline and check them one by one, for example:

Find out who you are: Are you a person? Do you identify yourself with the name and the body you inhabit? Or are you something else?

Belief: Check all your belief systems and see if any particular belief is not serving you anymore, then work on it to eliminate that belief.

Behavior: Evaluate your behavior pattern and see what improvement or changes need to be made. You don't need to ask someone to tell you about your behavior. You should be able to tell yourself about your behavior, you know yourself better than anyone else.

Desires and Attachments: Every human being has many desires, attachments to worldly objects, and events that it's difficult to come out of it. Start recognizing your desires and attachments and figure out whether it's a necessity or just a wantedness.

Emotions: We live our entire life in contrast to emotions, all the way from happy/love to sorrow/anger, etc. Notice those emotions, find out a way to overcome those emotions, and stay in complete bliss all the time.

Love: We all love something. It can be a person, place, or thing, but this type of love comes with a condition. If you love someone, you want to make sure that the person loves you as well. Otherwise, you are unhappy, or you become happy when you get things. That's not the love I'm talking about here. It's the true unconditional love to yourself, the Source, others, and everything.

Knowledge: Most of us have gained knowledge through family, culture, education, experience, etc. but, how far has this knowledge taken you, and in what direction? Is this knowledge taking you close to the Source or away from the Source? You need to enquire within yourself and find out. Sometimes the knowledge that is instilled within you isn't enough and you want to acquire more. The best thing is to do research on various ancient scriptures, spiritual books, spiritual articles, and websites to find out some of the enlightened beings who existed before, or still exist even today, and learn from them.

Self Evaluation

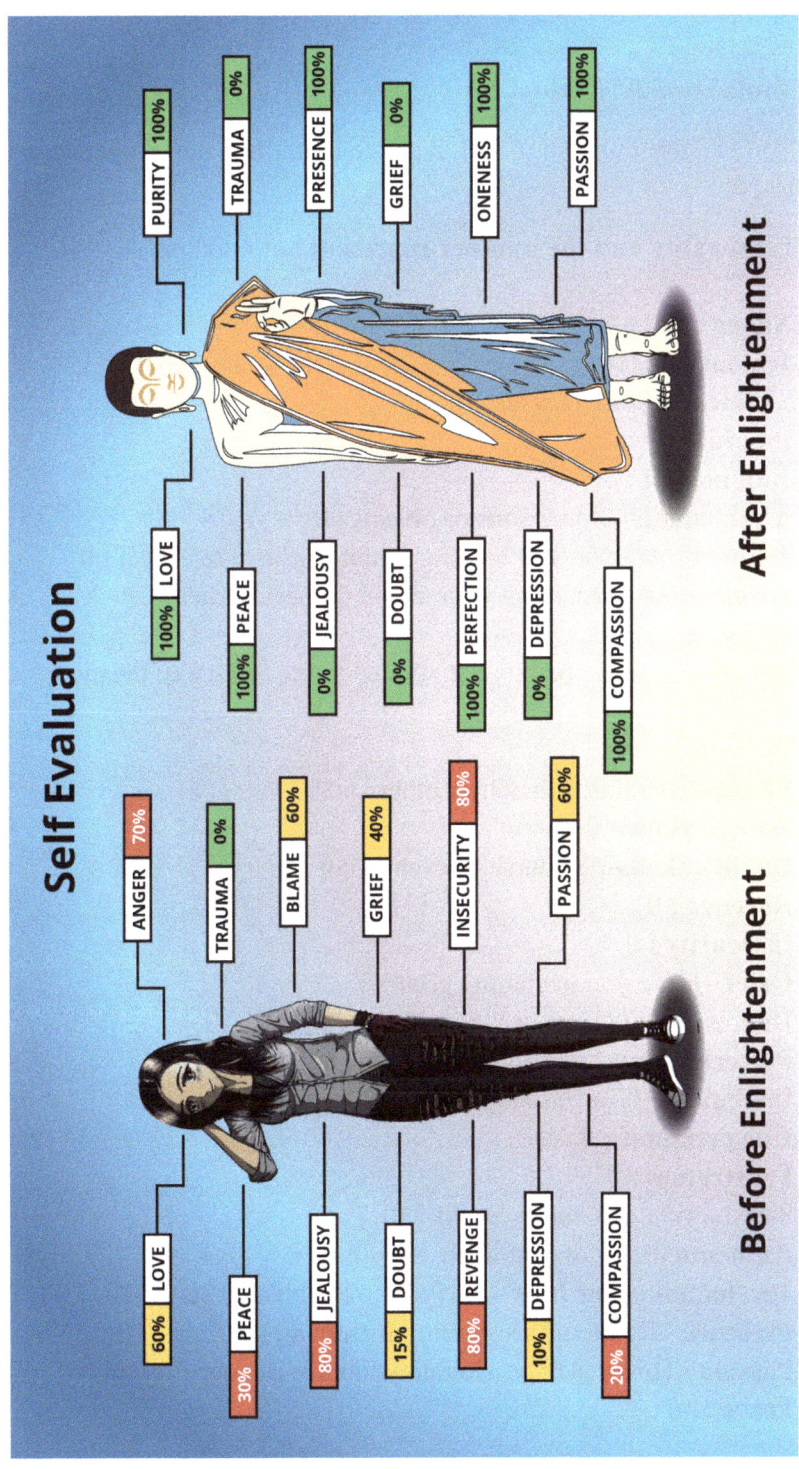

After Enlightenment

PURITY	100%
TRAUMA	0%
PRESENCE	100%
GRIEF	0%
ONENESS	100%
PASSION	100%
LOVE	100%
PEACE	100%
JEALOUSY	0%
DOUBT	0%
PERFECTION	100%
DEPRESSION	0%
COMPASSION	100%

Before Enlightenment

ANGER	70%
TRAUMA	0%
BLAME	60%
GRIEF	40%
INSECURITY	80%
PASSION	60%
LOVE	60%
PEACE	30%
JEALOUSY	80%
DOUBT	15%
REVENGE	80%
DEPRESSION	10%
COMPASSION	20%

Tools For Self Evaluation

You can use this tool to self evaluate by rating yourself between 0 to 10.

Personality and the number represent Set marker

Anger : 0
Jealousy : 0
Shame, Guilt or Regret : 0
Dominating others : 0
Judgmental : 0
Attachments - To persons or objects : 0
Trauma - Are you still holding trauma or have release it : 0
Forgiveness - Forgiving yourself and others (0 means forgiveness) : 0
Beliefs - Clearing beliefs not aligned to the Source (0 means cleared) : 0
Prone to worry : 0
Blame - Blaming yourself or others : 0
Hate or Rage : 0
Doubt - Doubting yourself or others : 0
Revenge : 0
Insecurity : 0
Grief - Have you overcome grief : 0
Depression : 0
Powerlessness - Are you feeling powerlessness : 0
Insecurity - How insecure are you? : 0
Unworthiness : 0
Frustration : 0
Satisfaction or Contentment : 10
Authenticity - How authentic are you : 10
Joy, happiness or bliss - Are you in the blissful state : 10
Presence - Being in the present moment all the time : 10
Passion - How much passion do you have in your life, source : 10
Peace : 10

Compassion : 10
Pure Unconditional Love : 10
Oneness Do you find oneness in everybody and everything : 10

Note: Use this self evaluate tool quite often so you can check your progress.

Study

Once you have done the research and the evaluation of yourself, the next step is to study. This is the stage to start working on your goal as a project kickoff.

You know what you need to study. Be dedicated to it and don't get distracted with worldly matters; it exists whether you are there or not. The focus should be on you and the Source. If you already have noted down the books or material that you want to study, start studying.

Hear

During your research, you would have noted down the list of masters or seminars that you want to hear about. It could be a particular master, teacher, transformational spokesperson, etc. whether that particular talk is live or virtual.

Listen to their perspectives about what they are saying about this reality, the Source, or You. Don't judge whether they are right or wrong. Use your discernment, take it if it makes sense to you, or drop it.

Think

Your next steps should be about thinking about this vast subject. There will be so many questions raised in your mind, like what to study, hear, or follow a particular master. Does it make sense? Should I follow this path or another path? What if…? and so on? The mind plays a critical role in this particular step, and it's necessary to think and come to a conclusion on which path you want to follow; use your inner guidance to decide.

Absorb

Absorb and digest the knowledge that you have learned so far. Try to look at each aspect of the knowledge you acquire and notice your inner responses towards it.

Meditate

Meditation is an important step in this whole process. The inner knowing occurs when you go within to find out who you are and your connection to the Source.

Be

Now is the time to *Be* that light that you have always been. So with clear understanding after doing all your inner work, it's time to *Be* in the state of pure bliss, love, peace, compassion, and one with the Source/everything.

Stay

Once you have reached that state of self-realization, stay in that state forever without external objects affecting you, even though what you access through your senses and what you are, are different.

*Note: Also check my website **LivingLibrarian** . It contains information on various topics on spirituality published by various masters and teachers. You can research there as well.* Also, it contains all the necessary tools, including the evaluation tool.

The next chapter will explain more about structured frameworks and processes that can be used for your transformation to the path of self-realization.

5

IKCRL STRUCTURED FRAMEWORK AND PROCESS

As a profession, I've been working on frameworks and processes for a long time.

So I thought, why can't I come up with some type of similar framework and process that can help in this path of self-realization?

The entire book is written and arranged according to this framework.

I hope it serves you well.

Part 1: Inquiry

The first step that any person who wakes up, will begin to start inquiring about everything, the reality, and who they are. They want to know more about the Source, or All That Is.

IKCRL FRAMEWORK

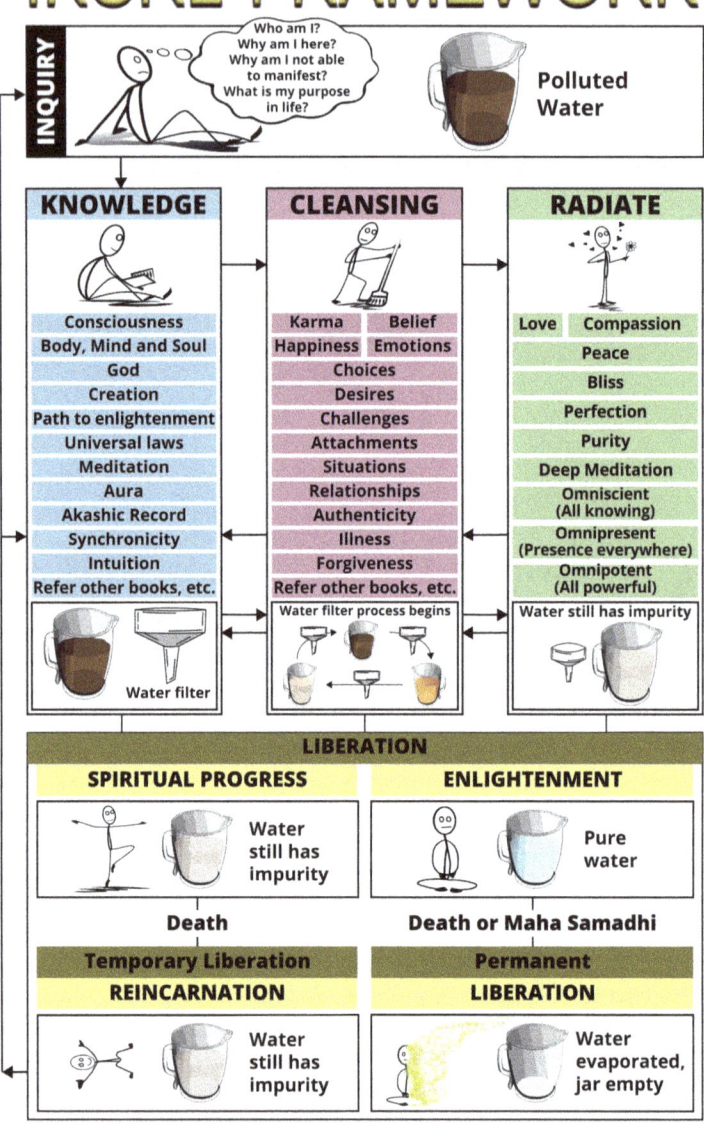

Try to look for an answer or might find people come into your life, with certain world views or intuitive connections that you don't understand logically yet you feel it in your 'gut' so to speak. We could find a topic or thought that persistently pushes through your consciousness, and you will find yourself thinking, 'I wonder how that started. I wonder what that means? Is there any meaning to this life? What am I doing here?'.

You tend to look for an answer externally during your initial awakening, but as you dig deeper, you realize the answer is within you and the journey is to go inward to find those answers.

Part One of this book deals with this inquiry and answers some of the basic questions. It aims to deal with the approach and process that you can take to reach the state of self-realization.

Analogy: Imagine that there is polluted water in a jug. The water does not realize it is impure. This analogy relates to yourself. You are in a sleep state without realizing how much built-up emotions, limitations, and disconnection from the Source you have. But once you start waking up, you start inquiring about everything.

Similarly, the polluted water knows it is dirty and needs to clean itself up.

Part 2: Knowledge

Knowledge is power. Power needs to be understood before you can grasp it, and your growth can begin. In this second section, you will gain a deeper understanding of spirituality, with a valuable comprehension of who you are and what your connection to the Creator is. Guided by the ultimate truth, it shall take you beyond all materialistic nature, ignorance, pain, and suffering. This will bring you closer to the Source, leading you to the path of enlightenment.

Analogy: Contaminated water realizes it needs a filter to clean itself.

In other words, the water is you, and this filter represents the knowledge you now seek.

Part 3: Cleansing

This third stage is where you start cleansing physically, emotionally, mentally, and spiritually based on your understanding of who you are. It is similar to doing practical's once you have understood the theory to become a master of it.

Analogy: The contaminated water starts using a filter to clean up itself until it becomes pure water again.

People over time develop various coping mechanisms when cleansing themselves. Cleansing can be physically done by exercise, healthy eating choices, or being outdoors. Emotionally you could work on your fears, past traumas, or angriness. Although, the one that's the most difficult to understand and come to terms with is mentally cleansing ourselves. Our habit of thinking clearly dictates our way of living and our sense of handling things in the outside world. Our outward circumstance is most often a reflection of our inward battles projected overtime at a constant vibration. So, a good mental impression is the key building block to overcome most of the unwanted situations. For our spiritual growth, it opens up a new Pandora box of new knowledge and understanding; bringing it closer to the divinity existing within us.

In part three the book provides a practical approach of dealing with issues, suffering, challenges, attachment, people, etc. and hence helps you in clearing all those negative emotions that are suppressed for years; bringing you closer to oneness.

Part 4: Radiate

After you have finished inquiring, gaining knowledge, and cleansing your body/mind, it is time to go much deeper within yourself and radiate the qualities of the Source. This includes unconditional love, compassion, bliss, peace, perfection, and purity in every part of your core being. Thus, transcending you beyond this physical reality.

Part 4 of the book indulges you in the feeling of Sources qualities. As you start doing this daily (along with deep meditation for long periods), your body, mind, and soul will come into complete balance and the Source qualities will start reflecting within you.

Analogy: The polluted water is using very refined filters to clean further until it becomes pure water again.

Note: Seeking a master's initiation and guidance on your spiritual progress will help you progress faster.

Part 5: Liberation

There are two kinds of liberation that can happen in this life:

1. Permanent liberation
2. Temporary liberation

Permanent liberation occurs when you are naturally enlightened and leave the body through death or Mahasamadhi. You will be liberated from the cycle of birth and death and ultimately merge with the Absolute; becoming one.

Analogy: Enlightened State - The water realizes the purity of itself. *Liberation* - When pure water is heated, it starts evaporating and ultimately turns into steam. The jar then becomes empty. Similar to steam, we turn into pure awareness and become liberated from the body forever.

Temporary liberation: If a death occurs in between your spiritual progress, you will temporarily leave your body in this life, reincarnate again with a new life, continue where you left off on your spiritual growth. This cycle continues until you become enlightened and permanently liberated from the cycle of birth and death.

Analogy: The polluted water still needs to be cleaned further to become pure water again.

Part five of the book, discuses about liberation and how the process of reincarnation works.

This ends part one and the process of spiritual inquiry.

PART II

KNOWLEDGE

Knowledge is power. Power needs to be understood before you can grasp it, and your growth can begin. In this second part, you will gain a deeper understanding of spirituality, with a valuable comprehension of who you are and what your connection to the Creator is. Guided by the ultimate truth, it shall take you beyond all materialistic nature, ignorance, pain, and suffering. This will bring you closer to the Source, leading you to the path of enlightenment.

Analogy: Contaminated water realizes it needs a filter to clean itself.

Water filter

In other words, the water is you, and this filter represents the knowledge you now seek.

Part two deals with the basic understandings of who you are. It provides the knowledge required to gain insight into your creation

6

TERMINOLOGY

B efore we begin, let's define a few terms that are necessary for the following chapters.

Energy, Vibration, and Frequency

Energy: The universe is created entirely of energy. Each of us is vibrating at a particular frequency range that makes us unique.

Vibration: Vibration is the oscillation of an object.

Frequency: Frequency is the rate at which the objects move and is calculated in cycles per second.

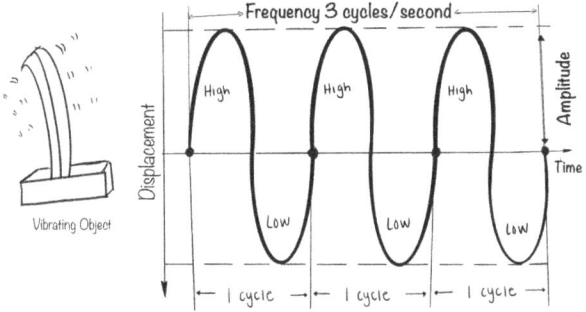

At your core, you are ultimately energy or consciousness. Suppose, when you look inside your body, you find organs. Within those organs, you find tissues, cells, and molecules. Inside molecules, you will find atoms. Go deeper into those atoms, and you'll find energy.

You are a Being of energy, including the trees, animals, ocean, stars, galaxies, etc. Everything in the universe is energy or a form of consciousness and you are part of it.

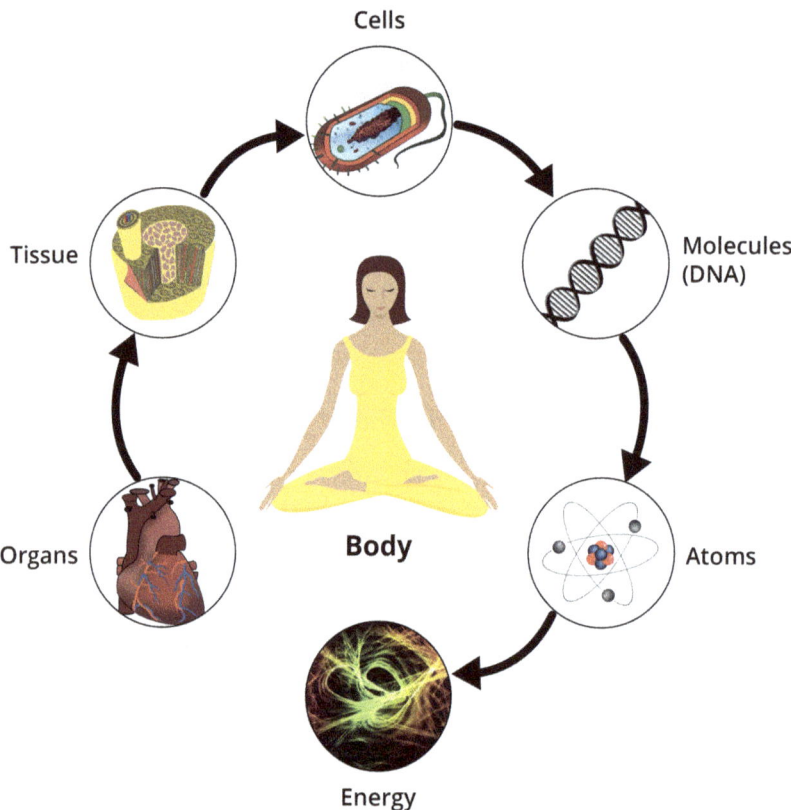

What is observed from your bodily eye represents a vibrational interpretation. You, the plants, animals, and stars feel solid because of natural vibrations. What makes you unique from everything else is, the rate of your vibration and frequency.

For example, If you set an ice cube outside, it would melt and become a liquid. If you heat the same water, it would evaporate and turn into steam. The steam is the same substance but has transformed its property based on the vibration of its molecules. The substance represents consciousness/energy, and these three states represent objects.

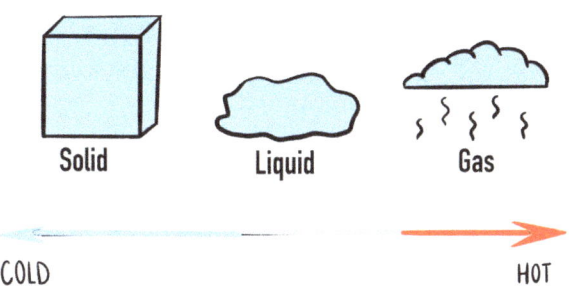

Even your thoughts, emotions, and feelings are energies that are vibrating at a particular frequency.

Resonance

If an object's rate of vibration is known, then it's possible to cause an object to vibrate. Suppose when an external stimulus of an identical frequency is introduced, a harmonic resonance occurs. It will naturally respond to that frequency.

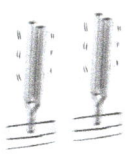

Setting two tuning forks with similar vibrational rates close together demonstrates this. If you strike one fork, the other one will echo it. This effect appears when people tuned to each other and they resonate off each other's frequencies.

What is consciousness?

Various definitions for consciousness are available in philosophy, science, and spiritual perspectives. Below is one of the definitions:

"Consciousness is an awareness of yourself, of your thoughts, memories, emotions, sensations, and external environment. Your conscious experiences are altering continually. One moment your concentration will be on reading this chapter, but that focus may shift to the memory of a discussion with your children. Perhaps your thoughts drift to plan for a vacation. Before long, attention is captured by how uncomfortable your chair is. Conscious thoughts can change drastically from one moment to the next, even as your perceived experience of it feels smooth and effortless."

How do we know we are consciousness?

When you are reading this book, you know that you are awake and in a wakeful state, now suppose you are sleeping and dreaming, even though your body is still laying in bed. You exist and are interacting in the dream world with places, objects, events, etc. What does it clarify with this experience? You exist even without a body, so the body is not you.

Imagine you are in a deep-sleep state. You are unaware of your organic body. Unaware of your mind. Since you are not dreaming, you don't recall anything and are in a complete void.

When you wake up, you know you were in a void or, you are aware of having had dreams. What is common in all three states is conscious awareness.

You as a Self is aware of all three states; the wakeful, dreaming, and deep-sleep states. This unchanging awareness of Self is who you are at the core.

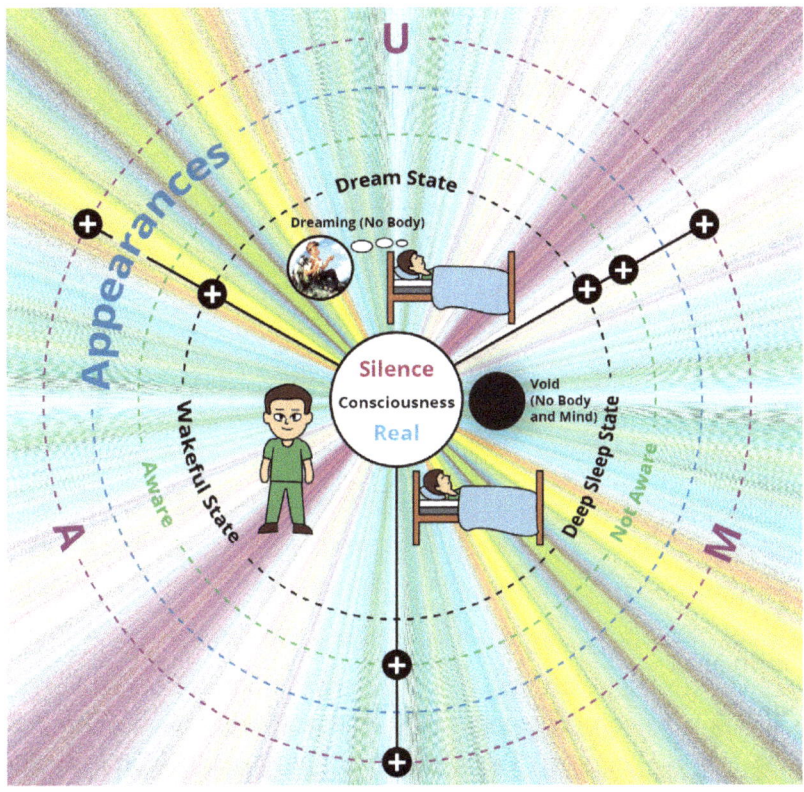

CONSCIOUSNESS (SELF) = Physical experience + Subtle experience + Causal experience.

Consciousness (Self) = Wakeful state (Aware) + Dream state (Aware) + Deep sleep state (Not Aware).

All three states i.e wakeful, dream, and deep sleep states are appearances in front of consciousness. The only real is You as a Self or Consciousness.

7

WHO AM I

Who am I

When somebody asks who you are, your response to them is, "I am Jack" or, "I am Nancy." You associate yourself to the body and the name, but do you think of yourself as just the name and physical body, nothing else? You aren't just a fragment of what you believe to be; in fact, you are so much more than that.

Example:

If there is a pot made of clay, can it exist without a clay?? No, without clay, the pot cannot exist because that's the essence of it.

Clay
(Consciousness)

Pot
(You as Physical
Identity)

Likewise, your consciousness(the clay) lives and identifies yourself as your name (the pot).

Another example:

Imagine you are sitting in the passenger seat and your chauffeur is driving the car. Say you meet someone and they ask you, "Who are you?". Would you respond back by saying "I'm the car"? No, you would most likely respond "I'm the passenger".

Similarly, the passenger is you as Self (soul, the consciousness), and the chauffeur is your mind, the engine is an astral sense, and the car is the body.

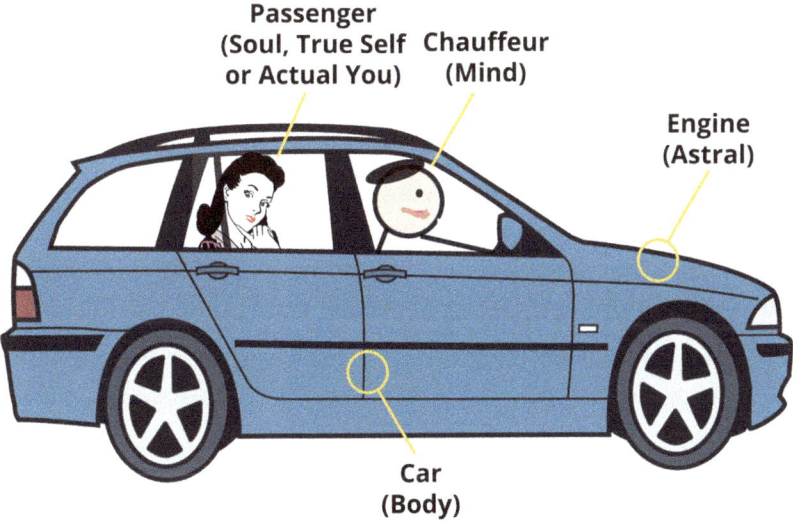

Passenger
(Soul, True Self **Chauffeur**
or Actual You) **(Mind)**

Engine
(Astral)

Car
(Body)

In essence, you are an expression of Source energy (*All That Is*) which is infinite and eternal. So, you're the passenger (Self / Soul / Being). You're an individual consciousness experiencing the denser third-dimensional planet earth.

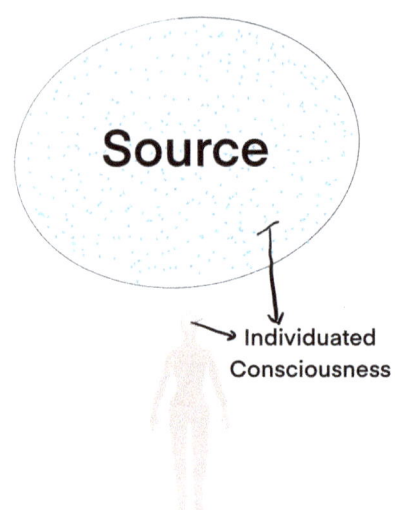

You're the soul; a consciousness. When you descended from the Source to lower dimensions, you started wearing these covers on the way. They are mental, astral, and physical bodies that are necessary to survive in these dimensions. In essence, you are a combination of these bodies, and souls, operating with limited awareness at present. Once you have a realization, you know that you are Pure Consciousness.

Physical, Astral, Mental Body, and Soul

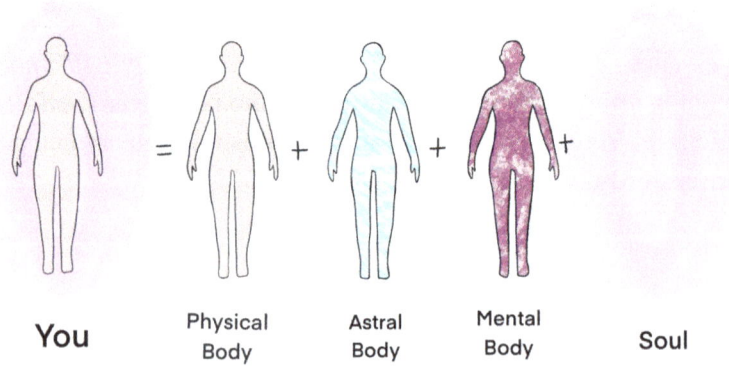

Physical Body

You associate yourself through the physical body by interacting with the world you live in, and the body is the only way by which you exist in this physical universe.

The physical body has a life force energy called Prana / etheric vital body. It draws energy from outside the physical realm and maintains the life of the body. As long as you have Prana, you are alive in this physical world. Upon death, the physical body created from the first density matter stays and merges back to earth. The rest, astral, mental, and soul goes back to the higher planes.

Astral Body

Within this physical body, there lies another body called the Astral body. The Astral body has senses similar to physical senses like touch, sight, hearing, and smell. These astral senses are internal. You use these internal senses while you are dreaming or imagining something.

In an astral state, you hold your perception in the senses, with the same mind and soul. During the night when you are dreaming, you use this astral body to travel. The average lifespan of the astral body is almost one to three thousand physical years. Both physical and astral senses are merely internal and external organs or equipment, powered by consciousness.

Mental Body

The next cover is the mental body or the mind, which is more subtle than the other two bodies. The activity of the mind is to think, conceive, create, rationalize, and process. All concepts are created or expressed by the mind and experienced through the astral and physical body.

You can categorize the mind into:

- The Physical Mind
- The Higher Mind

The Physical Mind

This is the mind of everyday thinking. The mind is concerned with reason and logic. It's your temporary personality that you have for this life and is very dependent on the orderly function of memory.

Memory is an impression of a thought-form that is registered in the universal field of Akasha. When you remember something, the elements are withdrawn from the associated impression in Akasha and reproduce the thought in the form of memories.

The Higher Mind

Ideas and concepts originate from a higher mind region. When you're experiencing a deep state of meditation, ecstasy, or contemplation, you embrace a higher mind, which is a home for your imagination, innovation, and invention.

All physical objects that you see today originally came from concepts in higher minds. You can accomplish spiritual progress when you tap into this higher conscious mind.

A portion of the mind function is *Intellect* and *Ego*. Other terms for the mind include the conscious mind, the subconscious mind, and the superconscious mind. This is explained in the upcoming chapters.

Soul

The soul is an individuated consciousness/Self, a spark of the Source that exists in your body. The soul is the one that's driving this life through the mind, astral, and physical bodies.

A small part of you exists as this personality, and the remaining portion of you still exists within the Source. In other words, you are a subset of the Source and that is your true nature. The rest is merely a cover that you wear to have experiences. But, you're so engrossed in this physical world that you have forgotten your True Self and identify yourself with the body you inhabited.

8

SOURCE OR GOD

Common questions asked by people:

- *Is there an intelligent source in this universe?*
- *How did the entire creation occur?*
- *What is that source, and where can I find it?*
- *What is God?*
- *Where is he/she/it?*

These questions have been asked for millennia, and we continue to ask them even today. The answer to these question are unexplainable from a human perspective, yet the closest answer society can come up with is as follows:

- *God is All That Is; the source of all creation and can only be experienced by dissolving in it.*
- *God is an energy essence with infinite unconditional love.*
- *God is an infinite/eternal ocean of pure knowledge, consciousness, and bliss.*

- *God is Omnipresence (everywhere), Omniscient (all knowledge), and Omnipotent (all-powerful).*
- *God is the Infinite Existence of Knowledge.*

In simple terms, God is an energy essence, a self-awareness, a knowing repository of all knowledge, and all experience. God is infinite in intelligence, a creator of *All That Is,* and *All That Will Ever Be*. God exists as:

- *Unmanifested God*
- *Manifested God*

The manifested God is light, and the unmanifested God is the source of light.

Analogy: The violin is like the unmanifested God. When you play, it is the manifestation of God.

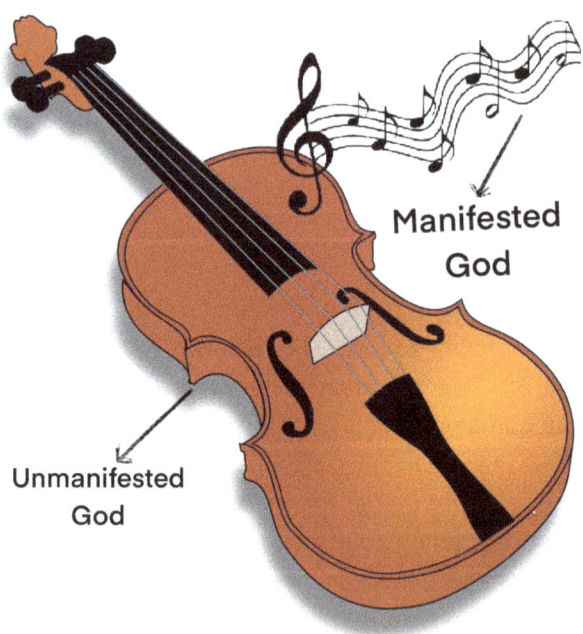

Manifested God emerged as an ocean of light, a subtle form of energy. This subtle energy was condensed by lowering its vibration to create the boundless ocean of consciousness, which is a divine matter that is present in all of Creation.

This is one of the best explanations that swami Sarvapriyananda gave in one of his talks that convinced me.

God is Infinite, Existence, and Knowledge.

God = Infinite X Existence
God = Infinite X Knowledge

Let's go through one by one.

Infinite

Infinite is vast i.e there is no limit.

Infinite = Vast = No limit

To understand vast or no limits, you need to understand, what limit means. Let's add three attributes to the limit.

Limit in Space, Time, and Object.

Limit in Space

An object is limited in space.

Examples: There is a cup on the dining table; and it occupies a small space in that area. The same cup is not present in other rooms, your friend's place, or even in your backyard.

Cup   No Cup

Another example could be when you're reading a book in your living room. You aren't in your office nor jogging in the park. Therefore, your presence is limited to that space in your living room.

These two examples give you a view of limits in space.

Attributes of God is No Limit in Space

Say there is something that has no limit in space. This would be a way of saying there is no place where God doesn't exist, and that is one of the main attributes of God.

Limit in Time

If you use a similar example from above, the cup and you. The cup is not going to exist forever, one day it will be destroyed.

Cup   Broken Cup

Like the cup, you won't survive forever. You are born as a baby, play during your childhood, work while an adult, relax in your old age, and then eventually die.

There is a limit in time for the cup and you.

Attributes of God - No Limit in Time

God has no limit in time and exists forever. Even before time and even after time. This is another attribute of God.

Limit in Object

A cup is also limited to its identity and can only be a cup.It cannot be a pan nor pen.

Likewise, you cannot be your spouse or kid. You are limited to yourself and not another person's physical body.

Attributes of God - No Limit in Object

God has no limitations in objects. There is nothing in the universe that is different from it.

Let us apply infinity to existence and knowledge.

Existence

God =Infinite X Existence

Existence is reality. So when you apply no limits in space, time, and object; to existence, it becomes infinite existence. Things that exist forever.

But now, the question that arises in one's mind is, if existence is reality, from a physical perspective, is everything real?

Example: The cup, yourself, plant, pot, table, etc. are limited in space, time, and object. Then how does God, the infinite existence, exist in all of us?

The answer to these questions, you need to take a step back and view them from a different perspective. In the picture above, you see a person, a table, a pot, a plant, and a cup exists. You realize that there is one commonality in the image; it puts your attention on existence. Humanity is all one ocean of existence if you apply infinity to this, then that sense of existence is **omnipresent**.

Example: Clay can be used to create a pot, jar, sculpture, plate, etc. once the material has fulfilled its purpose, it is destroyed and becomes clay again. Pure Existence is similar to clay, manifesting in time, space, and objects for the experience. When that experience is over, it merges back into Pure Existence. Nothing in the universe can be there without existence. Existence is non-dual or in other words, a sense of oneness.

Knowledge

God = Infinite X Knowledge

Knowledge is pure consciousness.

Example: When you are reading a book, that is knowledge. When you are thinking or watching something: that is knowledge. Everything that you do in your day to day life, for example, wake up, eat breakfast, go to work, read books, walk in the park, watch movies, etc.. all these activities you are aware of, has one commonality i.e awareness/consciousness.

Another question arises in one's mind. *All this knowledge is limited in space-time and objects?*

Example: When I was younger, I studied and learned about algebra. As time passed, I don't recall much about algebra. The information I had was limited in time. The knowledge that I have now is not the same knowledge that the people around me have. Then how does this infinite knowledge exist in all of humanity?

You need to take a step back and look again. What is similar in all of these examples? The consciousness that is underlying in each object that lights up the unchanging one. Pure consciousness is common to all of these, and all knowledge is grounded in this consciousness, which has no limit in Space, Time, and Object.

Therefore, it gives you the understanding that *God is Infinite, Existence, and Knowledge.*

We are trying to explain God, which cannot be explained, but only felt within yourself. In essence, God is everything. His presence exists everywhere, and there is no place where he does not. We are all part of that existence.

❧

9

CREATION

There are numerous different perspectives about creation explained in various scriptures and spiritual books. Although, there is one commonality in all of these materials; the creation happened because the Experiencer (Source or Pure Existence), wanted to know more about itself to the fullest extent. The Experiencer did this so that it could continually strive to evolve with a greater capacity of love by experiencing through its very own creation.

Overview

At the beginning, where there was no time, there was only Supreme Consciousness, Source, or *All That Is*. It was intelligent, loving, self-aware, and wanted to experience its true nature by creating a process that would generate the creation and understand itself to the fullest extent.

It started to individuate itself into many consciousnesses, giving them free will and asking them to explore, create, experience their creations, in return, they had to share what they had learned. The experiences they report would become a part of it and would know more about itself. Ultimately, growing in experience of itself because of their creativity.

The source started splitting itself into many parts. One part being itself, and the remaining split into many individual consciousness/awareness.

Example: Imagine the Source is the complete puzzle, and the individual consciousness (pieces) are part of that puzzle.

Each Source started desiring a specific type of experience that they knew would result from the creation they create. Let's say Source One started creation by splitting itself into experiencer and experience.

- One experiencer became many experiencers, by individuating itself into many spirits/souls. Thus, creating an experience of singularity, and at the same time being whole.
- The experience was created through creation. The Source One created our universe in such a way that the Souls can experience from the highest dimensions to lowest dimensions (where we are at present), This allows us to play around in this grand scheme of creation, to evolve and expand.
- The creation happened in a blink of an eye.

Individuated Souls

Experiencer

Source

Experience

Dimensions,densities,
Universes, planets,
Time, and space

Few souls volunteered to explore the creation by leaving the Source and taking adventurous trips to different planes, dimensions, and densities, experience the creation and then return back to the Source. Those volunteers started planning their trip to explore by creating roles for each group based on certain natural laws that exist through creation. One of those individual souls were You. You were aware as an individual, or whole, at the same time.

Volunteers

- Group 1 acted as a smaller version of the Source for the particular realm they occupied.
- Group 2 became Guides, Angels, Fairies, Masters, occupying different planes, densities, and dimensions.
- Group 3 became explorers of these planes, densities, and dimensions.

Natural Laws

- Each density and dimension have their own set of natural laws.
- Each dimension has a certain vibratory level, and they go from subtle forms at higher planes to denser forms at lower planes.
- Space and time were created in the first three planes, physical, astral, and mental. The laws of karma and duality exist in the first three lower planes.
- And other natural laws.

Density and Dimensions

Density

Density is the vibratory level of the atoms in an object. If the rate of vibration is low, it is considered gross or denser. If the rate of vibration is high, it is considered subtle or less dense. In general, density defines the level of consciousness or the level of evolution of the soul.

Dimension

A dimension is a means of organizing different densities based on their level of consciousness. Some call it a different harmonic level. Each dimension has certain laws and principles that are specific to the frequency of that dimension. Access to a particular dimension depends on the rate at which you vibrate and the level of evolution you have achieved.

Each density brings some insight to the soul from which it gains knowledge and wisdom through experience.

1st Density: Minerals, rocks, air, chemicals, dust, etc. They are the building blocks for other densities.

2nd Density: Bacteria and animals are intact with the ecosystem when compared to humans. We try to destroy the ecosystem rather than develop a symbiosis with the ecosystem.

Density	Examples	Physical / Non Physical	Dimension
1	Fire, Water, Minerals, Rocks	PHYSICAL	Height, Width, Depth & Time
2	Plants, Animal		
3	Humans, Other 3rd density physical beings in the universe		
4	Light Beings or Semi Physical beings (Our next Evolution)	SEMI PHYSICAL	Height, Width, Depth & Time is fluid
5 & 6	Semi Physical being with more spiritually evolved		
7 & above	Ascended Masters, Angels, Non physical beings such as Arcturians, etc	NON PHYSICAL	

3rd Density: Are human beings or other physical beings.

The first three densities are in one harmonic level. Everything you physically see, touch, and experience, are in the same harmonic level or dimension.

The 4th density is a higher harmonic level than the previous three densities. Some beings are already in the 4th or some will be going to the 4th density. This is our next stage of evolution.

The *4th*, *5th*, and *6th* densities are at higher harmonic levels, and the beings are more semi-physical than 3rd density beings like us.

The *7th density* and above are all non-physical beings.

Realms and Planes

According to Sant Mat and other traditions, the various planes of existence are described below. Note that some of the descriptions are in a metaphor.

Physical Plane

The physical plane of this universe is the lowest projection of a source that is guided by the medium of a universal mind. All physical matters exist in this plane.

Astronomers estimate this particular physical universe is approximately 12 to 14 billion years old, and earth is around 4.5 billion years approximately. The law of karma also applies to this plane. At the end of the cosmic cycle, the physical plane gets destroyed.

Astral Plane

This is the second plane of creation. It's medium is concrete emotional energy. This is the second closest plane to our physical plane. The entire physical universe gets its source of power (driving energy) from this plane, including all ideas.

There are fewer ground rules to follow, compared to the physical plane, in terms of constraints that we have on earth, for example, time is more malleable, or nonlinear in this plane, we can go forward or backward in time.

THE GRAND SCHEME OF ALL CREATION

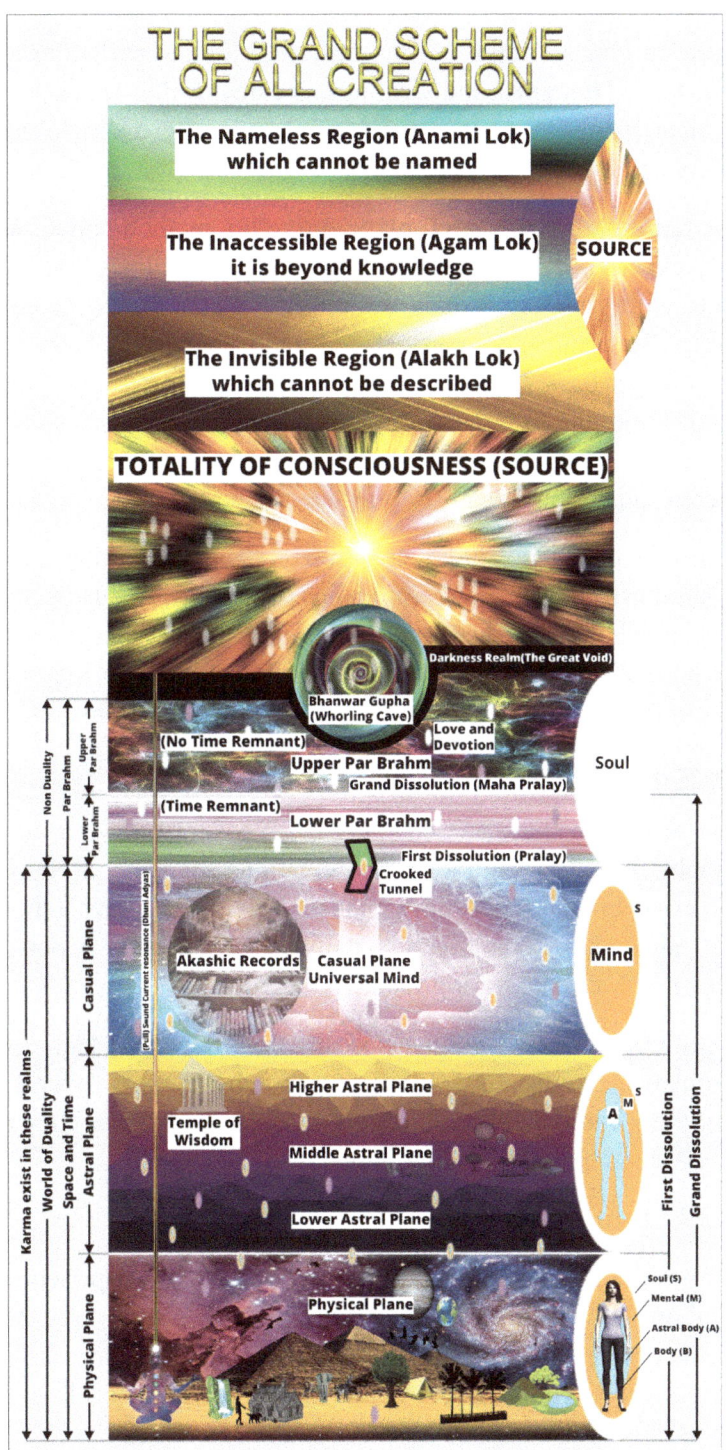

The Nameless Region (Anami Lok) which cannot be named

The Inaccessible Region (Agam Lok) it is beyond knowledge

SOURCE

The Invisible Region (Alakh Lok) which cannot be described

TOTALITY OF CONSCIOUSNESS (SOURCE)

Darkness Realm(The Great Void)

Bhanwar Gupha (Whorling Cave)

(No Time Remnant)

Love and Devotion

Upper Par Brahm

Grand Dissolution (Maha Pralay)

Soul

(Time Remnant)

Lower Par Brahm

First Dissolution (Pralay)

Crooked Tunnel

Non Duality

Upper Par Brahm

Par Brahm

Lower Par Brahm

Casual Plane

[Pull] Sound Current resonance (Dhani Adyat)

Akashic Records

Casual Plane Universal Mind

Mind

S

Higher Astral Plane

Temple of Wisdom

Middle Astral Plane

Lower Astral Plane

A

M

S

First Dissolution

Grand Dissolution

Karma exist in these realms

World of Duality

Space and Time

Astral Plane

Physical Plane

Physical Plane

Soul (S)

Mental (M)

Astral Body (A)

Body (B)

Based on your vibration level, you can go to that particular plane in astral. Thoughts and feelings create reality quicker than physical planes. Fear can create evil as easily as love creates beauty and joy.

You can travel to the astral plane through a method called out of body experience, or Astral Travel. Some techniques allow you to travel with your astral body through the planes of existence and reality. Between your physical body and your astral body, there will always be a connection through a silver cord. Parts of the astral world are co-created through the individual consciousness. One can see the astral world as beautiful mountains and valleys, whereas other beings can see it as devastated land.

Even in astral planes, there are jobs or assignments that we take on similar to what we do in our physical plane. We help others, take on roles to safeguard portals, doorways, to other planes. At the end of the cosmic cycle, the astral plane gets destroyed. Within the astral plane, it is subdivided into three sub-planes.

Lower Astral Plane

This section of the plane contains the repository of your densest thoughts, negative emotions, and creations. Imagine if you have anger or guilt and focus more intensely; it then becomes a thought form and takes on a life of its own. We are such a powerful creator and we take it for granted.

In some scriptures, this plane is also referred to as Hell. Some fragmented souls are trapped in their own world of mind/imagination and are currently living in this plane. They have no recollection that they are trapped by themselves.

Middle Astral Plane

Every night when you go to sleep and dream, you experience the astral world, and this is the place that you usually go. Many worlds and realms exist on this plane that it's an utterly different universe of its kind. It operates at a higher energetic level.

There is a replica of our planet earth at an energetic level that Includes replicas of countries, cities, buildings, roads, etc. There are areas where you create your own world, sort of like a child playing with a sandbox.

Some communities still exist that would have been our past society on planet earth. Or, some communities would be our future society on planet earth. You are allowed to travel to these communities based on their invitation or request.

Higher Astral Plane

After death, you come back to this plane. This is where your consciousness is focused upon between lifetimes. Often you discover your loved ones, or fragments of loved ones, who have passed before existing here.

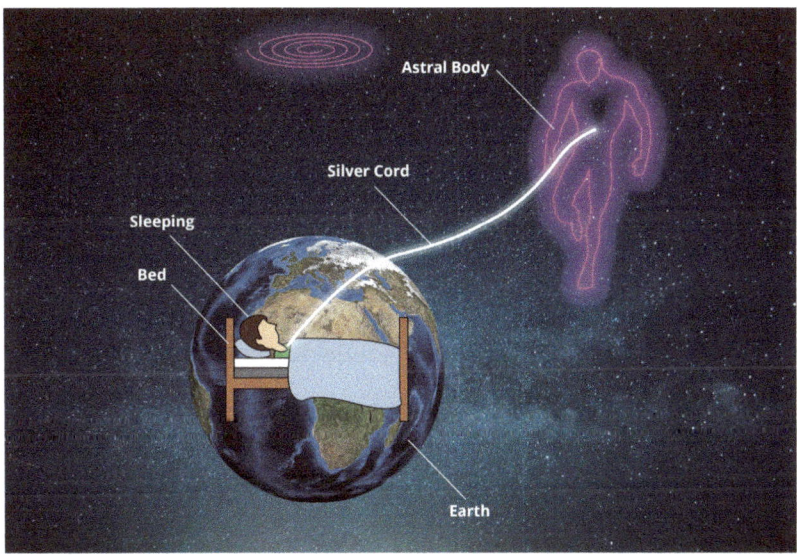

You will remember all the past lives that you ever had, and will find out more about your karma that has accumulated over your lifetimes.

Mental plane

The third plane of creation is a medium of concrete intellectual energy. It's the origin of the Universal Mind and the area of memory, from this region, all individual minds are derived.

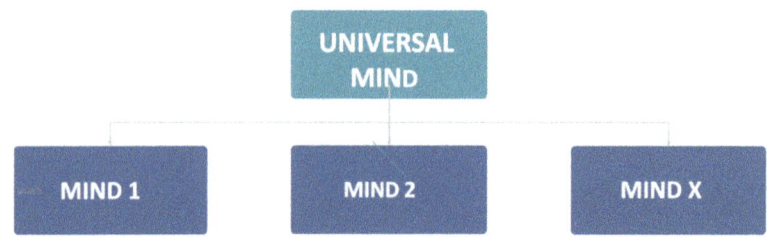

The understanding of the mind, the astral, and the physical planes are shaped here. Within this plane, there are many sub-planes: the Causal Plane, Mental Plane, Etheric Plane, etc. The Akashic Records exist in this plane, where all your past and future life records are stored. Not only, it contains records of physical planes but also the lives of astral planes as well. This is the place where you go when you meditate and visualize. Your thoughts originate from here and are used to create your physical reality.

It's the source of all philosophy, moral teachings, aesthetics, etc. All things that you see today in the physical world originate from the concepts of this plane.

The soul is still mixed with a subtle form of matter, a Causal body.

The first dissolution occurs in this region and below. All planes below will be wiped out, and follow a period of darkness equivalent to the life of the universe. After darkness, a new creation happens again, and the process continues.

Par Brahm (Beyond Mind)

Between mental and Par Brahm, there is a region that the soul has to pass through called a crooked tunnel, which can ward off souls from progressing further. Imagine it's a twisted shape and the soul cannot see what is behind the other side unless the soul reaches the midpoint of the tunnel. Once you pass through the tunnel, you reach timelessness, a stateless state, where you will discover your true self. Your soul, the one which is powering all the other states below it (Causal, Astral, and physical body).

Par Brahm is non-duality, there are no opposites. All opposites or dualities are created below Par Brahm. In theory, Par Brahm above is non-duality, and below is duality. Free from all Karma and rebirths. You'll find out that the script (past, present, and future) was written by yourself, as a soul, to have an experience and evolve out of that experience. There is no experience in this plane, all experience exists in time and space and in causal and below. A remnant of time still exists, and it's a timeless zone. The soul is an individual rather than a total oneness.

The Par Brahm splits into upper and lower planes. One attached to the totality of consciousness (which is absolute and no time remnant), and the other attached to the causal plane (which has a residual of time).

The Grand Dissolution happens at the lower part of Par Brahm, which has remnants of time but not the upper part of Par Brahm. So, only the upper part of the Par Brahm is left. During dissolution, all inhabitants of all of those planes to be dissolved, are drawn up to a higher plane. When the creation happens again, we occupy the planes and experience them all again. It is similar to, during night, when you go to sleep, you are not aware of your body nor the environment. Such as the bed, room, house, or the world. This is similar to dissolution, but in the morning when you wake up, you bring all your senses back and automatically follow your routines.

Darkness Realm (The Great Void)

Above Par Brahm, there is a layer of darkness. It is called the void or the dark realm. The souls are not to dwell upon this region for their protection and can cross only with the help of the master.

Bhanwar Gupha (Whorling Cave)

In between Par Brahm and Totality of consciousness, there is a cave called Bhanwar Gupha (an analogy). All souls have to travel through this cave to reach the totality of consciousness on the other side.

Many souls have been trapped in this timeless Bhanwar Gupha permanently. It's due to their level of consciousness even though they are free from their physical, astral, and mental bodies.

No soul has ever crossed this realm without the help of another soul. The one who has already reached the other side and is in awareness with a continuous connection to the totality of consciousness/Source are called perfect living master.

The Totality of Consciousness (Oneness, Source)

This is the region of the Source; the spirit reigns supreme. The total absence of matter. Free from destruction and death, an individual soul regains full awareness and becomes one with totality. One becomes many, and many become one. Some of the higher vibration qualities that come from this plane are Love, Intuition, Compassion, Oneness, and Unity.

It's indescribable from our perspective. To give you an idea so you can understand in physical terms, it's like a collection of islands. Each island belongs to an individual soul. The interweaving ocean is made of souls; and all souls are intermingling with each other.

Souls who have left the Source to experience other realities and came back to the Source are called VANCE (pronounced as once). Souls who never left the Source are called HANCE. Each soul can experience individuality, and at the same time, be whole on their island of a true home.

Alakh: Which cannot be described.

Agam: It is beyond knowledge.

Anami: It cannot even be named.

The ultimate creator, or Source, can go to those regions of experience on his own.

Q&A

Why are we not able to see life on other planets?

Beings of higher density can only see density beings below, or lower than them, not vise versa. That is one of the reasons why we are not able to see life on other planets. You, as a 3rd density being, try to look for life on other planets, but not able to find any because that particular planet may have life forms above the 3rd and/or 4th density.

There are certain exceptions where higher density beings reduce their vibratory level to such a degree that other density beings lower than they, can physically see them.

Why would the Source destroy what it has already created?

The Source would uncreate when:

- It has completed its job of experiencing.
- It's objective is not met and would require changes in creation.
- A complete change of direction is required to make it more efficient.

How do we achieve spiritual growth?

As a human being, the knowledge and wisdom learned through experience, creates spiritual growth.

A High-Level Summary

- Consciousness, when becoming conscious of something, becomes creation.
- Consciousness creates and experiences universes.
- When consciousness wants to experience its creation from a different perspective, it becomes a soul.

- When consciousness wants to explore different realms of dimensions, or reality, it adds a costume of mind and body, thus creating space, and time to explore.
- Consciousness creates an experience by the principle of duality. Light and dark, proton and electron, life and death, etc.

In the next chapter, we will go through the path to enlightenment.

10

PATH TO ENLIGHTENMENT

All paths lead to one destination, as all pathways lead to one Source. There are various paths one can choose to take to become enlightened, but ultimately, it all leads to union with God.

The following are some of those paths mentioned in:

- Vedanta scripture,
- Teachings of buddha,
- Sant Mat tradition,
- And others.

Vedanta scripture

In Vedanta scripture, they have mentioned four paths.

- **Bhakti yoga:** The Path of Devotion.
- **Raja yoga:** The Path of Discipline.
- **Jnana yoga:** The Path of Knowledge.
- **Karma yoga:** The Path of Action (Duties and Responsibilities).

Bhakti Yoga - The Path of Devotion

Bhakti Yoga is the path of pure love and devotion to God. It's the process of inner purification and transforming your egoistic love with pure love by pouring holy thoughts into your mind. It's usually accomplished through prayers, chanting, studying of holy scriptures and worshipping the ultimate divine God.

Raja Yoga - The Path of Discipline

Raja Yoga is the path to maintain control over your mind by bringing it still and calm. Through this, the Self will be revealed. To attain this self-knowledge, one has to develop a strong will power by persistent practice of meditation, mantras, and other techniques.

Jnana Yoga - The Path of Knowledge

Jnana Yoga is the path, where ignorance is eliminated through the light of knowledge or wisdom. Through knowledge, one can burn away impurities in the mind and, at the same time, enlighten the inner consciousness. Thus ultimately realizing that you and the Source are one.

Karma Yoga - The Path of Action

Karma Yoga is to perform selfless action without any attachment to the outcome of the result. Due to your ignorance, the ego is born and has created a wall between your Personal Self and True Self. It binds yourself to this world through attachments.

So by performing selfless action without any attachment, you overcome ego identity, and all action is seen as an offering to the divine. You ultimately release yourself from all attachment through non-attachment, based on the action performed.

Even though there are four paths, they complement each other, and everyone has all these characteristics in them. Some are more predominant than others, so choose what resonates with you.

Approach to Vedanta

There are three main approaches to Vedanta.

- Advaita by Sri Adi Shankaracharya, Non-Duality.
- Vishishtadvaita by Ramanuja, Non-Duality with qualifications.
- Dvaita by Madhva, Duality.

Advaita

- Atman (soul) and Paramatman (God) are all the same. There is no duality between God and the soul.
- God / Atman or consciousness, is the only truth, and the rest is His illusion (Maya).
- Enlightenment (Moksha) is achieved by removing ignorance regarding your misidentification with the five koshas (physical, energetic, mental, intuitive, and bliss layers) and Maya (illusion).
- It emphasizes Jnana Yoga as the ultimate path to enlightenment and others such as Bhakti, Raja, and Karma Yoga as a means to knowledge.

Vishishtadvaita

- God and Self are the same, there is no duality, but it's characterized by multiplicity.
- The illusion, or the creation of a diversity of life forms, is just a mere reflection of God. When you see your reflection in the mirror, in the same way, you are seeing the entire illusion is a reflection of God.
- It emphasizes Bhakti Yoga as the ultimate path to enlightenment. Karma and Jnana Yoga are sub-processes of Bhakti.

Dvaita

God and his creation are two distinct and eternal realities. The liberated soul may come to his presence but never merge into him. Moksha is attained through a loving union with the eternal God.

Teachings of Buddha

Buddha has preached four noble truths to his disciples that can end suffering and ultimately lead to nirvana (enlightenment).

The truth of:

1. Suffering (Dukha).
2. Cause of Suffering (Samudaya).
3. End of Suffering (Nirodha).
4. The path leading to the end of suffering (Magga Marga).

1. Suffering (Dukha)

There are two types of suffering.

Physical suffering: Mostly due to age; it leaves a man with physical issues and eventual death, bringing grief to others.

Mental suffering: Pain from loneliness, depression, anger, and frustration.

2. Cause of Suffering (Samudaya)

The cause of suffering is due to desire and greed to attain name, fame, or worldly possessions. This eventually gives rise to anger, greed, fear, and pain. Old age comes to everybody in life.

3. End of Suffering (Nirodha)

The end of suffering is possible by deliberately avoiding desires and cravings in which one can find contentment in life.

4. The path leading to the end of suffering (Magga Marga)

There are the eightfold paths to end suffering which ultimately lead to Nirvana.

The Eightfold Path

A person mostly suffers due to a yearning for the fulfillment of their desires. When they realize this, the person is said to gain a better understanding of their path. This eightfold path of wisdom is directed towards ending suffering and reaching for enlightenment.

The eightfold path is categorized into three qualities:

Wisdom (Panna):

Right Understanding
Right Thought

Morality (Sila):

Right Speech
Right Action
Right Livelihood

Meditation (Samadhi):

Right Effort
Right Mindfulness
Right Concentration

LET us take a closer look at each of the eightfold paths.

1. Right Understanding

- Right understanding is to see things as they are.
- Change is the only constant; this is the fact of life.
- Happiness comes from within and not from outside.
- All things are impermanent in this world.
- One must not focus on one's yearnings.

This kind of understanding will enlighten you and cease longing for happiness.

2. Right Thoughts

- One should be able to recognize between right and wrong thoughts.
- Your perception of reality influences your thoughts. If your perception of reality is deformed, then you may end up giving rise to harmful thoughts.
- Your thoughts directly influence your mental state. It's crucial to understand that having the right ones can lead to the elimination of harmful thoughts and motivate you to develop kindness, compassion, and detachment.
- Remove these harmful thoughts from their roots forever.

3. Right Speech

- Being mindful of your speech is very important. You should weigh your words before you speak them.
- Avoid false, harsh, and mindless speech.
- Always use honest, kind, nurturing, and worthy words.

4. Right Action

- Cultivate the right action in your daily life that can bring peace and happiness.
- The right actions will result in purifying your karma.
- Avoid doing wrong actions that can bring harm, disharmony, or sufferings to others.

5. Right Livelihood

- Earn a living righteously; and not through negative or illegal activities such as arms, drugs, prostitution, exploitation of animals, or other such activities.

- Your mind and heart are affected by the nature of the work that you choose to do.
- Make a living in a way that brings peace, compassion, and kindness within yourself.

6. Right Effort

- You need to realize that no one but yourself is responsible for your awakening, and you must do it for yourself.
- Make an effort to avoid harmful qualities from rising within yourself, such as; anger, greed, and jealousy.
- You should make an effort to develop good qualities that have not arisen within you already. Traits that are harmful, and habitual should be eliminated and should develop qualities such as love, compassion, kindness, peace, and wisdom.
- Be sure to maintain the good qualities that you already possess.

7. Right Mindfulness

- Mindfulness means your capacity to be consciously aware in the present moment.
- Through controlling your mind, you can overcome suffering and becoming a slave to negative emotions such as anger, jealousy, and greed.
- By being aware of your body, feelings, mind, and mental qualities, you will be able to bond with life.
- Your body should be well taken care of; focus on your breathing as a way to achieve calmness.

8.Right Concentration

- Your mind always wanders around and is greatly influenced by the external environment. To bring the mind under control, you should concentrate on yourself. This can be achieved by practicing meditation.

- Meditation brings peace and serenity within yourself, which brings your mind under control.

Sant Mat tradition

In Sant Mat tradition, there is a spiritual practice called Surat Shabd Yoga. (Surat: soul, Shabd: sound current, Yoga: union). You practice by going within to discover your True Self and attain, the enlightenment which ultimately reunites you with the Absolute Supreme Being. More details about this practice in Chapter 52.

Conclusion

There are many other paths apart from the ones mentioned so far. But it is up to each individual to choose the pathway that their soul yearns after. If we focus carefully on what those scriptures are mentioning, there is more commonality in all of them, and they are all saying the same thing, which is ultimately union with the Creator. So if we compare the path with this book, then I would say that this is a hybrid version specifically focusing on Raj Yoga in Vedanta or Sant Mat tradition, which ultimately is to go within to get enlightened. Of course, during that process, you go through clearing some of the internal issues that we all have. This is later mentioned in the next few chapters that relates to Jnana or Karma Yoga, in Vedanta or the suffering mentioned in Buddhist teaching.

∼

11

UNIVERSAL LAWS

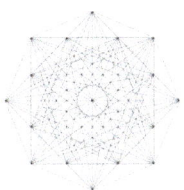

1. Law of Divine Oneness

This law states that we are all connected with everything around us. This includes you, others, plants, rocks, animals, planets, galaxies, the universe, etc. Since we are all energy of the same Source, everything you do, think, feel, believe, act, and your emotions have some effect to a certain extent on everything. This law can also be stated as "One Is All, or All Is One".

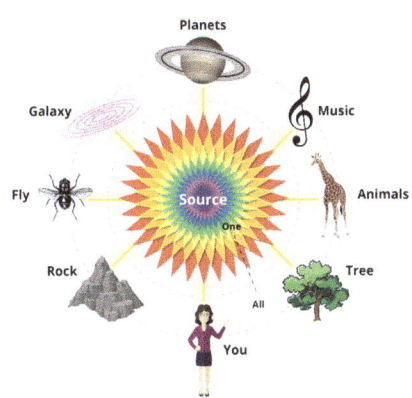

2. Law of Vibration

Everything is energy; you, others, plants, rocks, animals, planets, galaxies, the universe, etc. Each of them is vibrating at a particular frequency, including your thoughts, feelings, and emotions. All of these frequencies have unique energy signatures. The quality of your life is dependent on your vibration.

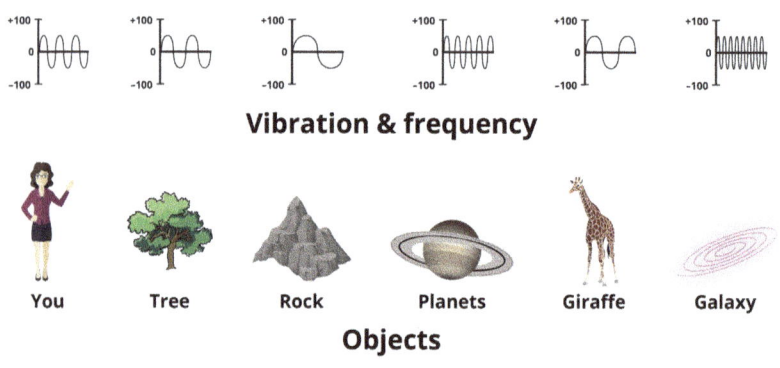

Vibration & frequency

| You | Tree | Rock | Planets | Giraffe | Galaxy |

Objects

Thought + Emotion = Feeling

If you are happy, blissful, excited, or in love, then you are emitting a high vibration. If you are depressed, angry, sad, or scared, you are emitting a low vibration.

3. Law of Action

This law states that you need to take action to accomplish something. An action is an energy in motion, and since you live in a physical world, it is necessary to achieve a goal/target. Sometimes inspiration can come from your inner self or it can guide you through feelings; it is imperative to take action before it fades.

 For example, you get inspiration to write a book so you take action to start writing it. This book was written based on the inspiration I received one day while I was walking in my backyard, but I didn't take action at that time.

The second time came while I was meditating. I thought it was too complex and time-consuming. As the days passed by, in a conversation I had with a friend, the inspiration came again, through him, asking me to write a book to help himself and others. Immediately, I took action the next

day to start writing, and now, you are reading this book. As I said, inspiration can come from anywhere.It can be from your friends or a slogan from an outside billboard.

My key point is to take action based on your feelings. Say that you want to win the lottery, but in order to win, you need to take action to buy a lottery ticket.

4. Law of Attraction

There is a saying that 'like' attracts 'like'. This law states that you attract people, objects, and events in your life based on the energy you emit through your thoughts, words, feelings, and actions. Positive energy attracts positive energy, and negative energy attracts negative energy.

It can also be stated as what happens in your inside world will reflect upon the outside world. It means that what you think, feel, or say will reflect in your outside world. Suppose if you always think and feel angry, sad, depressed. Then, you will meet angry, sad, or depressed people.

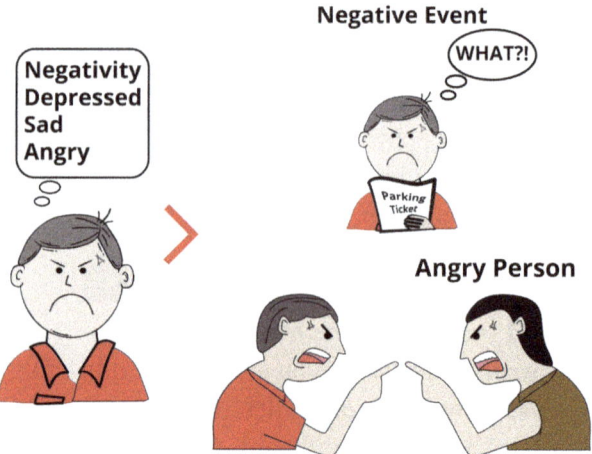

Events will happen that match your feelings. This type of event will be dependent on whether your feelings are negative or positive.

On the other hand, if you are thinking, feeling, or believing in positivity, then you will meet corresponding people who are in that positive attitude or a positive event.

5. Law of Cause and Effect

There is a saying *"we reap what we sow"*. This states that every action has a consequence or reaction. The thoughts you think, the words you speak, the actions you take, or decisions you make, are actions that create effects. Known as the law of karma, the effect can occur in days, years, a lifetime, or in extreme cases, another lifetime. Suppose you have a business and have cheated people of their money. One day, you have that effect of somebody cheating you. Or, you lose all your money and file for bankruptcy. If you have done good things in life like helping people by providing money, shelter, or food, the effect would be that people start helping you. The money keeps flowing. This is called cause and effect. More details can be found in chapter 28 : Karma.

6. Law of Free Will

This law states that everyone has a choice to choose whatever they intend to do. You cannot decide for others as they have free will to decide themselves.

7. Law of Compensation

This law states that you will receive what you give to others. The compensation can come in many forms. The good things you do will eventually come back to yourself, matching the same energy in the forms of good friends, money, support, things, etc.

Suppose you are taking care of your plants as a child every day. Then one day, the plant will compensate you with lots of fruits. This is just one simple example. Say you are helping poor people, eventually the good you do will bring you something in return.

8. Law of Perpetual Transmutation of Energy

There is a saying *"change is the only constant"*. This law states that everybody has the power within them to change the conditions in their lives.

Since everything is changing and nothing is constant, everybody can make a change in their life, whether it's related to money, events, or diseases. You are the creator of your circumstances, and you just need to rearrange the way you think and empower yourself.

Suppose you have been doing negative things to people, and one day you realize the people that you affected. You don't have to be in that regret mode; you have the opportunity to make changes by becoming more positive and doing good things going forward. Avoid resisting change that leads to struggle; instead, embrace the change.

9.Law of Relativity

This law states that everyone will face challenges. These challenges will make you stronger, and strengthen your light within. No matter how bad the situation or the suffering is, there will always be another person who has it worse off than you; it is all relative.

10.Law of Polarity

This law states that within everything, it contains the opposite of itself: *light vs. dark*, *above vs. below*, *negative vs. positive*, etc. One aspect of quality that cannot be experienced without the existence of the opposing aspects.

11. Law of Rhythm

Everything is energy. It vibrates and moves according to its rhythm. These rhythms establish cycles, patterns, seasons, etc. For example, the rotation of the planets, stars, galaxies, the seasons we have every year, and the waves are moving in a rhythm one after the other.

12. Law of Gender

This law states that everything has masculine (Yin) and feminine (Yang) energy. The law itself is the basis for all creation and should remain balanced in everything.

ASCENSION

Where are we and Where are we heading to?

Everything in the universe is operating in cycles, like the cyclic rotation of the earth on its axis and the revolution around the sun, the rotation of the solar system, the galaxy etc., thus all moving in a cyclic motion, obeying the universal laws. Similarly, all life forms inhabiting the planets will go through many evolutionary cycles during their existence.

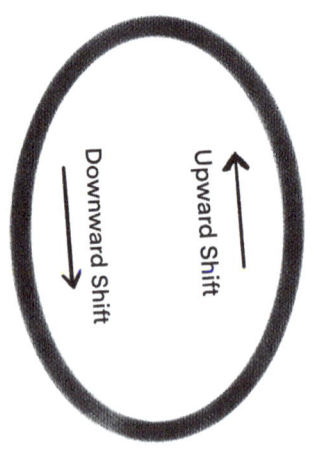

During each cycle, humanity will go through a shift in consciousness, passing both downward and upward shifts. Currently, humanity is in an upward shift and is moving in the direction of Ascension. So Ascension is a natural evolution process of our soul to return to its natural state in a higher dimension.

Ascension (3D to 5D shift)

Ascension is a shift in consciousness by becoming aware of your true self, who you are and integrating your human self with your divine self. This is currently happening on our planet, you and the earth (Gaia), are shifting from 3 dimensions to 5 dimensions (3rd density to 4th density), and are in a transition period. That's why you see so many souls (around 7.7 billion) taking birth at this time; everyone is aware at a deeper level that, they have come here to participate in the ascension graduation.

The earth is already moving in the direction of 5D and asking all the inhabitants to join its journey. But now it is up to you to choose whether you want to stay in 3D or move along with the earth to 5D. It's important to remember you have free will; and it's your choice to make the move.

This is not the first time an ascension has taken place here on earth. It has happened many times in history. But the difference of this time, which has never happened in the entire history of the cosmos, is that, for the first time, both the planet and the inhabitants are shifting together at the same time.

There are many galactic beings, and other beings, who are currently watching, how humanity is doing; they are providing assistance as much as they can. Since the ascension will also help them grow. (Remember, everyone is part of the same Source).

Photon Belt

As the earth rotates around the sun, the entire solar system rotates around a particular star in the Pleiades called Alcyone. It takes 26,000 years to complete a cycle. During each cycle, the solar system enters a particular region called the photon belt. The photon belt is nothing but photon energy, which is a collision of anti-electrons (positrons), causing enormous energy in the form of photon light particles. This affects all planets and all the humans alive at this time. We have already entered this belt somewhere between the last 25 years.

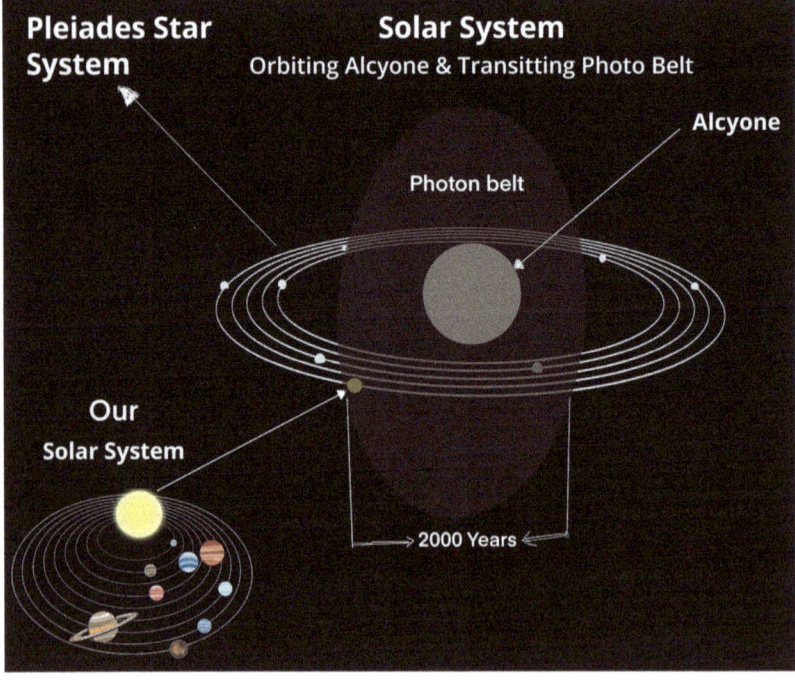

This ocean of light reaching out to humanity has an impact on each person. It provides them a boost in their evolution, but it's entirely up to each person how well they integrate this energy and clear out all their negativity, toxic beliefs, etc. An important part is also recognizing themselves as a part of Source, becoming whole again, and working in love, peace, and harmony. These are all parts of ascension.

Cycles or Yugas - Another Perspective

Time is one of the prominent measurement systems that we use in everyday life. Time is based on a yearly cycle of the earth's rotation around its axis and the sun.

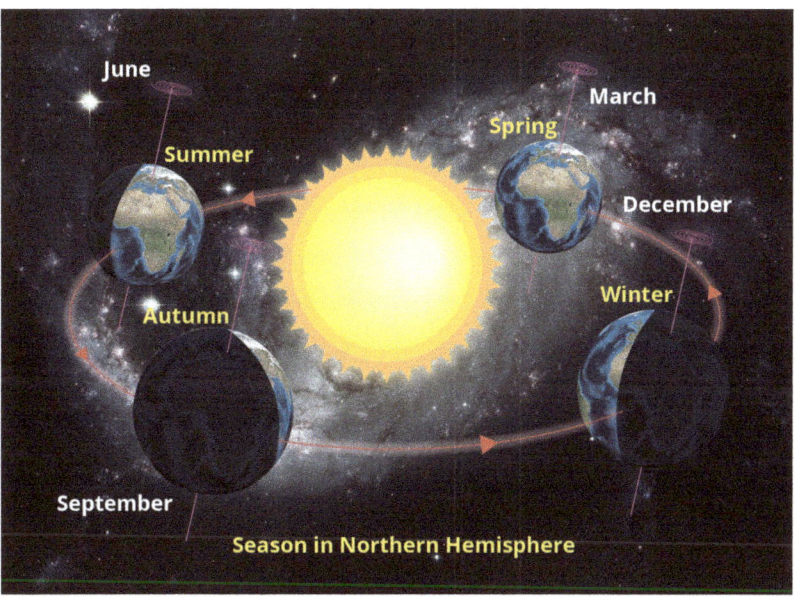

However, there is another cosmic time measurement that many rishis from ancient India have written about called Yugas. One of the recent master, Yukteswar, (1855-1936) from India, has written about Yugas, it's based on the rotation of the sun with its dual star (* yet to be found) in a circular motion across each other and around the galaxy.

*Note: May be Alcyone as specified in previous perspective. Both perspective have difference of 2000 years.

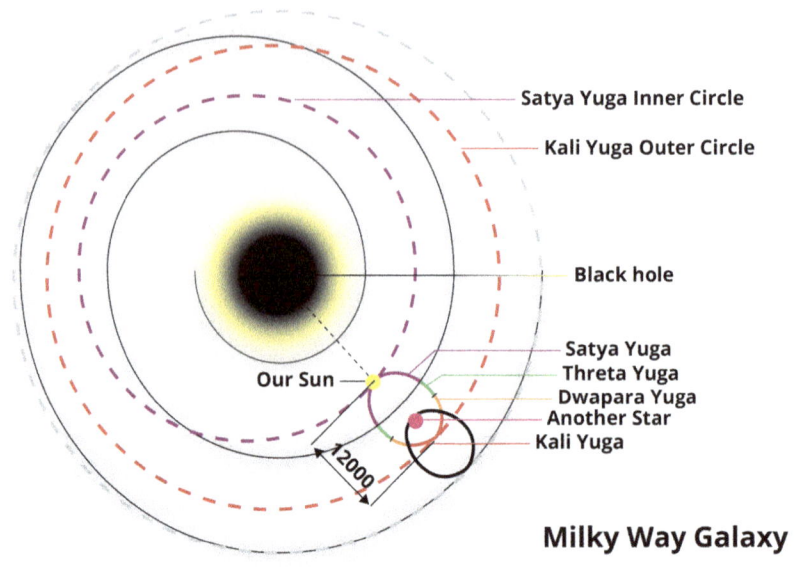

Milky Way Galaxy

Each circular motion with its dual star takes 24,000 years.

The descending part of the circle takes 12,000 years and is called descending Kalpa. The ascent takes 12,000 years and is called ascending Kalpa. Based on this circular motion, they are divided into four yugas:

- **Satya Yuga** is when our sun is closest to the grand center of the galaxy. The period of this yuga is 4,800 years descending and 4,800 years ascending.
- **Treta Yuga** is about 3,600 years descending and 3,600 years ascending.
- **Dwapara Yuga** is about 2,400 years descending and 2,400 years ascending.
- **Kali Yuga** is about 1,200 years descending and 1,200 years ascending. This is when the sun moves the farthest from the grand center of the galaxy, occured around AD 500 that was the end of descending.

From AD 499, the ascending started and are now in Dwapara Yuga in 2020.

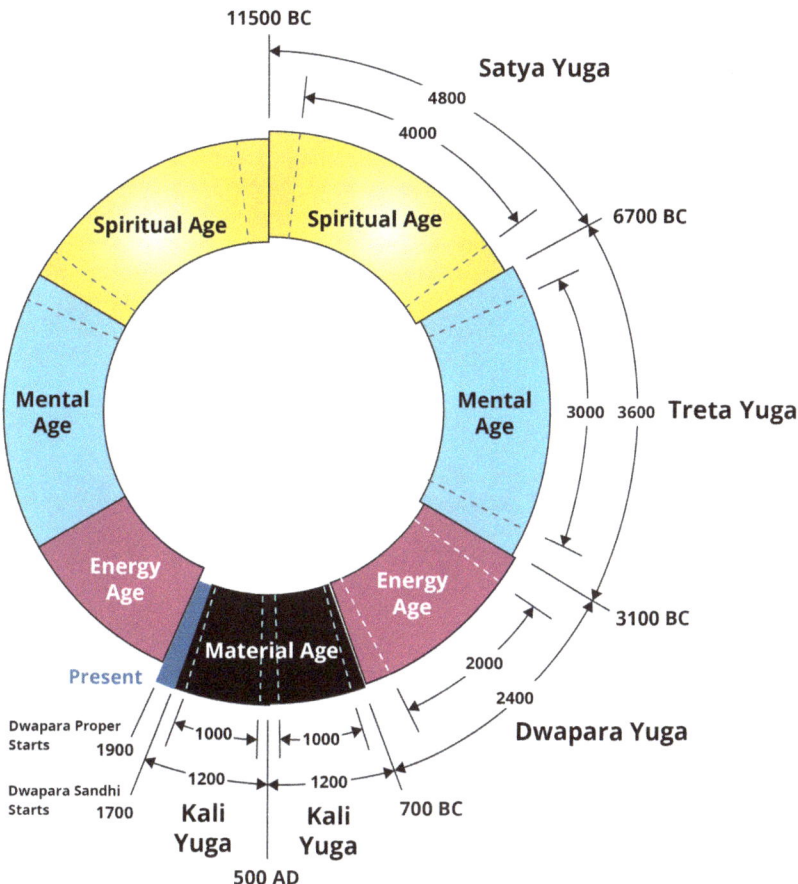

You may be wondering, what does this have to do with you or the human collective?

This has everything to do with you, and these cycles have a major effect on the collective consciousness. As the sun began descending from Satya Yuga, humanity started losing their grasp of spiritual knowledge. By the time of entering Kali Yuga, the human intellect was so diminished that humanity could not comprehend anything beyond the gross material world and far away thought of being spiritual.

Now things are heading back to ascending and have passed Kali Yuga and we are in Dwapara Yuga; slowly the lost knowledge of who you are, is coming back.

Characteristic of 5D Earth (Gaia) and 5D human

Some specific characteristic of 5D earth and humans are:

- We will become the light body using silicon as the primary building block compared to the dense physical body based on carbon that we have now.
- We will know who we are and how we are connected to everyone and everything.
- The foundation of this reality is formed based on love.
- We will be working in unity, rather than separation, and in complete harmony and peace.
- We will start operating from our hearts rather than our minds.
- There is no corruption, chaos, manipulation, or control of any human.
- A heightened sense of perception, intuition, and deep knowledge is our natural state. Telepathy will become our mode of communication with each other.
- Time will become more flexible and malleable. Apart

from the past, present, and future, we can also move around timelines or other dimensions such as parallel reality.

- We won't have to use our memory to access knowledge. There will be a deeper understanding and knowledge with all of us.
- We will know all our incarnation selves across various timelines.
- Our thoughts will be manifested as objects, music, art.
- There is no pollution; the planet will be full of vibrant colors and natural resources.
- There will be new colors, sounds, textures, at an unimaginable amount more than you can think of at this moment.
- Full transparency; nothing can be hidden. Everything is always aligning with the truth.
- Stronger energy centers. There will be a 5th-dimensional chakra system which will be hovering around in our energy field.
- We will be part of the Galactic community.

Ascension Symptoms

- Withdrawing from lots of physical responsibility such as: not running around behind money, power, etc. You will feel as though you don't belong here anymore.
- Feelings to stay out of the crowd and city life, looking for a simple life, and you will have a desire to be with nature.
- You always want to be in the same frequency of people that resonate with you.
- Not interested in participating in any part of 3D social media or news that lowers your vibration.
- There will be some energetic upgrades causing temporary physical symptoms such as headaches, digestive problems, etc.

- You will have an urge to change your diet plan and lean more on organic and natural diets.
- At times it can trigger emotional turbulence, showing you the need to make an effort to clear out those emotions.

What changes are we seeing today, and what we need to do?

During this transition period, many things are happening in your life, the nation, or even the whole world. The high-frequency energy that is coming into the earth's atmosphere is bringing out all the negative emotions, traumas, and shackling the belief systems that are deeply buried within all beings. This has started showing up more frequently. It allows you to reflect and heal your emotions/karma before moving to the next stage of consciousness evolution.

Know that you cannot carry those 3D types of emotions, traumas, and beliefs to 5D reality. This is not just happening for humans. Even nations with all their past karmas like all the wars, pollution, viruses, and controls over other nations are getting cleared away. That is why you are seeing so much chaos everywhere.

You should also know that Time is an illusion, and everything is happening in the PRESENT moment. Yet it is difficult to comprehend using our 3D mind. Ascension reality already exists; once our consciousness has fully absorbed and integrated into this higher frequency of light, then it will expand beyond belief in Time into a PRESENT moment. You will start regaining your innate ability to simultaneously perceive and interact with more than one reality.

As an individual, your consciousness is bouncing around between these two worlds at this time. That is why sometimes you are vibrating high and sometimes low. It is easy to manifest when you are in 5D and becomes difficult when you are in 3D. You will also see you are not able to hang out with your old friends anymore who are still operating in a 3D mindset, or they would have vanished from your life as you move up in frequency.

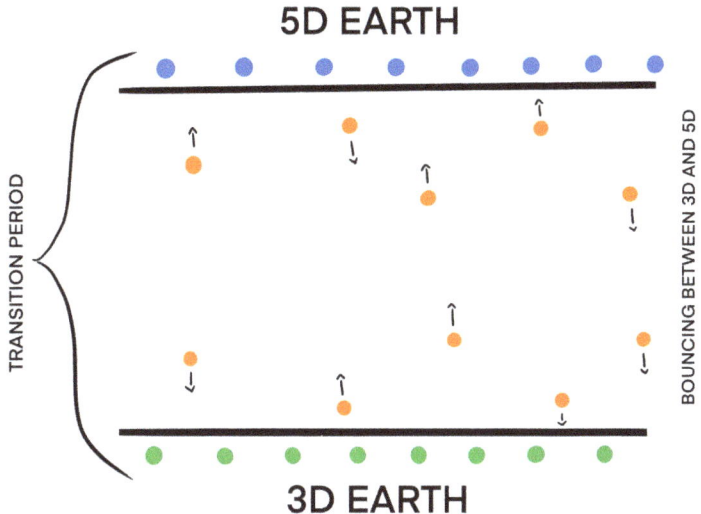

What you need to do:

- Let go of your 3D identity by surrendering your false identity and embodying a greater aspect of your higher self.
- Let go of all your physical accomplishments, pride, or status in the world. These attachments will hold you down to 3D.
- Become unified with everyone and everything. Realize that you are all one and connected.
- Discard all the false ideas and beliefs that are no longer required; see yourself as a being of light and love, that is what you are.
- No longer respond to life from the place of worry, fear, or doubt.
- Raise your vibration and frequency by healing all your unresolved emotions and traumas.

- Meditate and maintain a higher vibration at all times.
- Try to be of service to each other without any expectations.
- Live life as if you are in 5D.
- Keep your energy field clear and always align with the Source.
- Reunite and become one with Gaia; take care of the planet, stop polluting, recycle, and preserve nature in all its life forms.

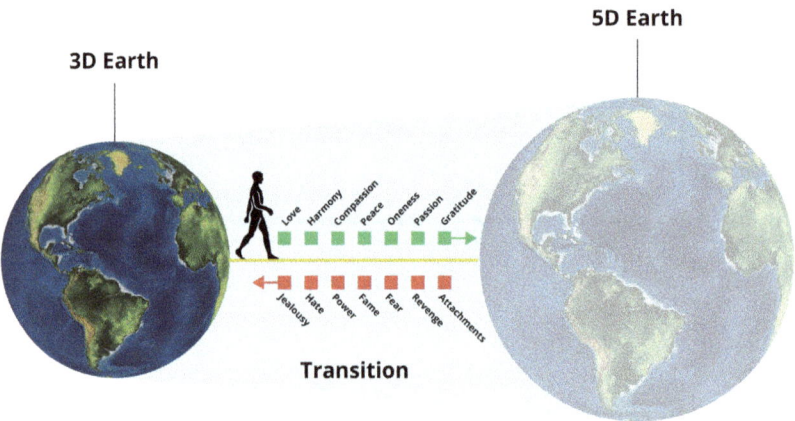

How Ascension is going to play-out

Nobody is sure how the ascension is going to play out since this is the first time it's happening at a mass consciousness level where both the planet and humanity are ascending together.

There may be various scenarios such as:

You will be ascending along with your human bodies and transforming them biologically into light-beings, in order to remain in the higher dimensions.

Or

You may drop your 3D physical body through the process of death, and occupy a new light body in 5D earth.

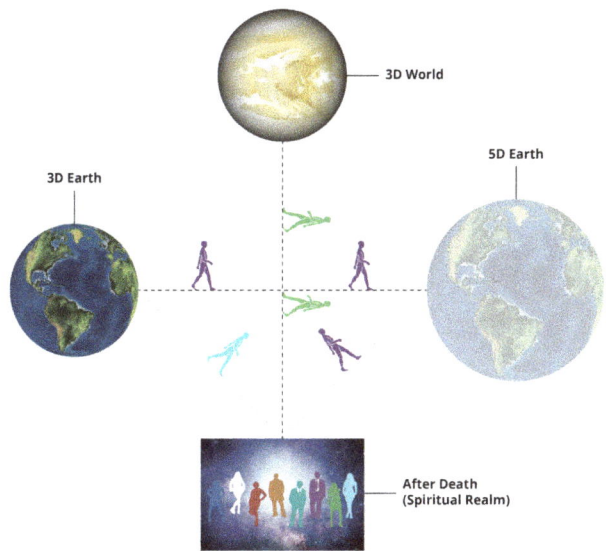

It's important to note, those who do not want to let go of the 3D reality, who are happy in playing the same old games of duality, power, fame, fear, limiting beliefs, controls, attachments, etc. will be able to move to other 3D reality planets. Earth will be a 5D planet, and only inhabitants with higher frequency who can resonate with Gaia can live in that new environment.

How can you prepare for this shift happening?

First of all, you need to examine your limiting beliefs. Look at the stories that you have been holding onto all these years and the expectations that have caused disharmony in you.

Release all those that don't serve you anymore by understanding who you are and open your heart through love, gratitude, and forgiveness to yourself and others.

Note: Some say you need to be at least 51% service to others, then to Self in order to move to the next level of their spiritual growth.

13

SOUL, OVERSOUL, HIGHER SELF, AND PERSONAL SELF

Oversoul

An Oversoul is a collective consciousness of multiple souls. All Souls belonging to that one Oversoul works on a particular theme set by the Oversoul. For example, the theme can be *love* because the Oversoul wants to understand love from all perspectives.

Analogy: Imagine the Oversoul setting up a theme to build a city as shown in the image.

Soul

A Soul is an energy essence of who you are at an individuated consciousness level. Suppose the Oversoul chose love as its theme; then one of the Souls could choose a life to understand *how to love others when you are not loved*. Similarly, other Souls would choose a love theme to understand which can include: parent's love, unconditional love, cheating, etc.

. . .

Analogy

The Soul chooses to build a community inside a city.

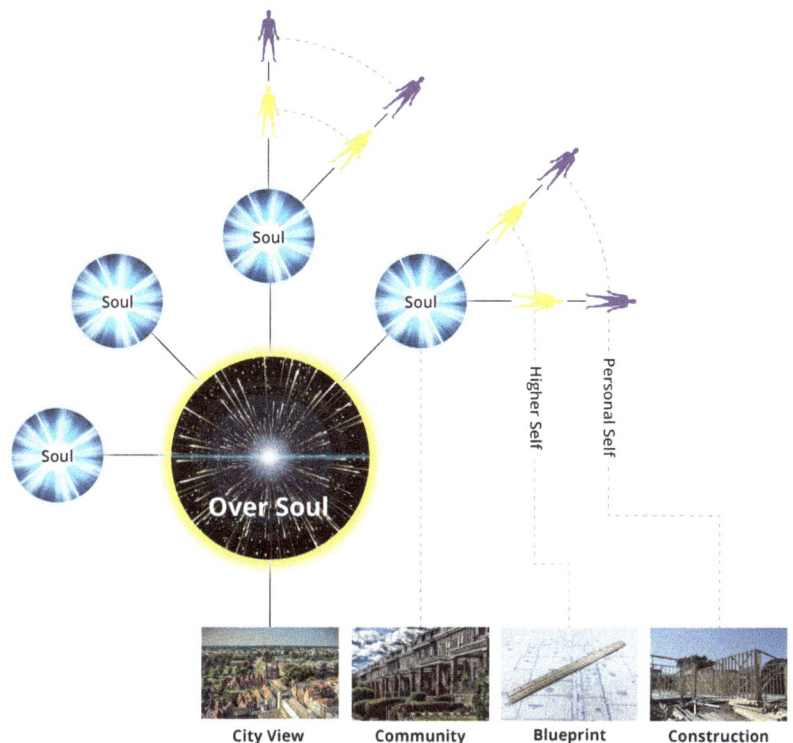

City View | Community | Blueprint | Construction

Higher Self

The higher self is an aspect of yourself that has reached the highest state of consciousness. Imagine yourself as a physical being that has reached the enlightened state with all the best qualities, wisdom, and knowledge.

This is what you aim to become. Like the example above, if your soul has chosen the life *to love others when not loved,* your higher self would have accomplished that task and would become a master in unconditional love.

Analogy: The higher self already has a building plan. In other words, a blueprint of the exact dimensions to build the house in the community.

Personal Self

This is you at your current personality. In this particular life, you are in love with someone and you have noticed that there are some ups and downs because of misunderstandings, bad communication, etc. Your higher self has mastered unconditional love already. If you don't know what to do, you can turn inward to your higher self and seek some guidance. Not only has the higher self mastered unconditional love, but it also has access to the other-self of your previous lives, future lives, or concurrent lives going on in the present.

Analogy: Your Self has started building a house. You have built the house half-way and now you are not sure if further construction will fit the lot that you are constructing.

The next thing that comes to your mind is to look for a building plan and decide how to move forward. In the same way, when you have issues in your life, you can touch base with your higher self to get some guidance.

14

MEDITATION

What is Meditation

Meditation is silencing the Body, Mind, and Intellect. Accomplished through withdrawing your attention from experience to the experiencer, or from the outside world to the inner world. Meditation is one of the common tools that have been used for many centuries to quieten the mind and access higher consciousness.

During meditation, when you withdraw your scattered attention from the outside world, you are immediately confined to the body. As you focus your attention on the third eyes center, which is behind the two eyes, you slowly start withdrawing from the body. For the first time, you realize that you are not the body.

By further withdrawing your attention even from the senses, you realize that you are the mind. And as you go beyond the mind, you come to realize that you are the soul and part of the same Source that everybody and everything is connected to.

Benefits of Meditation

Some of the benefits of doing meditation are:

- Your awareness expands to cosmic limits.
- You become a more peaceful and loving person to yourself and others.
- Cleanse your entire system thoroughly of all impurities and negative qualities.
- You will rejuvenate your body and become healthier.
- Physical and mental stress will reduce.

- The efficiency of the body, mind, and intellect will increase gradually.
- At an advanced level of meditating, you perceive better intuitive powers.

Meditation Method

There are various methods to meditate.

- Silent Meditation- as the name implies, is meditating in a silent state.
- Mindfulness Meditation- the flow of one thought to another.
- Spiritual Meditation- prayers.
- Focused Meditation- through mantra, sound, and pleasant thought.
- Movement Style Meditation- focus on breathing.
- Visual Meditation- visualizing light, imagination, guided by someone.
- Guided Meditation- is a process by which one or more participants meditate in response to guidance provided by a Master or trained practitioner.
- Other forms include walking in nature, playing instruments, painting, etc.

How to Meditate

1. Sit comfortably in a chair or a Padmasana position: *Lotus position.*
2. Pray to the Creator/Source/All That Is/I Am. A prayer like, "*I am praying to calm my mind and shower your blessings*" or something like that.
3. Mention a specific request, but it's up to you whether you want to mention one or you can skip this step.
4. Take a few deep breaths.

5. Gently close your eyes and face forward, relax your legs, hands, neck, shoulders, and facial muscles.
6. Visualize a bright white light entering from the top of your head crown chakra and filling all parts of your body. Let that light expand outside your body, protecting you completely.
7. Now focus your attention on the third eyes center, which is behind your two eyes. After some time, you will notice that your awareness of your body is withdrawn, and your mind is still.

Initially, meditate at least 20 minutes daily. When you start to progress further, increase the meditation time up to two to four hours daily.

While meditating, I get so many thoughts, what should I do?

If your mind chatters too much during meditation, it doesn't matter initially because it can bring you some great insights. Note down the thoughts that come to you and become aware of what's important to you.

You can also determine your vibration by paying attention to your thoughts and emotions that your mind brings. So let go of any sense of perfectionism and instead focus on the benefits. As you start doing meditation daily, gradually these thoughts will start diminishing.

My Experience

I have been doing meditation for many years now. In the initial days, I used to get many thoughts during meditation, but as I started practicing with full determination, the thoughts have been reduced drastically during meditation, and as a byproduct, the intuition started rising.

Sometimes, I get some insights, symbols, or an unknown person/being pops up in my mind's eye. Once in a while, I've no recollection of my body or mind. For example, in one of the meditations, a symbol or some sort of

instrument shows up in my mind's eyes. It was hovering in front of me, and the inside wheel was rotating.

During those days in 2012 while I was learning and practicing some of spiritual knowledge I gained, I saw the benefit that it provides for the body and mind. So, I started initiating satsang with few kids and adults at that time. This was to make sure that I don't forget that knowledge, and also to show others the benefits that they can also achieve.

Kids meditating in one of the session.

15

MIND

Conscious, Subconscious, and Superconscious Mind

Our mind can be categorized into three sections:

1. Conscious Mind
2. Subconscious Mind
3. Superconscious Mind

CONSCIOUS MIND

You are aware of the conscious mind, and it deals with the daily activity that you engage in during your waking state. For example, when you wake up, the activities that you do such as drinking coffee, working out, dealing with clients, your boss, playing with your children, etc. are engaged through your conscious mind at that particular moment.

Subconscious Mind

The subconscious mind is your inner mind where your beliefs, memories, and emotions are stored. It records everything that you experience in your life, including your childhood experience, or your past lives, and stores in your subconscious mind.

All your beliefs, thoughts, actions, likes, and dislikes, are all stored in this area of your mind. You would have noticed while driving from work to home, that sometimes you don't even know how you reached home without being aware of all the roads and turns you took, but somehow you reached home safely. This is the subconscious mind that took control while your conscious mind was not active.

Superconscious Mind

The superconscious mind is the higher mind, or you may also call it the higher self. All your inspiration, intuition, and wisdom comes from this area of your mind. Your awareness enters the superconscious when you are in deep meditation without any thoughts, emotions, and in stillness with complete bliss, love, and peace. This area of the mind contains information about your in-between lives.

Ego

Ego is your accumulated personality that has formed throughout this life and many other lifetimes. You have two distinct personalities: one from ego and the other from the soul. Each of them has unique characteristics and were created to perform as one aspect of your Being.

The Ego was created for survival instincts in this physical world, whereas the soul was the driving force of your Being. Although, as time passed, the ego-personality took over and became in charge of interacting with the world today. The soul then became a dormant observer.

To understand what aspect of your Being is interacting with the world today, you need to know the characteristics of Ego and the soul.

EGO

- The Ego is a personality aspect.
- Love is limited and conditional.
- Service to self.
- It contains both positive and negative qualities: Positive qualities are limited and based on conditions. Negative qualities are jealousy, fear, hate, anger etc.

SOUL

- The soul is a divine aspect.
- Love is limitless and unconditional.
- Service to others.
- The qualities of source exist in soul such as Compassion, unconditional love, peace, joy, and fairness.

The ideal nature of your Being will be when you eliminate the negative aspect of your ego and expand the positive aspect of the Ego from limited to unlimited, condition to unconditional, working in that direction until it allows the complete aspect of the soul to manifest through it.

Brain and Brain Waves

The mind controls the brain and is composed of:

- The right hemisphere: focuses more on creativity, imagination, intuition, art, rhythm, music, etc.
- The left hemisphere: focuses more on logical thinking, reasoning, analytics, sequencing, computation, linear, etc.

Most people who are more spiritual tend to use more of their right brain than the left brain.

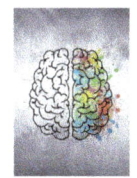

Brain Waves

Brain waves are electric impulses and characterized by the frequency of neuronal firings in our brain. There are four brain waves:

1. Beta waves
2. Alpha waves
3. Theta waves
4. Delta waves

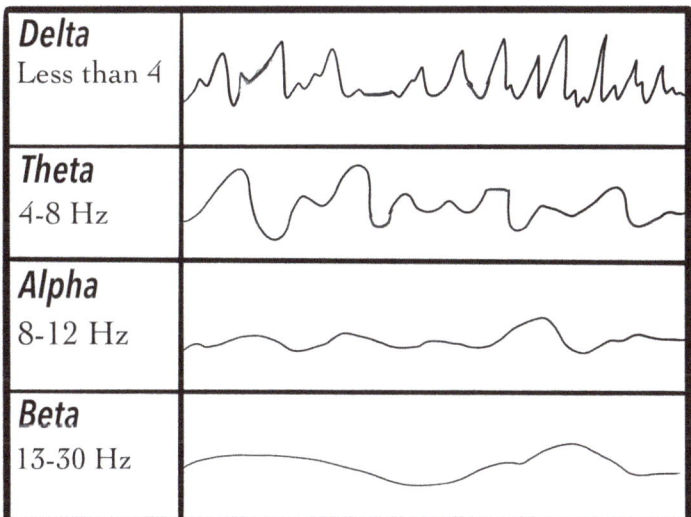

Beta Waves

- It is predominant when you are in a waking state and consciously processing your thoughts.
- The brain waves pulsate between 13 to 30 cycles per second.

- Your inner voice can be dimly heard when you are in a waking state.

Alpha Waves

- When you are in a relaxed state, you shift to the alpha state. This is the state where you are in-between conscious and subconsciousness.
- The brain waves pulsate between 8 to 12 cycles per second.
- During the alpha state, you are more conducive to accelerated learning, problem solving, creativity, inspiration, motivation, etc.
- It is easier to hear your inner voice during this time.

Theta Waves

- You reach this state when you experience deep meditation, creativity, or during deep sleep.
- The brain waves pulsate between 4 to 8 cycles per second.
- During this state, you focus primarily on your inner self and maintaining a conscious contact with your physical body and the outside world is difficult.
- During the Theta state, you are more conducive to peace, transformation, mystical truth, etc.

Delta Waves

- You reach the delta state when you are in a dreamless and deep sleep level.
- The brain waves pulsate between 0.5 to 4 cycles per second.
- During the Delta states, you are more conducive to divine knowledge, miracle healing, intuitions, oneness with the Source, insights, etc.
- Practiced yogis can consciously achieve this state.

As a human being, our brainwaves fluctuate depending upon the status of our brain activity. When you are making an action-oriented decision, you are in beta mode, and your perceptions calibrate to the third-dimensional reality. When you are relaxed and in a creative mood, you are in the Alpha state. Your perception is between the fourth and third-dimensional reality. When you are deeply spiritual, your perception is between the fourth and fifth-dimensional reality. When you focus on your non-physical reality, your perceptions would be from your higher selves, and you will be able to live all realities at once.

16

TIME

Time in our world is a man-made illusionary marker created based on the rotation of our planet around its sun. It exists on our planet so that it's possible to keep track of all our past, present, and future events that we all agree upon. Nowadays, we often see that time is becoming more malleable.

For instance, when you are deeply involved in doing something that you enjoy, you often wonder, *time flies so fast,* and the same is true when you are bored in doing something. You feel that time has completely stopped or slowed down.

In other higher dimensional realities, the concept of time is different. They use the concept of focusing their consciousness on a particular event that they are interested in, to experience at that particular moment. Whether it can be in the past or future from our human perspective, they can jump into that time to experience it.

Imagine, you as a human being, linearly experience events as shown in a horizontal line. Whereas, higher dimensional beings experience time in the PRESENT moment. All events are happening in the same PRESENT moment, as shown in the vertical line. They focus their consciousness on any moment that they want to experience, whether it be the 1960s or the 2020s, they go right to that time and experience it. Similar to turning to any page number in a book to read and not reading linearly, chapter-wise.

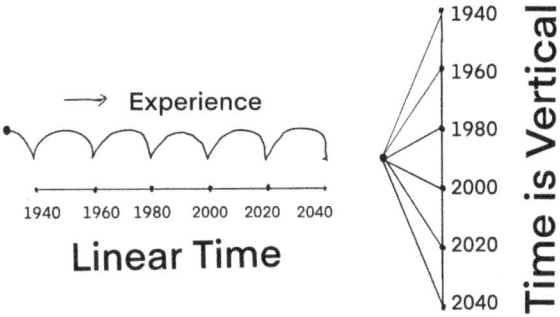

Can you manipulate time according to our needs?

Yes, it's possible. Suppose you are in the office and worried about reaching school on time to pick up your children. Instead of worrying, why don't you see yourself reaching there exactly on time? Remember, everything is based on your vibration, and time becomes more flexible when you are in that high state of vibration; things happen according to your needs.

You will notice that traffic is clear or you will be guided to alternative roads with less traffic, or perhaps, you are riding smoothly without any red lights. It takes some practice to change and adapt to this type of concept, but it is achievable.

Timelines

A timeline is a path where there are beginnings and endpoints. In between starting and the endpoint, you can mark events that have happened. For example, you can create a timeline about your life.

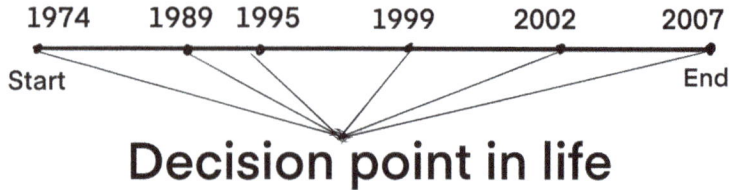

Decision point in life

Multiple Timelines

You are under the impression that you follow one particular timeline in your entire life, but as your awareness starts expanding, you realize that you are a multidimensional being. You live across various timelines, but are aware of one at a time, where your consciousness is focused upon.

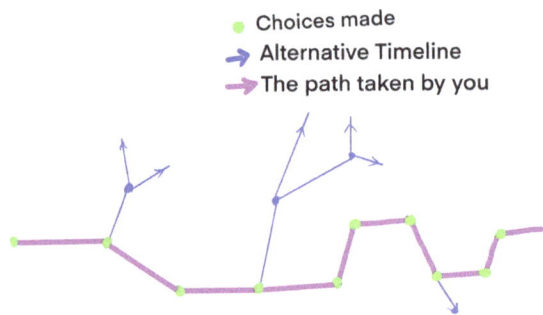

For example, during the year 1989, let's say, you were deciding whether to study medicine or engineering. You finally made a decision that you want to pursue engineering; and you continued that path. Although, as a soul, it wants to experience everything to the fullest, every possibility, choice, and scenario, that its human counterpart comes across while making decisions in their life. So another part of you will continue to pursue medicine and follow that path in another parallel reality or parallel universe.

In general, every decision and choice that you make will have another part of your fractal living in the reality which you never chose to pursue (blue lines); so, infinite realities and timelines exist.

Choosing Timeline

There are infinite timelines with every possibility and probability existing right now. It is up to you to choose what timeline you want to be in by knowing the very fact that you create your reality. As you work on your emotions and raise your vibration, focus upon the thought that you want to manifest in your life.

By taking action with your highest excitement, you will automatically jump to that timeline where the thing that you want to manifest already exists.

You are capable of choosing the timeline that you want, whether it is for material things, peace on earth, or anything else. You can create and choose the one that you prefer to live in.

You can also project your consciousness to different timelines. You project to the ones you want to explore before physically moving to that timeline and bringing that information back to check whether you are in alignment with it or not. This allows you to create a new one that you prefer to have.

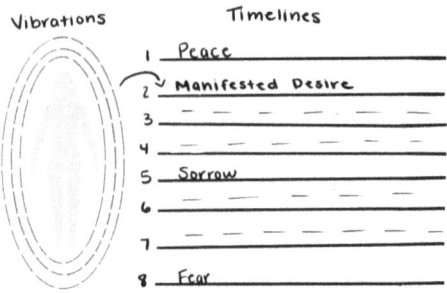

This concept also explains that everybody can have whatever they wish for. For example, when two persons are competing with each other, only one person can win. What happens when they are at a higher vibration and in complete alignment with their thoughts, feelings, and actions at the same time? In that case, both of them will win since each of them will follow their timeline where that individual is a winner.

Merging Timelines

This is going to be complicated to explain, but I'll do my best.

Example: Joe is in the afterlife, and he decides to take a journey to be born on earth. He plans his life path and the mission that he wants to achieve when he is there. Once he is born, he has no recollection of his plan, and he has a free will to choose whatever path he wants to take.

Every time he makes a new choice, whether he makes that decision as per his life path or against it, a fractal of Joe will split at that moment and continue on that path when the actual Joe doesn't want to take that path.

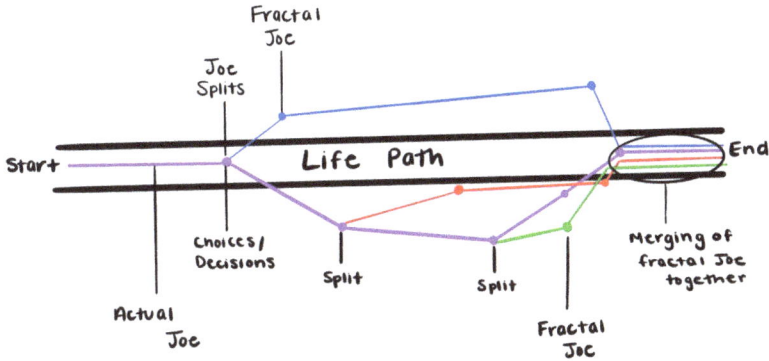

During his life, he makes countless decisions and choices. So there could be multiple fractals of Joe following different timeline, but, at any moment, Joe is aware of only one timeline where his consciousness is focused upon. As Joe starts making better choices and following his life path, some of his fractal timelines will begin merging. Joe can feel the experience that his fractal had at the energetic level, even though the actual Joe didn't experience it. You will have this type of experience often like when you have some feeling not to take the road you usually take and choose another road that day. Later you realize that you made the right decision of not taking that road since there were multiple accidents, and that road was shut down.

In this scenario, one of your fractals would have taken that road and would have experienced the accidents. But as you merged, you were able to access that incident energetically and were able to make a better choice of not taking that road.

Similar to individual timelines, there are collective timelines at a city, nation, or planetary level. As the consciousness of the people expands, the choices and decisions they make at the group level will affect the collective timeline as well. Some timelines will start merging, or new timelines will start creating at a collective level, affecting the memories that you used to hold.

One of the best examples would be the Mandela effect. Many people believe that Nelson Mandela died in jail, while others believe he lived several years after his release. Another example would be the fairy tale movie *"Snow White and the Seven Dwarfs"*. Depending upon the timeline that you focus on, there are two versions of this. She either asks the magic mirror,

"Mirror, Mirror on the wall, who's the fairest of them all?" or, *"Magic Mirror on the wall, who's the fairest of them all?"*

17

SYNCHRONICITY

S ynchronicity is something that you intend and believe. Ultimately it shows up in your reality very soon. It can be in minutes or within a few days, depending upon the intensity of the feeling that you have at that moment.

For Example, when you're thinking of a person and suddenly a phone rings and it's the same person who is calling you on the other side. Your immediate reaction would be *what a coincidence*, but it's not, this is synchronicity.

Nothing in the universe is a coincidence; everything happens according to nature 's intentions. We 're all connected, so the outer reality showing up to you is just a reflection of what's going on inside of you.

Synchronicity is common in my life.

Synchronicity is a common occurrence in my life. I might be thinking about something, and suddenly I look at my watch, and it would be showing one of these times 11:11, 12:12, 5:55, 4:44, or 3:33. I start laughing at it because earlier even I used to think *what a coincidence*, but I know now, it's a type of message or response that the universe is providing to me synchronically.

Even while I was writing this book, there were so many synchronicities happening that it was hard to believe myself. Let me specify a few synchronicities that occurred while I was writing some sections of this book, and have never told anyone what I was writing at the time.

Cold

In one of the examples, I wrote about the cold and how it affected me. After writing it, I went out and sat in my backyard. Suddenly my son's friend came to enquire about my son and sat in front of me. While he was waiting for my son, he started a conversation with me about the weather and specified that he doesn't like the cold, and how it affects his body. I was stunned. Why would he talk about the cold all of a sudden? It was synchronicity.

Music

While I was writing about music, how it affects your vibration, my daughter came and asked me to purchase speakers to hear music since she cannot hear properly through the phone.

Illness

While writing on the topic of illnesses, I heard one of my friends becoming very sick and they needed treatment.

Alexander

I was writing the story of Alexander the Great as one of my examples, and suddenly I got text messages from my friend about Greece.

Death and Reincarnation

One night I had just finished writing a topic about death and how few people will go through the tunnel experience. After writing, I went to the kitchen to have my dinner, my kids were watching some cartoons in the living room which is right across from the kitchen.

While I was eating, suddenly, in the cartoon, they were showing a tunnel experience that one of the characters was having. I was stunned to see this, and thought, *what a synchronicity that the universe is showing me*.

Time for Ascension

I just finished writing the topic, *Time for Ascension* and went to bed to sleep. My wife suddenly asked about the time, and how it works from a metaphysical perspective.

Perspective

I was beginning to write a chapter on perspective before I started typing, I just thought, let me check YouTube and see what's going on today. The first thing that popped up on the front page was *Coronavirus: Perspective from the Spirit Realm*.

Create your own reality

I was writing about this topic, *Create your own reality,* in my office room, and at the same time, I heard a conversation going on with my spouse and one of her friends over the phone. My spouse was talking about how *you create your reality* and trying to explain it to her friend. She didn't even know I was writing about this topic.

Samadhi

While I was researching and writing about this topic, my daughter saw my meditation diary on the bookshelves. She was curious to read what I had written. While reading the diary, she showed me the content written nine years ago. I was stunned to see there were two synchronized themes that I had written about when I was in a meditative state.

1. Thoughts about writing a book.

2. The meditative experience that I had and specified about merging with the environment.

I don't remember wanting to write a book, and I was writing on the very same topic of samadhi state. Also, the journal entry was in May 2011, which is the same month as I'm currently writing about this topic.

How can you use synchronicity to your benefit?

Synchronicity works on the basis of your intent and belief. If you ask with intent and believe without any resistance, the guides, or your higher self, will come back to you with some kind of sign.

It can either be the number plate of the car stopping next to you, a billboard sign or a friend talking to you about it. You will immediately know it's a sign you got back from higher intelligence.

You can practice it:

1. Think of any number and notice how many times it shows up during your day.
2. Parking lot synchronicity. You'll often go to a shopping mall, and there will be no easy access to parking. But this time, go with the intent that you will find a parking spot, at the right moment. When you are there, believe in it without any doubt and notice what happens.

Practice this until you become an expert and know for sure that things happen synchronically.

18

MASTERS (GURUS OR TEACHERS)

For simplicity, I will refer in this chapter as Master, instead of specifying Master or Gurus, or Teachers every time.

Spiritual Masters

When the student is ready, the Master arrives synchronically. So if you are a seeker and truly seeking spiritual growth, the Master will show up at that right moment, whether they are physical or non-physical beings.

At one point in your life, you always want someone who can guide you spiritually and help you overcome the issues, situations, problems that you are facing. If you seek with true intent, there will be someone who comes to your life at the right time and guide you.

It doesn't mean that they are going to appear on your doorstep. It means you may be introduced to them while randomly watching a YouTube video, and you felt like meeting them in person since the message was very uplifting to you. Or, your friend could have come across a Master and introduced that Master to you as well. So there are various avenues that a Master could be introduced into your life.

A few important points to keep in mind

How do you know if a particular Master, Teacher, or Guru, is the right one for you? Go according to your feelings. The attraction of pure love from the Master will start pulling you from within yourself. You know, they are the right one for you at that moment.

There are so many Masters in this world that no two Masters are the same. Their levels of knowledge and achievement vary based on the spiritual progress they have made so far. So a Master can take you to a certain level in your spiritual progression based on that particular Master's capacity.

After that, you may have to look for another Master who can take you further in your spiritual growth, and maybe another until you find a perfect living Master who knows everything and has been in all levels of planes and dimensions, operating from the totality of consciousness (All That Is) in his current human form.

Nowadays, you notice that there are so many non-physical beings who are currently helping humanity by communicating through individuals who are channelers. Non-physical beings can interact with a human persona. The messages that they provide are uplifting and will help you in your spiritual progression. They can be your master or guide as well.

Note: Beware of any monetary spending with the services provided by many spiritual groups. Use your judgment before spending and ask yourself whether they are helping you or taking you for a ride?

19

COLLECTIVE CONSCIOUSNESS

L ike the individual consciousness, there is a collective consciousness that shapes the physical reality. This collective consciousness is constantly fed by everyone, living on this planet based on thoughts, feelings, beliefs, and actions enabling all at a planetary level to move forward in evolution and spiritual growth beyond the limited capabilities.

You have noticed some scientists who are working on similar problems will find the solution at the same time, even though they don't even know each other and have never shared any information, why? Because of collective consciousness.

Collective consciousness is something similar to having a Wikipedia in the clouds. Everyone has access to it, and it's constantly being added to, or updated by users. Some users may add content, some users make updates, and others read content to gain knowledge.

Collective consciousness is constantly fed by each person. You interact either in uploading or downloading mode all the time. So the world where you are today is completely based on the current collective consciousness, and what the future holds is also based on what everyone as a collective thinks. Everything is within humanity's own hands to create the future.

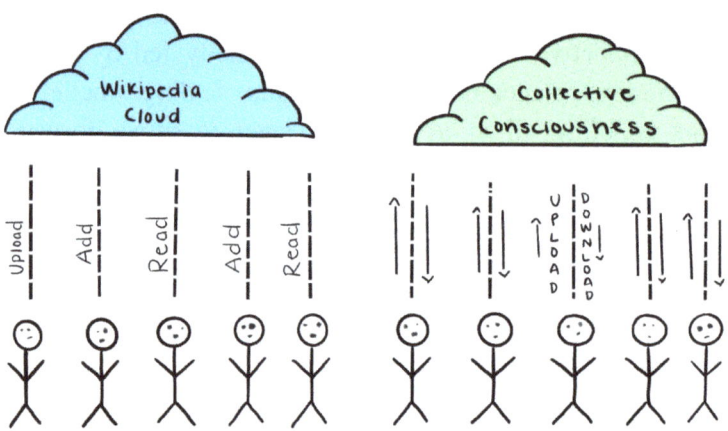

How to change the collective consciousness for the betterment of all?

If enough people hold the thought and intention to change the world for the better, then in no time, you will see things changing to that intent. The intention is not just constrained to the physical bodies. It affects the part of the collective consciousness, which in return shapes the physical reality.

Example: If enough people reach the target that humanity has not reached before, and hold that light for others to join, then there won't be much time before the rest of humanity catches up to the new target.

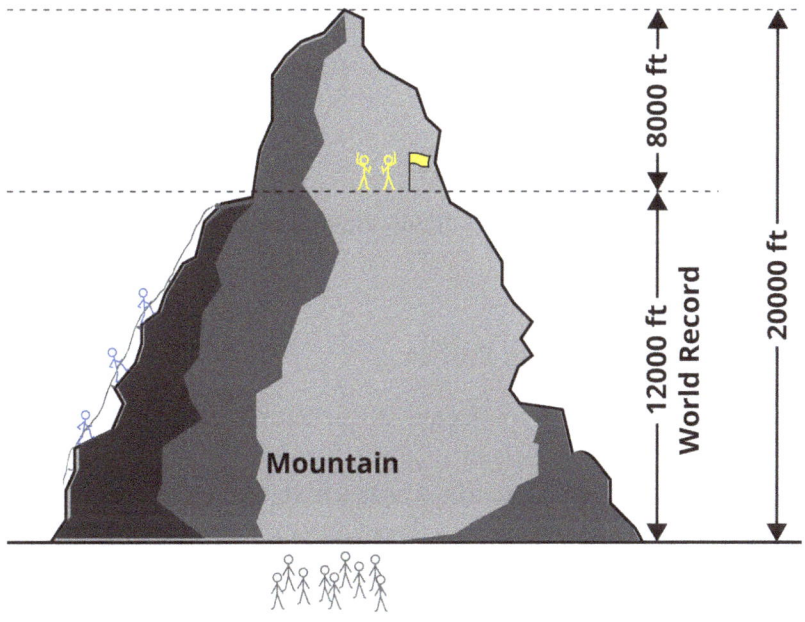

Let's say 10,000ft is the world record for climbing a mountain. This information is now stored in our collective consciousness. Whenever any new person tries to climb to that height, he either makes it to 10000ft or less than that; it becomes hard to go further than 10,000ft.

Suppose a few people with self-determination and confidence try to reach 12,000ft and succeed, it then becomes a new record and gets stored in our collective consciousness. Now, the rest of humanity has the option to reach even higher. You will notice that it becomes easier for most of humanity to reach 12,000ft, which was very difficult earlier when no one reached more than 10,000ft.

The collective consciousness holds at 12,000ft, and if enough people try with full confidence and determination to reach 20,000ft and succeed, in no time humanity will reach the top of the mountain.

The ultimate goal is to know who you are and to find oneness in everything. If enough lightworkers reach and hold that torch for the rest of humanity to join, then soon, you will notice the rest of humanity catch-up. You will see a different physical reality where all enlightened souls walk on the streets in complete love, peace, and harmony.

Collective consciousness effects

There were a few experiments conducted related to the collective consciousness.

Global Consciousness Project:

This experiment was conducted at Princeton University under the direction of Roger Nelson using a Random Number Generator (RNG). Under normal conditions, the RNG produces 50% - Zeros and 50% - Ones, but under lab conditions with the intention set for either value, it delivers results that are not 50% - Zeros and 50% - Ones.

So when they placed RNG across the globe and started collecting data, they would notice a change in the patterns when there were any global events taking place before or after the event occurred. It happened on September 11th, when the twin towers attack occurred. They noticed that randomness went away slightly 2 to 3 hours before the time of attack until some time after the attack. This shows that a great event synchronizes the feelings of millions of people, and it gives a clue that it's possible to change the world according to a wish if enough people feel it.

Maharishi Effect

A study was conducted by Maharishi University on how a small percentage of people (1% of the total population) can change the world by holding a group meditation.

A large group of people practiced Transcendental Meditation during the intervention period of 2007-2010 and found a significant decrease in the crime rate during that period. This shows that a group of collective consciousness using meditation techniques can produce a measurable result in improving the quality of life.

Is it possible to heal someone using collective consciousness? Try this experiment yourself. If someone is sick, try gathering some friends and family members who have the same intent to heal that person. Pray or meditate at the same time, and see what happens.

∼

20

CHAKRAS

C hakras are like energetic centers and provide life force energy to the physical body.

The connection of our physical and non-physical bodies are connected and energized through chakras.

There are seven major chakras and many minor chakras that connect to the major one.

Root Chakra (Muladhara)

Color
Red.
Location
The base of the spine near the anal region.
About
It's about grounding yourself by connecting your energy to mother earth and providing stability to survive.
1 Dimensional energy is part of your awareness.
Element
Earth.
Characteristic
Survival, Grounding, Security, Safety, and Basic Needs.
Physical
Hips, Knees, Spine, Feet, Intestines, Legs, Vitality, Stamina, and Strength.
Imbalance
When imbalanced, you feel insecure and are always in survival mode.
Excessive negativity.
Ego loves to be in this place.
Eating disorder.
How to Balance
Be grounded as often.
Do meditation.
Try to do earth-related activities. For example, going out in nature for a walk, gardening, cooking, etc.
When balanced, you feel accomplished and at peace.
Healing Stones
Stones, Ruby, Quartz, Rhodonite, Garnet, and Coral.

Sacral Chakra (Swadhisthana)

Color
Orange.
Location
Just beneath the Naval.
About
It's about your identity as a human.
Creative energy.
Sexuality and reproductive capacity.
Connecting to energy of plant kingdom.
Element
Water.
Characteristic
Emotions, Feelings, Sexuality, Reproductivity, and Relationships.
Physical
The bladder, Fluid Functions, Lower Back, Ovaries, Testicles, Womb, and Uterus.
Imbalance
Being ruled by emotions.
Dependency on others or substances.
Either an over or lack of sexual desire.
How to Balance
Withdraw from too many indulgences and direct that energy into your heart. Enjoy while you are working.
Try to be creative; for example, painting, pottery. When balanced, you will be in enjoyment, wellness, and abundance that life offers you.
Healing Stones
Agate.

Solar Plexus Chakra (Manipura)

Color
Yellow

Location
Stomach area or upper part of the belly.
About
Sense of Persona Power, self-confidence.
Element
Fire.
Characteristic
Clarity, Will/Personal Power, Leadership Quality, Taking
Responsibility of Oneself, Independence, and Self-Discipline.
Physical
Digestion, Stomach, Gail Bladder, Pancreas, Liver, and Nervous
System.
Imbalance
Issues with the digestive system.
Excessive authority, control over people, and environment.
Misuse of power and lack of clear direction.
Helplessness or Irresponsibility.
How to Balance
Regain your will power and know that you are part of the Source
energy. Open your heart with love and compassion.
When balanced, you feel a sense of confidence, personal power,
and ability to make the right decisions.
Healing Stones
Yellow, Gold Tourmaline, Citrine, and Tiger's Eye

Heart Chakra (Anahata)

Color
Green.
Location
Center of The Chest.
About
This chakra is all about expressing love and compassion to
everything. It includes a love for yourself and others
unconditionally.
Element

Air
Characteristic
Love, Compassion, Forgiveness, Transformation, and
Relationship.
Physical
Hands, Arms, Breathing Circulations, Heart, Lungs, Fingers,
Ribs, and Immune System.
Imbalance
Jealousy. Fear. Emotionally Down.
Holding Grudges. Overly Defensive.
Issues with the Heart.
How to Balance
Work with the breathing exercise.
Appreciate everything.
Show compassion to yourself and others.
Forgiveness.
Express your Gratitude.
When balanced, you feel love and will have compassion for
everything happening in your life.
Healing Stones
Pink Quartz, Clear Quartz, Green Calcite, Emerald, Malachite,
and Tourmaline.

Throat Chakra (Vishuddha)

Color
Blue.
Location
The base of the Throat.
About
It's all about communication and personal truth.
Element
Aether or Akasha.
Characteristic
Expression, Truth, Communication, Purpose, and Ideas.

Physical

Throat, Jaw, Lower Neck, Vocal Chords, Thyroid, and Lungs.

Imbalance

Lack of control of speech.

Not listening to others.

Fear of speaking.

Lies.

Shyness.

Secretiveness.

Lack of purpose in life.

How to Balance

Express with full clarity and truth.

When balanced, you will speak with love, kindness, and truth.

Healing Stones

Aquamarine, Lapis Lazuli, Sapphire, and Turquoise.

Third Eye Chakra (Ajna)

Color

Indigo.

Location

Forehead between the two eyes.

About

It's about opening your reality beyond this physical world.

Element

Light/Inner Sound (Vibration).

Characteristic

Intuition, Vision, Psychic Abilities, Creativity, and Connection to Wisdom.

Physical

Eye, Ears, Nose, Lower Brain, Upper Neck, Pituitary Gland, and Sinuses.

Imbalance

Feeling stuck.

Lack of vision.

Lack of clarity.

Delusional.

How to Balance

Meditate.

Follow your instincts.

Ground yourself to the earth.

When balanced, you will be in tune with both the material and the spiritual worlds.

Healing Stones

Amethyst, Fluorite, and Sugilite.

Crown Chakra (Sahasrara)

Color

Violet.

Location

Top of the head.

About

It's our spiritual connection to the universe.

Element

Time and Space.

Characteristic

Awareness, Realization, Bliss, and Presence.

Connection to higher dimensions.

Transcendence of Limitation.

Physical

Cerebral Cortex, Nervous System, Pineal Gland, Upper Brain, Skull, and Skin.

Imbalance

Disconnection from spirit.

Disconnection from physicality.

Closed mindedness.

How to Balance

Balancing other chakras will bring you closer to experience spiritual connection in your crown chakra.

When balanced, you feel a state of enlightenment and complete oneness with everyone and everything.

Healing Stones

Calcite, Diamond, Moonstone, Opal, and Zircon.

21

PSYCHIC ABILITIES (INTUITION OR SIXTH SENSE)

P sychic abilities have an innate ability to connect to higher realms and receive information.

You live in a multidimensional universe, where the information may come from any non-physical consciousness beings such as:

- Guides who have been with you since you were born.
- A higher self.
- The Source or Universe.
- Higher-dimensional or other planetary beings.

You wonder why only certain people have those abilities. Everyone is born with psychic abilities and it is predominant during the early stage of your childhood. As you start relying more on your physical sense and stop using your internal ones, you start weakening your psychic abilities.

Apart from that, some choose to shut down because of fear and the situations they faced in previous lifetimes. Few of them ignore it completely, and for others, it is blocked due to the life lesson they choose for this lifetime or they are not evolved enough to responsibly handle the gift. As you raise your vibration, with some practice, you can regain this ability.

Clairvoyant, Clairsentient, Clairaudient, and Claircognizance.

Each of us is inclined to one of these psychic abilities or sometimes a combination of these, but one of them will be more prominent than the rest.

Clairvoyant

The ability to receive messages through the mind's eye in the form of visions, images, or symbols. Visions can be direct answers to questions you would have asked in higher realms. You may be more inclined to clairvoyant if:

- You see color, symbol, pictures, or objects during meditation or when you close your eyes.
- You always dream and remember things about your dreams.
- You are more creative in arts or graphic design.
- You have a good imagination.

Clairaudient

The ability to hear messages through spiritual or physical ears. You are more often inclined to clairaudient if:

- You hear voices.
- Often you hear ringing or buzzing sounds.
- You are a good listener.

Clairsentient

The ability to sense messages through feelings, downloads, and energy fields. You are more often inclined to clairsentient if:

- You perceive even the subtle change in the energy around you.
- You feel the emotions and feelings of others, including plants, animals, or surroundings.
- Sometimes for no reason, you become more emotional.

Claircognizance

The ability to know things spontaneously. You are more often inclined to claircognizance if:

- You will know about stuff that you did not read, listen to, or learn about.
- You get creative or inspirational ideas.
- You know whether someone is telling the truth.

Real Incident

This happened during the 1990s. A man and woman who loved each other very much got engaged. One weekend, the man came home from his job in the wilderness working on roads and dams, to his fiance. He hadn't eaten all day trying to get his work done so that he could spend the weekend with her.

When he arrived at the house, he found that all his friends had surprised him for his bachelor party. He went along with them, and within a few hours, partying on an empty stomach caught up with him. He ended up admitted to the hospital for alcohol poisoning. His friends phoned his fiance on the landline and let her know the news, and said they would call her when he was to be discharged. They apologized profusely. She was saddened but soon fell asleep again, waiting for the call.

Back at the hospital, the man woke up feeling a lot better after they pumped his stomach. It was 4 am, and he wanted to go home immediately. So he signed his discharge papers and got out of bed. He didn't think to phone his fiance; he already knew she would be there soon intuitively.

From her perspective, she woke up at 3:30 am. There were no cell phones that were easily accessible in those days, only had landlines to contact each other. She hadn't received a call yet. But, she just woke up and knew it was time to go. She got in her car and drove to the hospital.

He walked out of the hospital and stood outside at 4 am. He waited for five minutes, his fiance then pulled up in the car and picked him up. All he wanted to do was go home and spend time with her.

This shows how intuitive they are.

Third Eye (Pineal Gland)

The pineal gland or the third eye is a small gland that is located right in between your two eyes and the center of the brain; it is said to be the seat of the soul. It's a portal to communicate with higher consciousness beyond this physical reality.

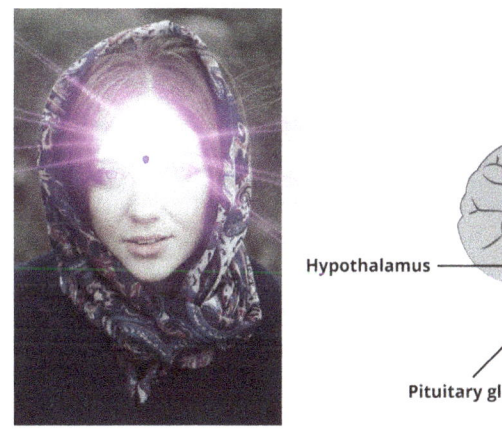
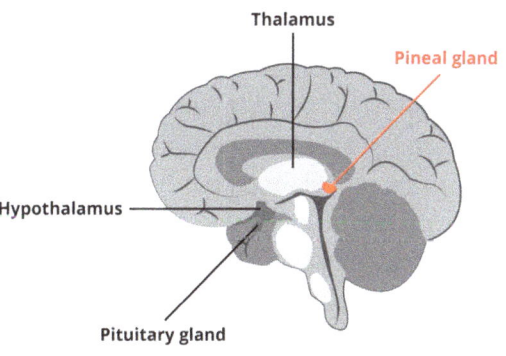

The pineal gland's function is to secrete the hormone melatonin (responsible for sleep), and other N-DMT (hallucinogen thoughts) compounds. Over time the build-up of fluoride inside the cells of the pineal gland will impair the function of it.

There are various things to do to strengthen the pineal gland through detoxification, proper nutrition, and practicing techniques such as:

- Focusing your third eye during meditation.
- Breathing and visualization exercises.
- Certain supplements are also helpful such as Melatonin, Phenibut, Spirulina, and Chlorella.
- Natural products such as oregano oil, neem extracts, raw cocoa, raw apple cider vinegar, etc.
- Balanced organic fruits and vegetables.
- Essential oils.
- Acupressure on the third eye spot.
- Binaural beat music, especially for the third eye.

What is Channeling, and how does it work?

Channeling is nothing but communicating and receiving information from any non-human consciousness and expressing it.

Your non-physical beings such as your guides, or Higher Self, will send information as energy. This energy, when received through your mind, gets translated depending upon the path of least resistance. You are attuned to it whether it is clairvoyant, clairsentient, clairaudient, claircognizance. You will receive the information through the medium that you recognize and express it. The expression of it can be in the form of art, music, poems, writing, or speaking directly as a channeler.

How to Channel

Channeling is like an art that anybody can do with some practice. It's like learning a new language, and the important part in channeling is to trust the information coming in, without your ego or mind interfering and doubting it.

1. Sit in a comfortable place and do some deep breathing exercises.
2. Make sure you are grounded and in a relaxed higher vibration state.
3. Close your eyes and imagine a divine golden light is surrounding you, protecting you.
4. Do some prayer or any particular chanting that you prefer.
5. Connect to higher dimensional beings such as your Higher Self, guides, or Source by imagining you are on the ground floor of a 100 story building. Once you are in the main lobby inside the building, you see an elevator, and you decide to go inside. As the elevator goes upward, passing every floor, your vibration is rising higher and higher along with it as well. When it reaches the top, the elevator door opens, you meet your guides or Source.
6. Ask questions through your mind and note down the answers that come up. Don't think, just let it flow. *Note: You can also speak and record this on a recording phone app.*
7. Once you are done communicating with your higher dimensional being, provide your gratitude to them.
8. Come down again in the same elevator to the ground floor and slowly open your eyes.

As you start practicing daily, you can tweak the steps according to your needs. You can also directly connect to your guides without going into meditation or trance state, depending upon each personal strength.

How to be in tune with intuition:

1. Know yourself that you have the intuition to tune to your higher self.
2. Reach within, for the information that you need.
3. Interpret the information that you have received.

4. Follow that guidance that you received without doubting.
5. Acknowledge what you received from your inner guidance is the best one.

Also, note that the messages that you are looking for can come from any direction. It can be in songs that you are listening to, a message on a billboard, the number plate of a car, or many other things. The key is to be open to it; do not ignore it.

Note: Many channelers teach how to channel; you can join their courses and learn as well. You can check the details on my website Living Librarian

22

AKASHIC RECORDS

What are Akashic Records?

A kasha is a Sanskrit word, meaning ether: a primordial substance out of which everything is formed. Akashic Records is a multidimensional library that records of All That Is, was, and will be. Every thought, word, action, belief, and experience of yourself is imprinted in the akashic record during this lifetime.

Now imagine, not only this lifetime but all other lifetimes you have ever lived, or will be living in future as well, is recorded. (Note, time is an illusion in this physical world, everything is happening in the PRESENT moment).

To further extend this, not only you, but all other souls living in this universe and multiverse as well, are recorded and stored there as well; it's that huge.

To give you an analogy, consider a corporate company that stores all the business transactions in a database *(Akashic record)*. As an employee *(you)*, when you sell a product *(thoughts, words, actions, beliefs, and experiences)* to a client, you store that transaction in a database. Every client that you have dealt with, and plan to deal with in the future, is stored in that database. Now, all the employees *(all beings in the multiverse)* in the company are storing the information in the same database.

Where is the Akashic Record located?

The Akashic Record doesn't have some physical place precisely. It exists as quantum vibratory energy in the higher planes of existence and is guarded by powerful beings of light. So continuing with the same analogy, the company database is stored in a remote data center *(higher planes)* fully protected and guarded *(beings of light)*.

Is the Akashic Record continuously changing or is it stagnate?

The Akashic Record is continuously changing and evolving. As you change your belief system, master the life challenges that you face, and learn from them. The records automatically get updated and are available for the benefit of all. In the analogy, it is similar to updating the records all the time in the database based on a client's request due to situation change, address change, etc.

How to access Akashic Records

You can access Akashic Records by following steps with good intent and a little bit of imagination.

A few guidelines:

- Use your current legal name when accessing.
- Don't access it while intoxicated with alcohol or drugs.
- Maintain a time limit while accessing the record; maybe 15 to 60 minutes.
- Make sure to close the record once you have finished reading it.
- Avoid asking questions about when. Stick to yes or no answers since time is eternal and the free choice that you have in this physical world.
- Prefer to ask questions about why, what, and how.
- Make sure you have been grounding, before and after reading.
- Trust the information that you receive during the reading. During the reading, if you see blankness or emptiness, then note that the information is not available to you at that moment since it was meant for yourself to discover in terms of personal growth and experience.

1. Sit in a comfortable place and do some deep breathing exercises.
2. Make sure you are grounded and in a relaxed higher vibrational state.
3. Do an opening prayer or particular chanting that you prefer with words and sound; make sure you are acknowledging the force of lights, and asking for direction, guidance, and to know the truth with good intent and highest good for everyone connected in the record.
4. Close your eyes and imagine a divine golden light is surrounding you and protecting you as light is passing through your body slowly.
5. You can visualize yourself stepping into a big crystal building. You enter the main lobby, and you see an elevator. You take the elevator, and as the elevator rises, passing each floor, you are increasing your vibration and reaching a matching frequency of a vibratory Akashic Record that exists. Then it reaches the top; the elevator door opens.
6. You reach the realm of Akashic Record, and inside you will see the beings of light welcoming you. Ask them to guide you in accessing the Akashic Record.
7. Once you are inside and guided, sit comfortably in a beautiful chair. In front of you, you see a glowing crystalline light encoded the Book of Life. Think of a situation that you need insight on and will serve you in the present; open it. You will see the words, symbols, images, or pictures in actions. Go through it, and receive the information
8. Once you finish reading, close the book, and provide gratitude to the beings of light. Use the same elevator to come down to the ground floor and out of the crystal building safely into the present time and space.
9. Write down all the information that you received at the

moment, even if you did not understand the symbols or images. This will become clear at a later stage; or, you may ask your guides to help clarify what you didn't understand.

With a little daily practice and patience, you will ultimately learn to tune to the Akashic frequency and read the information for the highest good, wisdom, and truth.

23

AURA

What is Aura?

Aura is an electromagnetic field or Human Energy Field-HEF that surrounds the human body. It usually appears as a glow encompassing your entire body. Humans are not the only ones with auras; every living thing has one around it.

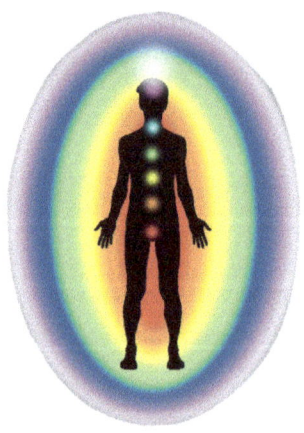

In an average individual, it will extend 8 to 10ft around the body. For some enlightened and ancient masters, it could extend around several miles from their physical body. Some could see the size, color, and type of vibration of an aura.

Children are very good at seeing and experiencing auras; those experiences are often translated into their drawings.

Auras are made of the following auric fields

The aura consists of seven layers or auric fields. Each one of the subtle bodies that exist around the physical body and has a unique signature frequency. They are interrelated and affect one another and the person's feelings, emotions, thinking, behavior, and health as well. Therefore, a state of imbalance in one of the bodies leads to a state of imbalance in the others.

The physical field

Vibrates at the lowest frequency of all fields, is visible to the human eye with training and changes according to health and wellbeing.

The etheric field

It's like a blueprint for the physical body. It usually has a grey appearance and changes based on how energy flows throughout the body. It handles the energy exchange between the universal energy field and the physical body.

The emotional field

It's one of the more colorful fields and changes hue based on the mood and wellbeing of each chakra. Stress and tension will affect the state of this field. It is more oval than the etheric field, which tends to follow the shape of the physical body.

The mental field

It is usually more spread out than the emotional even though it overlaps. It's visible as bright yellow around the crown of the head. In religious paintings, important figures are seen with a yellow halo, just like the mental field appears to those who can see it. It changes depending on how confused or focused you are, and benefits from work on the third and fifth chakras.

The astral field

It acts as a nexus between the physical and spiritual realms. It exists in its plane and the astral plane, free of the confines of time and space. It generates colors similar to the emotional field, but usually with a reddish hue. Benefits from work on all chakras.

The celestial field or spiritual field

It has access to all energies from the universe, appearing as pastel colors similar to those of the emotional field. It acts as a template for the etheric field in the physical plane.

The causal field

It is named causal because it has to do with the direction your life is going to take. It appears as pale gold; this field exists well beyond death and even into the next life. The energy here is used to direct our lower levels of existence based on a world without time or space. It's the equivalent of the mental field in the spiritual plane.

Characteristics of Aura

Increased perception and awareness of your aura begins with understanding basic properties:

- Every aura has a unique frequency.
- Your aura will interact with the auric fields of others, not only humans, but also interact with animals, plants, minerals, and other energy fields.
- The longer and more intimate the contact, the larger the energy exchange. The aura and the changes within it are a mere reflection of ourselves physically, emotionally, mentally, and spiritually.

Aura colors

Red: This color shows powerful energy, fire, and primal creative force. It's life-promoting energy that reflects strong passion, anger, love, hate, and unexpected changes. It affects the circulatory and reproductive systems. It can indicate an awakening of latent abilities/talents. However, too much red or muddiness can reflect overstimulation or imbalance.

Orange: A color of warmth, creativity, and emotions that indicate courage, joy, and socialness. It shows a huge amount of energy, stamina, creativeness, productiveness, and adventurousness. The shades can vary and can also indicate emotional imbalance and agitation. The muddier shades of orange can reflect pridefulness, flamboyance, worry, and vanity.

Yellow: This is the easiest color to see in an aura. It's the color of sunshine, happiness, optimism, and awakening psychic abilities. Yellow around the hairline indicates spiritual development, growing wisdom, ideas, intellect, sense of appropriateness, and mental clarity. Muddier shades of yellow can indicate being too critical, overanalyzing, and excessive thinking.

Green: This shows an increase in compassion, love, and a desire to assist others. Green is the color of balance and harmony. It reflects personal growth, heart openness, willingness to change, and transformation. The muddier shades could show possessiveness and fear of being unlovable, eventually leading to self-doubt and mistrust.

Blue: They are truthful, calm, and serious. A lot of blue shows a strong sense of purpose, sensitivity, and has a developed inner guide or teacher. It also indicates loneliness and a journey of coming home to a Higher Self or Essence. A darker blue might be a connection to the deep mysteries of spiritual life, intuition, creative imagination, clairaudience, and telepathy. Muddier shades reflect blocked perceptions and indicate melancholy, fearfulness, forgetfulness, and oversensitivity.

Violet and Purple: Displays warmth, transmutation, and a sense of leadership. It shows a blending of heart and mind integration of the physical and spiritual plane. It also indicates intuition, hyperactive imagination, visualization, and connection to the world of dreams. They might have the ability to lucid dream, astral travel, and other psychic abilities.

Gold: Reflective of dynamic spiritual energy, transition into true power, and has zero constraints from Ego. The color means connection to a higher power or God. It's a color of a higher mind with a deep knowledge of patterns/laws of the Universe. Gold around the hairline could mean a high spiritual development. They are inspired and devoted. The muddier shades indicate they are in a process of awakening a higher inspiration and have not clarified it within their life.

Pink: This color in an aura displays softness and a love for all others. It shows growing compassion, tenderness, kindness, and gentle nature. Along with more pastel colors, it shows a quiet and modest person. Muddier shades can indicate an emotional imbalance, suggesting they give too much.

Black: Seen as negative energy, but depending on the overall color and vibrancy of the aura, black shows they are embracing a higher level of peace. It can also indicate an imbalance or a literal blockage; specifically, if it's seen close to a body part, like near a knee, it can indicate a blockage/pain in that area. The color can also be a sign of death and rebirth.

Grey: It can show a spiritual opening in their inherited abilities, like intuition and creative imagination are awakening. Darker hues of gray can designate physical imbalances if seen next to areas of the body.

White: This, in an aura, reflects truthfulness and purity. An indication of energy that is cleansing and purifying itself. It reflects an awakening of higher creativity as well.

How to see Aura

Auras are more ethereal and look like wisps of smoke around your body. There are various exercises or practices to see Aura. One of them is to situate the person in front of a very softly illuminated plain white background. A color background will change Aura colors, so you need additional knowledge about combining colors. Some combinations of background and Aura colors may cause misinterpretation problems.

Choose one spot to look at, the middle of the forehead is a good area. This is the location of the so-called Brow Chakra or the Third Eye. In some cultures (India), they put a mark on the forehead. The mark in ancient times could mean the invitation to look and see the Aura. Look at this spot for 30 to 60 seconds or longer. After 30 seconds, analyze the surroundings with your peripheral vision, while still looking at the same spot.

Continuing the concentration is most important. Resist the temptation to look around. You should see that the background near the person is brighter and has a DIFFERENT color than the background further away. This is your perception of the Aura. The longer you concentrate, the better you will see it. Remember, concentration on one spot increases your sensitivity by accumulating the effect of the Aura vibration reaching your eyes. Next, you can try with animals and objects.

See your own Aura

Stand about 1.5 m in front of a decent size mirror. In the beginning, it is best if the background behind you is plain white, and there are no shadows. Illumination should be very soft and uniform, not bright. Follow the instructions above for seeing Auras. Practice for at least 10-15 minutes each day to increase your sensitivity and develop Auric sight. Remember that practice is required to develop Auric sight.

Using Technology to see Aura

Kirlian photography refers to a form of contact print photography, theoretically associated with high-voltage. It is named after Semyon Kirlian, who in 1939 accidentally discovered that if an object on a photographic plate is subjected to a strong electric field, an image is created on the plate.

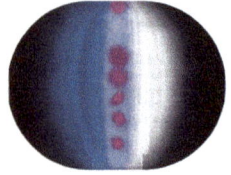 The image looks like a colored halo or coronal discharge. This image is said to be a physical manifestation of the spiritual aura or *life force* that allegedly surrounds each living thing. *This image was taken using the Aura photography of a person.*

24

PERSPECTIVE

Perspective is the driving force of life, and it creates experiences that lead to choices and make us unique. Without perspective, we would have been living like robots. Everybody would be following the same routine, same interest, the same choices, and life would have become boring with no intent to do anything. Perspective:

It can bring love, compassion, and unity when clearly understood.

OR

It can bring fear, chaos, hate, vengeance, war, etc. when misunderstood.

Let me give you an example of people's perspective about the situation of the Coronavirus disease that is currently going on worldwide, while writing this book (iMarch 2020).

Everybody has a different perspective on the same situation, and this is what I heard when I was listening to some of their perspectives:

- The virus has created a fear in them, it's a question of survival, and they are not sure what is going to happen to them if they catch the virus.
- Some of them hate the nation that started it, and they want to have vengeance.
- A few people think it's a conspiracy going on behind the scene, they think, there is no actual virus.
- A few people feel that the environment got a break from people polluting the planet because of the situation.
- Some feel this is the time to heal, to emanate love and compassion to everyone, and to conduct mass meditation.
- Even higher beings have their perspective as well.
- A summary version of St. Germain: "A Multi-dimensional Shift is Taking Place Within Your Being and Mother Earth. The virus and its impact upon the world are allowing humanity to recognize the presence of fear and negativity within their being, to recognize suffering, and to begin to create positive shifts within their beings to create something beyond fear and negativity, something that will empower all. The ascension shift taking place upon the Earth now is major, many have been waiting for this shift for lifetimes. As with any ascension shift, some souls choose to depart their physical bodies and return to the inner planes to be of service. This is a contract made by their soul before their birth and not a decision made by the personality. While the shift taking place due to the presence and impact of Covid-19 is occurring predominantly for the Earth. Each person will begin to recognize that the Universe of the Creator resides within them, therefore, they will bond on a deeper level with the dimensions of the universe residing within. This will offer humanity a glimpse into the fullness, completeness, and wholeness available to embody and express".
- A summary version of Sananda: "Humanity has to recognize the presence of the virus, acknowledge it and transcend beyond their physical self and truly understand

who they are. You are multidimensional beings, and peace is your true nature. Life is eternal and not to be afraid of a situation that is going to change."

What perspective do you hold?

Now, just imagine, this one situation has created many perspectives in all of us. You need to know that:

- Perspective is a point of view from one person/being or a group of persons/ beings.
- Always be open-minded and use your discernment when a particular perspective is presented.
- Don't get attached to a particular perspective and come to a conclusion that is the only truth, ignoring other perspectives. This has created separation and fights between people and even nations. Be open-minded and listen to all views that are presented and make your own decision on it.
- A perspective presented by one person can change over some time by the same person, as he grows during his life experience. Or your perspective can change over time. Note that change is the only constant, and the rest is always changing.
- All perspectives should be welcomed by knowing the fact that we are all unique in our way, and are part of the same Source. This is the way to bring unity, love, peace, and compassion in all of us.
- As an individual, you can evaluate each perspective based on some information, whether that perspective is uplifting you or making you down. If it is making you down, you can ignore that perspective rather than going against it, with an understanding that we live in a world of duality, and every one of us is in a different level of spiritual growth.

This book has its own perspective as well, the entire book was written based on some of my life experiences, and knowledge acquired through reading, listening, attending various spiritual retreats. The book contains a combination of both East and West spiritual teachings. So, it's just another perspective, use your discernment and the points mentioned above when reading it.

25

DREAMS

What Are Dreams?

reams are the reflection of your deepest emotional states that you hold in your life. They are inter-dimensional and provide a window of opportunity for us to explore during a sleep state.

As human beings, you are familiar with the physical world and the dream world. The physical world is something that you interact with every day when you are awake. Although the mysterious part is the dream world, where everything is non-linear, there is no beginning or end. What you remember is a particular scene or a sequence of actions taking place. So when you wake up from a dream, you wonder what does it mean?

How to interpret dreams

A similar dream can be interpreted in many ways by different people from their point of view. Of course, there are some universal common meanings to certain symbols, colors, or even scenarios. However, some may or may not represent actual meaning until it is completely dissected and understood. Only the dreamer who is dreaming would know it's true meaning if he or she can interpret based on their understanding of life in general.

A simple technique can be used to interpret a dream.

1. As soon as you wake up from the dream state, write down everything that you remember, every minute detail will help you to understand it better.
2. Where did the dream take place? In other words, what was the location of the dream? Was it in your childhood house, some desert, another dimension that you can't even describe?
3. What was the atmosphere or mood in the dream? Was it gloomy, romantic, bright, scary, etc?
4. How were you feeling or behaving in the dream? Were you worried, panicked, angry, happy, etc?

5. What were the elements involved in the dream? Were there crystals, animals, trees, a particular thing?
6. Were there reoccurring thoughts in the dream?
7. Was this a repeated dream?

Dream Example

"I'm sitting on a plane with another person and hear screams in every direction. The pilot begins to speak over the microphone and says the engine broke and to hold on tightly. I look out of the window terrified, and all I see is miles of sand covering the earth. I begin to panic and close my eyes, trying to calm myself down. The world finally tunes out, and I lose consciousness.

Next thing I know, I wake up to being surrounded by smoke and fire. I slowly and painfully try to get out of the plane to look for other survivors. I call their names loudly, screaming, but no one answers in return. I then start to walk out onto the vast desert, looking for anything that can help me. I call out again and begin walking for miles on end, searching continuously. Nothing greets me. There are no plants or animals. The blazing sun burning on my skin makes my head go hazy, and then the sky turns dark".

Let us interpret the dream from my point of view.

Location: Sky, Desert

The sky represents openness and freedom.

The desert represents loneliness and tiredness.

Atmosphere/mood: Bright, dark

The brightness became dark.

Feelings: lonely, sad, frightening, screaming

These are the lower vibrational emotions that the dreamer was feeling during the dream.

Elements: Plane, sand

In this scenario, planes represent flying up in the air. Sand represents Grounding.

Was there recurring thoughts: No

Was this a repeated dream: Yes

If this is repeatedly happening, it has some meaning to it and cannot be ignored.

Interpretation of dream

The dream is telling the dreamer not to be in a hurry to achieve the goal that he/she is seeking, and it can lead to disaster. Not to take everything for granted, try to slow down and calmly think when planning to achieve something; and be grounded.

The repeated dream is telling about the current situation that he or she is facing, a course of action that needs to change or it is a road to disaster.

What is your interpretation?

What is a Lucid Dream?

A lucid dream is a dream where the dreamer knows he/she is dreaming and can influence it with their thoughts in any way he/she wishes. It provides a sense of mastering the power of thoughts over matter, or ability, to influence events. For example, you can fly in your house, interact with planets, or touch a giant giraffe. Name it, and you can create it with your thoughts.

Usually, lucid dreams happen when you are in between sleep and wakeful state. You suddenly wake up from a dream or attempt to wake up, but you keep your eyes closed for some time and continue dreaming.

26

MANIFESTATION AND CREATING YOUR OWN REALITY

How to manifest what you want

You always manifest whether you are consciously aware of it or not. However, the question lies whether you are manifesting according to your desire or not. To answer this, you need to have a certain understanding of how the entire manifestation process works.

Basic Understanding

- You are part of Source energy in human form. Currently, you are living and operating in this physical world. The qualities and characteristics of the Source energy are within you.
- Everything is energy, including *you*, the thoughts, the feelings, things, etc. and are all vibrating at varying frequencies.
- When you desire something, a particular thing to manifest, you need to vibrationally match the frequency of the desire of what you want to manifest.

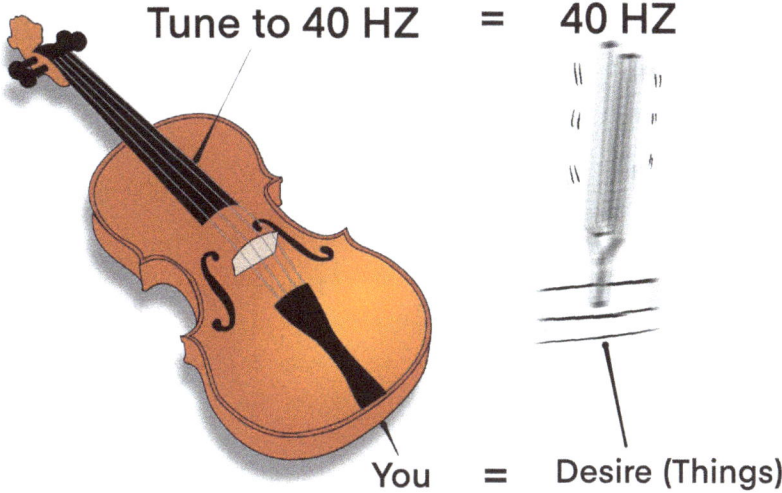

Tune to 40 HZ = 40 HZ

You = Desire (Things)

For example, to tune a guitar, you use a tuning fork and strike a specific note. You then tune the guitar to match that vibration. Similarly, imagining you as a guitar and tuning fork is your desire. You need to vibrationally match that desire to get what you want. The Source or universe always responds to you by your feelings and not by your words.

Belief

From childhood, you learned to believe in certain things based on your parent's belief, the people around you, or the society you were born into. Some beliefs may be favorable to you, and some may not. You need to evaluate every belief that you hold and check whether it makes sense to hold that belief based on your new understanding. If it is not sensible then try to take it out completely, there is no point in holding that old belief that can trigger resistance in your manifestation.

Example: *I'm not worthy enough to buy a new car*. This belief of you not being worthy may have been existing from childhood, or an experience that you had earlier in your life based on old understanding.

Time

You live in a physical world where there is some delay between the time you ask, and the time it takes to manifest in your life. The time variance is dependent on the vibration you are holding, and the resistance to it.

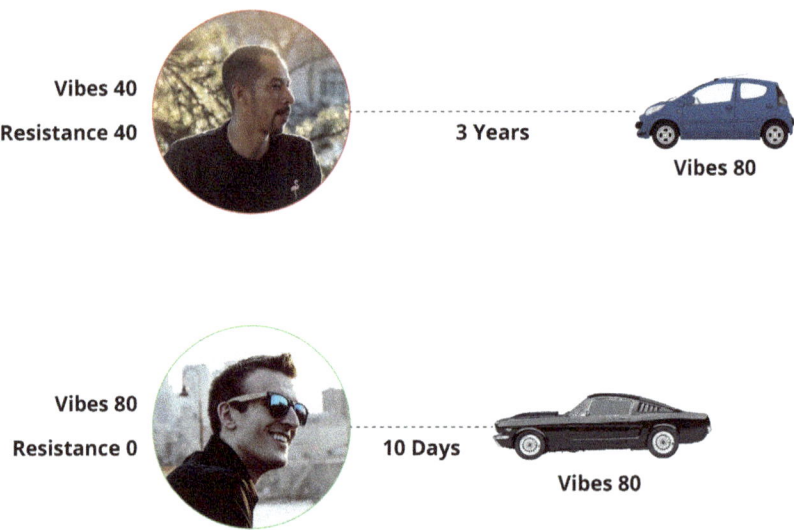

Vibes 40

Resistance 40

3 Years

Vibes 80

Vibes 80

Resistance 0

10 Days

Vibes 80

For example, if two people wish to manifest a new car. One person can manifest it within a few days, whereas the other may take even a year or can't manifest at all. This is based on the vibration they are emitting.

The process

A perfect being, aligned to Source energy or higher self is having a feeling and a thought to manifest something, they immediately take the right course of action and manifest the things they want.

But you are a physical Being, living in a physical world where your vibration is continuously changing. As you emit various ranges of frequency by your emotions throughout the day, it becomes hard sometimes to manifest the things you want.

The following steps will help you to manifest the things you want.

1. Have a clear understanding of who you are as mentioned above:

2. You get a feeling and a thought about something that you want to manifest in your life.

3. You start thinking about it, whether you want that thing to manifest in your life or not. You finally choose to manifest it.

4. As soon as you make that choice, the Source or universe will procreate with you and is manifested immediately. It exists in a certain vibrational frequency, so you need to reach that vibration to receive it.

5. This is the time where you need to be in a vibrational match with the desire you are seeking without any resistance. You can use few tools, such as checking your vibration, visualization, and gratitude.

When Aligned

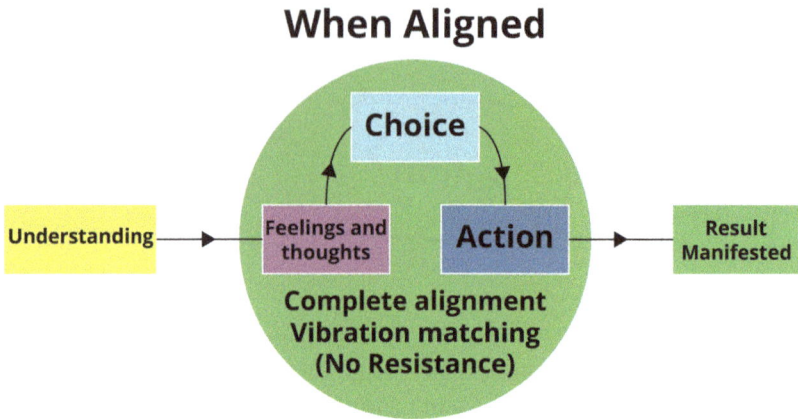

When Not Aligned

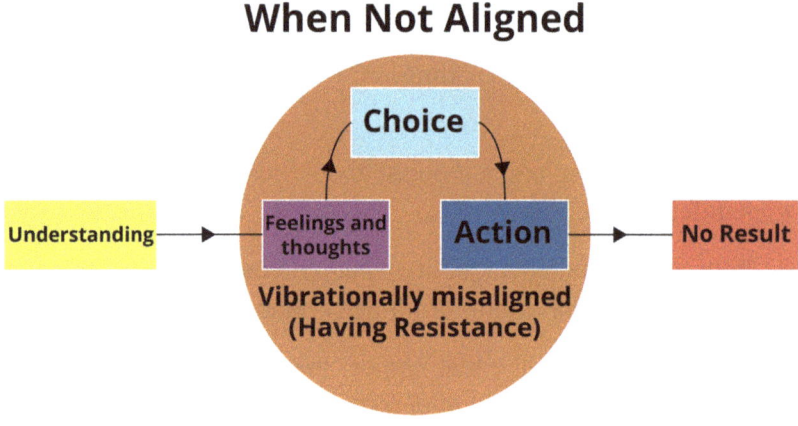

- **Check your vibration (feelings)**: to ensure you are not vibrating lower or have any resistance to your desire. For example, suppose you are doubting yourself, *am I going to get that, I doubt it's going to happen, I need to work hard to deserve that*, etc. These are self-imposed thoughts and conditions. It shows you are vibrating at a lower frequency with doubts, worries, etc. Take this out of your system by reminding yourself about the steps mentioned in the new understanding above. Keep checking your vibration and make every effort to maintain that higher vibration.
- **Visualization**: Imagine you already received the thing

that you wanted to manifest. Now, how do you feel about it? You may be feeling happy, excited, joyful, etc. Try to be in that feeling as often as you can because this vibration is in perfect match to your desire, and it helps to manifest sooner.

- **Gratitude**: When you are in gratitude, you are holding a higher vibration in your field and telling the universe, or the Source, that you are happy and thankful. That reflection of you will have a ripple effect, and the universe will be providing more and more to you of the same vibrational nature that you feel more gratitude towards. This is one of the ways you are raising your vibration to match that desire.
- **Attachment**: Don't get attached to the outcome of your manifestation or desire. When you get attached, you feel desperate to have it, so the vibration you are projecting is desperate, and the universe will provide more experience of desperation, which is not the result that you want.

When you are in that higher vibrational state, an opportunity can arise from any direction, so don't stick to your limited belief that it has to be presented only this way or that way. The Universe presents the opportunity to you in various ways, so be open when it shows up, and act on it by taking action without any doubt or hesitation. It is something like buying a lottery ticket (the action) to win (the desire) a lottery. Without buying a ticket, how could you win the lottery? Similarly, take action to manifest the desire that you are seeking.

If everything is in perfect alignment, and you did your part, then you will receive the thing that you want to manifest in your life. Once you receive it, provide your gratitude to the universe.

Personal Experience - 1

Let me provide my personal story on this. When I initially started learning and knowing about Spirituality, everyone was talking about manifestation during those days when the secret was recently released. I thought, let me try manifesting something, so I decided to manifest $30K. I did it according to the steps mentioned above, and within two and a half months, I received $32K through a tax refund, bonus, and other incomes. It worked out with less effort.

You can also start testing it out by manifesting simple things such as a $20 bill or a flower. See how long it takes to manifest. Since these are simple ones, you wouldn't have much attachment to the outcome of it.

Creating your own Reality

You always create your reality, whether you are aware of it or not. The outside reality that you see, experience, and feel, is just a mirror reflection of your thoughts and feelings. If you want to see the changes outside of you, you need to change yourself from the inside.

It is similar to standing in front of a mirror, asking your reflection to smile, when in fact, it is you who has to smile so that the image in the mirror will reflect you with a smile. So if you are in peace and harmony, the outside experience will reflect the same to you. Similarly, if you feel anxiety, hate, anger, then the outside will reflect the same to you.

How to change your existing circumstance or experience that you don't prefer:

1. Be aware of what's going on outside of you, the experience that you are having at present. Does the environment feel harsh, people being mean, your family keeps fighting, etc.
2. Accept that you have created all those surroundings. You may be wondering "why?" ! "I *didn't ask people to be mean to me. Or my family to fight!* For this", you need to

know that those surroundings exist because it matches your vibration. There is a saying that *'like' attracts 'like'*. You are attracting those people and circumstances based on your inner vibration, accept it.

3. You are now aware and accept the fact that you are the creator of your reality, and if you want to see the change outside, you need to first make changes within. So, the people, object, and circumstances are representing you as a mirror, and showing you what's going on inside you. You become a conscious creator and start making some changes within.

4. Check what's going on inside you. Are you always angry, worried, and unhappy? Then make some changes within you. Use some of the techniques mentioned in chapter 43 'Raising Vibration.'

5. Once you have made changes within, you will soon notice that the reality will start changing around you, and you will experience the things that you prefer.

Personal Experience - 2

Let me provide a short story that happened in my life, and how I used this technique above to resolve and continue to use.

I work in a corporate company where things change quite often. There will always be some restructuring happening, and/or employees moving around to different departments within the company. During one of the changes, I was moved to a new department and had a new boss. Initially, I was able to fit in, and they were matching my frequency as well. But as months passed by, a misunderstanding started happening between my boss, another team member, and myself. This was the first time in my entire career that I was facing such a situation, and we were having conflict about work-related issues. I knew it was not my mistake, and I was pointing to them as the culprit. I was so down that I wanted to resign.

During the worst time of it, it was the holiday season and I was going through the peak negative period of this conflict. So I took a break and went for a vacation to the Grand Canyon. While I was enjoying nature outside, I was thinking, *"why am I facing this situation?"* I soon realized the statement *you create your reality*. It doesn't matter whether you are spiritual, or if there are things you still need to let go/work on. The universe will show you the reflection. In this case, the reflection was my boss and colleague. I started thinking, what is within me that I need to work on, and I soon realized it was my ego that was dominant and causing this situation. Immediately, I started changing it from the inside. I accepted the outside situation as a mere reflection of what's going on within me. I began to work on myself by being completely in peace and harmony, even when the outside situation is still the same.

Within two to three months, I started noticing the change. There was some restructuring within the company again. A few people were laid off, and some people even left the company, including my boss and the colleague I had a problem with. I was then moved to a new department. All this happened within a year or so. When I look back at that situation, I thank them for showing and helping me in becoming a master of my reality. It doesn't matter whether they learned the lesson or not, what matters is whether you learned the lesson from this experience.

I've already changed and vibrating at a higher frequency than why do I still see the same reality and nothing has changed?

You need to understand that you live in a physical world where time exists. It takes a certain amount of time to reflect on the changes that you want to see outside. Until then, you need to maintain that higher vibration even though things are not according to your expectation. Think of it as similar to switching off a fan that was running continuously. It takes some time to stop, and it's not going to stop immediately. It's the same case with your reality as well, and it's not going to show up immediately.

27

ADDITIONAL CONCEPTS

Some terminology that is good to know.

Light Language

Light language is a universal language that is understood by all life forms in the universe. It consists of light photonic energy, sacred geometry, and encoded cosmic information.

There are multiple levels to it; you might sense them as a type of symbol or light that moves across in your mind's eye. You can feel the vibrations in the body by triggering your body at a cellular level and adjusting the frequency. You bring your attention to your divine Self. Therefore, you start opening up to new frequencies with an overwhelming sense of knowing about your True Self.

In general, any information that passes through your ego-mind, it tries to understand it first, and then warps to a form that is undoubtedly relatable to. However, one of the advantages of light language is that it bypasses the ego-mind.

The light language is gibberish, and the ego-mind cannot understand it. This untouched information enters directly into your body and triggers your soul.

Sacred Geometry

Have you ever noticed various shapes and patterns visible in nature, and wondered what it is all about? Is there some meaning to it? There are geometrical shapes across the cosmos with sacred meanings. It is believed that the architect is none other than the Creator itself.

All the ancient mystics and sages have applied meaning to those shapes. They believed that within those sacred geometries, it contained the secret of life, and everything arises out of it, including you, me, nature, universes, and the dimensions.

Flower of Life

The flower of life is the beginning. It's about life and everything. It embodies the life force energy that flows through us.

TREE OF LIFE

It is a concept of cosmic creation within which encloses various symbols.

Merkaba

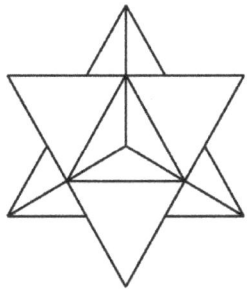

It's a chariot (light vehicle), believed to be used by ascended masters to transport to higher realms.

Yin Yang

It represents how positive and negative energy is connected and illustrates the dualistic nature of life.

Sri Yantra

It represents the cosmos, the human body.

Metatron Cube

It represents the building block of creation.

PART III

CLEANSING

This is the stage is where you start cleansing physically, emotionally, mentally, and spiritually based on your understanding of who you are. It is similar to doing practical's once you have understood the theory to become a master of it.

Analogy: The contaminated water starts using a filter to clean up itself until it becomes pure water again.

Water filter process begins

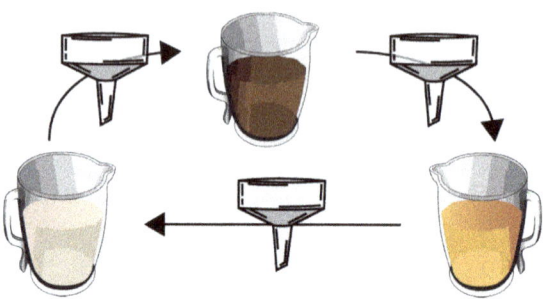

People over time develop various coping mechanisms when cleansing themselves. Cleansing can be physically done by exercise, healthy eating choices, or being outdoors. Emotionally you could work on your fears, past traumas, or angriness. Although, the most difficult to understand and come to terms with is mentally cleansing ourselves. Our habit of thinking clearly dictates our way of living and our sense of handling things in the outside world. Our outward circumstance is most often a reflection of our inward battles projected overtime at a constant vibration. So, a good mental impression is the key building block to overcome most of the unwanted situations. For our spiritual growth, it opens up a new Pandora box of new knowledge and understanding; later bringing it closer to the divinity existing within us.

In part three the book provides a practical approach of dealing with issues, suffering, challenges, attachment, people, etc. Therefore, it helps you in clearing all those negative emotions that are suppressed for years.

28

KARMA

What is Karma?

Karma is one of the universal laws that has been specified in most of the scriptures and is related to cause and effect. This law states that for every action, there is a reaction.

Whatever you put out will eventually come back to you.

- An action that brings merit will ultimately result in happiness. Action that brings demerit will result in sadness.
- It is possible to create karma through the mind by expressing free will.

- Karma is not a punishment. Suppose if there is no judgment about your thoughts or your actions, whether they are good or bad, then you wouldn't seek a reward or punishment for the act. Karma merely provides you the opportunities to gain more understanding by experiencing both sides.
- No one can escape from the law of karma. It applies to everyone as long as they are on the physical plane.
- One of the spiritual master used to say that if you have been born as a human, then you have both good and bad karma. If you had only good karma, then there are other places to stay, such as heaven. Whereas if you had only bad karma, then there are other places, like hell, in the lower astral plane.
- The law of karma applies to the physical, astral, and mental bodies but not to the soul. The soul is always free from karma.
- Karma is created only in human life, and there are many ways to lessen it; either through events, meditation etc.. You would do this in the physical, astral, and mental planes.

Types of Karma

Types of Karma

Kriyaman Karma

Karma that you create in this life through your choices I.e through free will. It's the only way to make Kriyaman karma.

For instance, if Neo robbed someone's house, karma is not going to come back in the same way as if somebody stole from Neo. Karma can come back in many other ways as well. Since Neo is vibrating at that level, he would inevitably experience similar consequences in nature. For example, it could be losing his girlfriend, receiving a fine in the mail, etc.

Prarabdha Karma

A portion of karma allotted to this life based on past acts done in previous lifetimes (a subset of reserved karma). It's an event happening without choice.

For example, Nancy is emitting positive vibes for a while. She is always happy, helping people, and loves her job. However, Nancy had a car crash while commuting to work. The question arises why did she create an event like that even though she was emitting good vibes and didn't choose any of it?. This is due to Prarabdha karma that she has taken into this life to clear it out based on actions performed in previous lifetimes.

Sanchita or Reserved Karma

The accumulation of Karma is set aside for allocation in a series of lifetimes.

For example, suppose Arun takes 10,000 dollars from Neil and intends to return it in a year. Suddenly one day, Neil dies and now Arun is not able to pay him back in this life. Therefore, the payback to Neil may go into Sanchita or Reserved Karma.

How to Release Karma

- The law of karma is applicable as long as you are in the physical world. To escape karma, you have to go within and beyond the mind to identify yourself (as the soul), and operate from that level without attachments to the physical worlds. This leads to karma not affecting those who have mastered it.

- Life always provides you an opportunity to make choices, and the choices that you make out of pure motives, love, and compassion instead of fear, hate, or anger will lead to balanced karma.
- A perfect living master can help. Any new actions performed in the name of the Master will not be binding. Since the masters are karmaless, their actions are not binding to them and they operate from the totality of consciousness. So, the only leftover is reserved karma, which the Master will take some upon themselves.

29

BELIEF

A belief is something that you believe or accept as the truth. You create these beliefs to anchor your understanding of the world around you. You can choose to believe in whatever you want to; it's called exercising your free will. However, sometimes you stick to your belief system to such an extent that you fight with others whose belief system doesn't match your own. Past histories have shown that nations have gone to war against each other due to their differences in beliefs.

Most of your beliefs would base off of:

- Parents belief
- Experience belief
- Facts belief
- Assumption belief

Parents belief

All parents' beliefs are automatically inherited or downloaded to the child subconsciously at birth. The soul knows this and chooses parents based on a belief system that it can work on to have that experience of belief. Also, the child holds all of its previous lifetime beliefs in its subconscious mind.

Things to Watch For

If the parents hold a restricted belief, then naturally, the child will also start holding that belief. For example, if the parents believe that they need to work hard to survive in this world. The child would then have that limited belief that she/he has to work hard to survive or else they will have problems. This limited belief will ensure that you have to work hard to survive unless you make an effort to change that belief.

Experience Belief

An experience belief is a belief that has embedded into a person's mind based on experiences. An experience can be either a positive experience or a negative experience. If the same experience happens many times, with the same results, then it becomes part of your belief.

Things to Watch For

Bear in mind there can be a catch 22. Experiences would have occurred based on certain beliefs that you already had. Those inherited from your parents can be created from the same experience again and again. For example, from childhood, you noticed your parents fighting with each other all the time. Those experiences become a belief that fighting is normal in relationships. Therefore, based on that, you attract that type of relationship and experience unless you replace it with a new personal belief.

Facts Belief

A fact belief is based on specific facts. For example, the earth is round, we have a day and night, and the sun rises from the east, and sets in the west.

Things to Watch For

The belief in facts can be modified. For instance, we studied from childhood that there are nine planets in our solar system. A few years back, this fact was altered to eight planets in our solar system based on a particular definition of a planet and its orbit.

Assumption Belief

A belief you assume to be truthful based on hearing or having been experienced by someone or yourself. It happens when you hear the news.

Things to watch for

For instance, you heard the news that a child drowned in the swimming pool when nobody was around. This news would have affected you so deeply that you start assuming or believing that having a swimming pool in your backyard is not safe. However, keep in mind that just because it has happened in their reality, it doesn't mean it has to happen in yours. Many people enjoy swimming in their backyard pool and are loving it.

Conscious Belief Vs Subconscious Belief

Conscious beliefs are something that you are actively mindful of. Like if you are overeating, you are aware you will put on weight. On the other hand, a subconscious belief is something that you are not aware of but exists in your subconscious. Such can include inheriting certain genes from your parents and other lifetime beliefs. It's easier to detect your conscious beliefs than your subconscious beliefs, but it shows up in your reality.

How to change your belief

You can start by looking at all your beliefs that you are holding on to from childhood till today. Examine these beliefs, and check whether they are making you sad, worried, frightened, and giving you anxiety?. Or, are they making you feel bliss, happiness, excitement, and abundance?. So notice, the experience created by these beliefs, If this is not what you want to experience OR if you have the same unwanted experience repeatedly, then eradicate that belief once for all and create new one that aligns to your true self.

For example, people have said," having more money makes you a bad person". Due to this belief, you are struggling too much to earn a decent amount of money that is sufficient for your standard of living. You have the belief that having too much is wrong. Therefore, the universe responds to that feeling and provide you with not enough money. Eventually, you are the creator, and the existence is just providing what you requested for. Once you realize the belief that is out of alignment, start replacing it with something like "money always flows easily in my life" or "having more money will make me a good caretaker."

Naturally, you want to see the proof before you make changes in your belief. But, the fact is, you need to believe in it first, and then it will show up in your reality. Sometimes, you see evidence through synchronicity as you slowly start making changes.

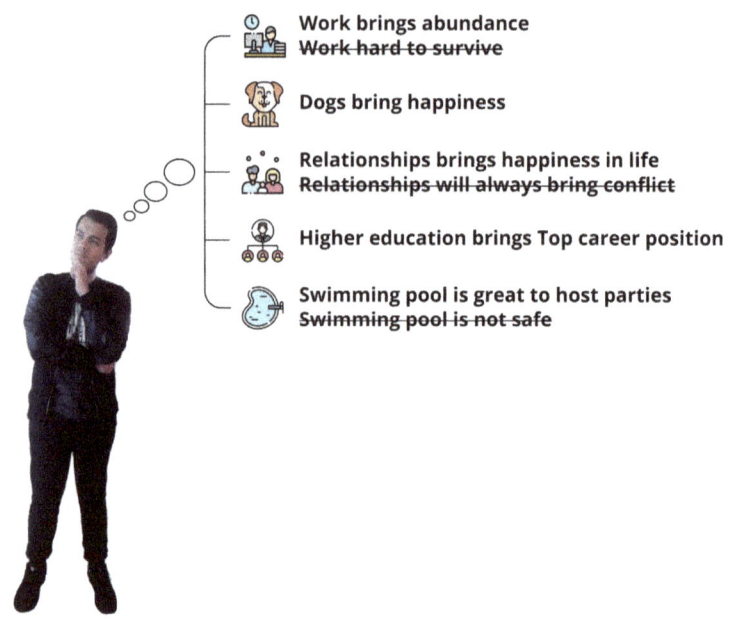

Work brings abundance
~~Work hard to survive~~

Dogs bring happiness

Relationships brings happiness in life
~~Relationships will always bring conflict~~

Higher education brings Top career position

Swimming pool is great to host parties
~~Swimming pool is not safe~~

Belief Summary

- Your thoughts and beliefs determine how you perceive your reality.
- Your beliefs should be in motion more malleable, easy to replace, and easy to let go; not fixed.
- You cannot achieve something new, whether it's an experience, inspiration, or idea, while you are maintain the old belief which is stale and not aligned to who you truly are.

 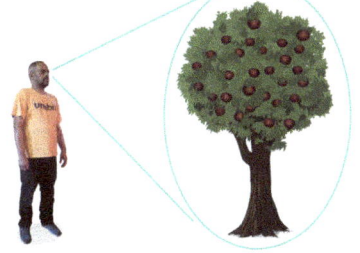

More beliefs – Narrow vision **Less beliefs – Wider vision**

- You are only able to see what you believe. If you add more beliefs, your visibility will become narrower. The more you release those beliefs, the more you will be able to see in front of you.
- If you focus on your ego side, then you get the same result every time that you believe in something. Instead, focus your attention on the Source and see how that power takes over to create a new experience or result for you.
- Remember, everything you believe is not a fact, just a perspective that you hold.

30

EMOTIONS

What are emotions

Emotions are byproducts of your thoughts or information received through your senses.

WHEN YOU HAVE POSITIVE THOUGHTS, like when you were a child playing with your toys or friends, you felt happiness, excitement, love, joyfulness, etc.

When you have negative thoughts, like remembering an accident that happened recently, your emotions could be sadness, anger, hate, revenge, etc.

A question arises whether your thoughts and emotions created the incident or the incident triggered them. The answer is both, but it happens in steps:

- Initially, your continuous thoughts create similar emotions in yourself and ultimately result in an experience. Since you are emitting that frequency, as per the law of attraction, you get that experience.

Negative Thoughts... + Emotions ▷ Experience

Sad

- When that experience happens, your senses send information to your brain and thus show up as an emotion. You keep thinking about that experience again and again. The result is a similar type of experience until you shift your thoughts and feelings.

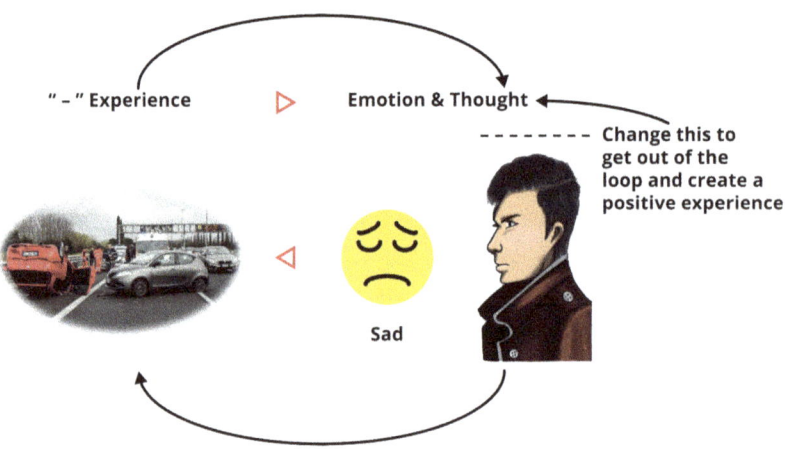

" – " Experience ▷ Emotion & Thought ◄

- - - - - - - Change this to get out of the loop and create a positive experience

Sad

Emotional Scale

Emotions are your Indicator

- Emotions are your indicator to let you know what your vibrational level is. Whether you are in a positive vibe or a negative vibe.
- Usually, these emotions, especially unwanted ones, seek your attention to be dealt with, released, and understood.

- Your feelings and thoughts dictates your experience. If this experience is unpleasant, it shows up again as an emotion. Especially if you start indulging in that emotion over a period of time, rather than coming out of it by changing your thoughts to something positive or pleasant one. For example, if you accidentally touch your hand on a fire, you feel pain and your immediate reaction would be to remove your hand from the fire, rather than keeping your hand in the fire and thinking *"why you are feeling pain?"*. It's the same with emotions; you need to shift to something that feels better rather than staying there.

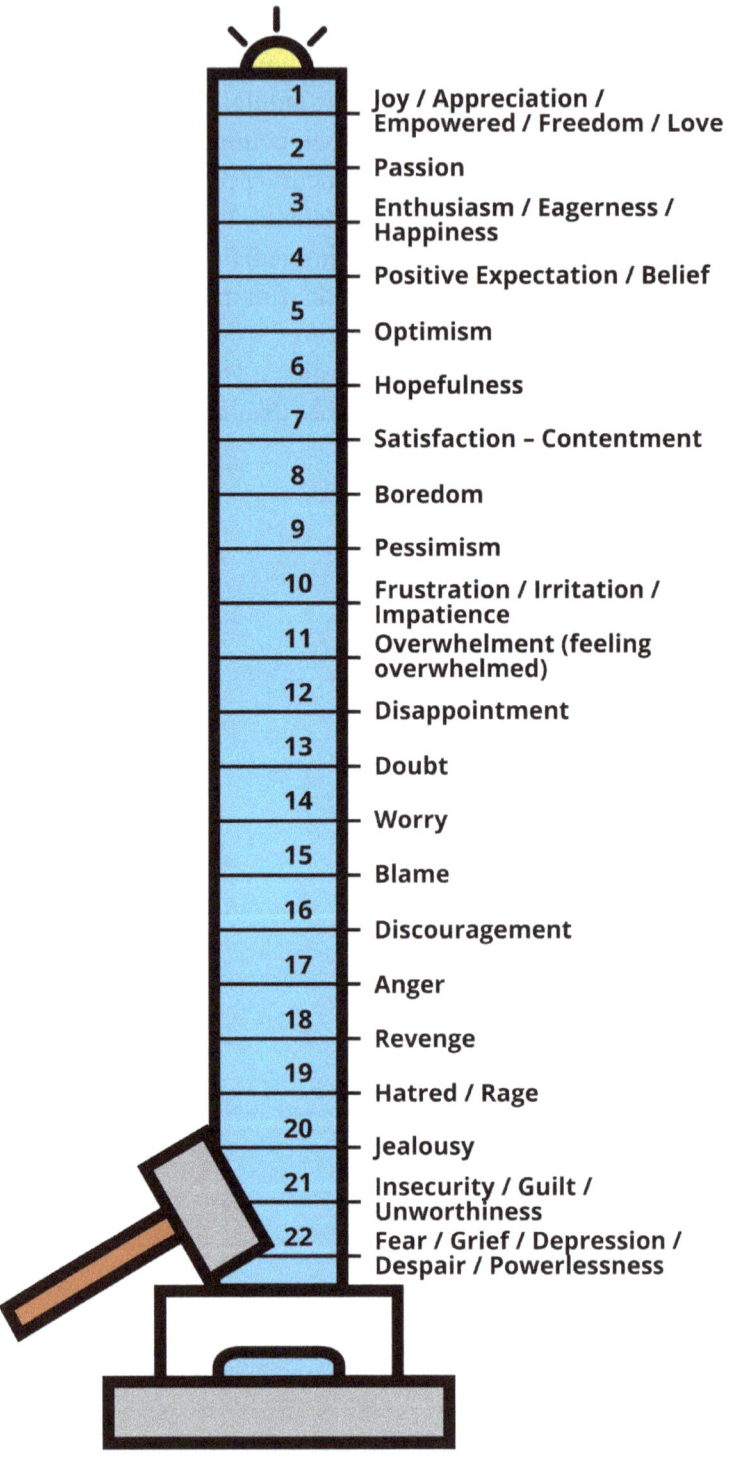

Source credit: Abraham, Esther Hicks"

Let's look at some examples. Suppose you are driving a car on a highway and the speed limit is 50 miles, but you are driving at 90 miles. You saw the speed limit but still continue to maintain 90 miles. In the next few blocks, a cop pulls you over and gives you a ticket. You saw the speed limit of 50 miles but you still stayed at a speed of 90 miles. Similarly, you know the emotion you are vibrating at any given moment, and you are still maintaining the same emotion.

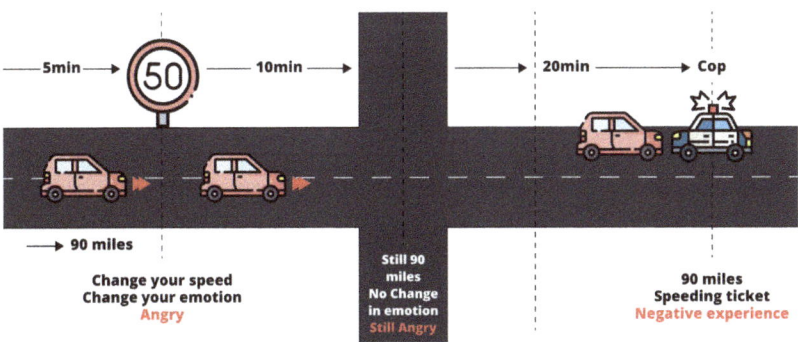

Supposedly in the same scenario, as soon as you see the speed limit of 50 miles, you shift your speed and bring it down to 50 from 90 miles, and you pass the cop without any issues. Likewise, when you notice emotions such as anger, you deal with it and move on; do not soak in it. Or you will have a similar experience that reflects that feeling which you don't want.

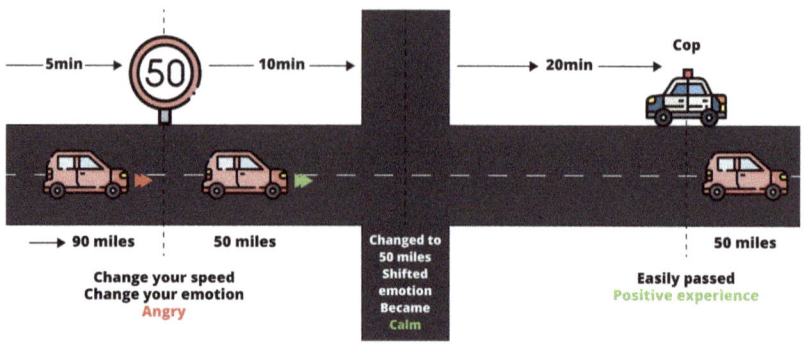

How do you deal with your unwanted emotions?

You can categorize emotions into short and long term, depending on how long it stays with you.

Short term

You can deal with unwanted short term emotions by focusing your attention on something that feels better to you. For example, instead of showing anger to others, when you get angry or upset, try to take a deep breath. By taking a deep breath, you start relaxing. You could also go out for a walk in nature, read some uplifting articles, or watch some funny comedy movies. You immediately diverted your attention from that anger and calmed your mind.

Long term

Long term unwanted emotions stay with you for long periods and keep popping up again and again. It remains until it has been dealt with and released. Some of these emotions are grief, depression, sadness, guilt, anxiety, fear, worry, or unworthiness. If not dealt with pretty soon, it shows up in your physical body as illness or disease.

Typically, you tend to deal with these emotions by either suppressing them or diverting your attention to something else. But actually, you should deal it with a clear understanding:

1. You know that you are a pure consciousness (a soul) by now after going through the previous chapters. Now, try to see yourself as that consciousness - it has zero effect on these emotions. Try to witness it without any attachment to it.
2. Emotions are not permanent. They come and go like a wave in the ocean. Viewing emotions based on who you are will release that negative emotion.
3. Perceive all emotions with equal sameness and witness it, rather than reacting to it by attaching it to your body and mind.

A Practical method for releasing unwanted emotions

1. Relax by taking a deep breath when you are angry.
2. Go out into nature. Nature is the best medicine. It brings you back to that higher vibration.
3. Do meditation, especially a guided meditation at the initial stage.
4. Talk to one of your trustworthy friends and express your feelings.
5. Write down your feelings.
6. Enquire within yourself; often those unwanted feelings seem to be unnecessary and not worth keeping. Since it is

trying to bring it to your attention, take that feeling from a positive point of view, learn from it, and release it.

What do we learn from it?

1. Thoughts and emotions create experiences.
2. Emotions are your indicators; they show what you are emitting at that moment. These unwanted emotions are trying to seek your attention, so try to deal with it and then release them.
3. You can deal with short term unwanted emotions by focusing your attention on something that feels better.
4. If unwanted long term emotions are not dealt with very soon, they may end up in your physical body as illness or disease until you reach a resolution.
5. Feelings will come and go like waves in the ocean; they are not permanent.
6. Witnessing emotions based on who you are will release those unwanted emotions.
7. Be vigilant about the emotions that show up.

Real Incident

This happened to one of my friends and it's her description below. It tells how she dealt with her emotions based on an unexpected incident.

"In a past life or situation, you have gone down that road, that is why you decide to go another way. The first time I realized how powerful it was, how life-altering it could be, it was scary.

Over 12 years ago, I learned to dive in South Africa in a small town that had a large seal colony; which meant a high number of great white sharks in winter. It was every divers dream to see great whites, but not mine. I was always happy and peaceful in the ocean. I loved to be on a dive with no expectations. I found that my happy place was the ocean.

One winter's day, a club diver wanted to go for a dive. He was twice my width and height, massive guy, and an experienced diver. I was the only Divemaster on duty, so I shut the dive shop and led the dive. It was a shore entry, which meant you walked in, put your fins on, and inflated your BCD (Flotation device), swimming on the surface of the ocean to the dive site, then together you would drop down on the dive site/reef. However, this day was a beautifully calm winter day; I can still remember it clearly. We made it to the beach in our full kit, the general place for our shore entry and walked in confidently.

I looked at my diving buddy and said, "We're putting on our fins and descending right now." "But why? We always drop on top of the dive site. I don't want to waste our dive time and air like this," He replied. I remember a feeling of utter dread at that statement, but I was determined, "No, we drop now. It's my call, and I'm Divemaster." So we did, at chest height, behind the breakers of the waves we put on our fins and descended below the surface. Side by side, we swam out to the reef underwater. When we reached the area that we usually drop to from the surface, I noticed a shape in front of us. The previous month, I had seen a school of dolphins pass by. You hear them first, then you see them underwater, and they're fast swimmers.

That day, I thought I saw the outline of a dolphin, it's back. However, as the tail swung into view of the animal before me, I realized the angle was wrong. My whole body froze underwater. The tail was up-right instead of horizontal. This was a great white shark and it was larger than my partner and I, about 2.5m or 7ft. My brain summarized it was a juvenile, a young male. My heartbeat started racing. I signaled to my buddy that there was a shark, and we sank to the bottom of the ocean. My mind worked on overdrive. Was this why I wanted to drop early in on the dive? I looked around me and realized this was exactly where we would usually descend.

Now, the protocol was to wait and see if it circled, and importantly, stay still. If you didn't see it in a few minutes, you could continue the dive, but if the shark circled, you canceled the dive. Ironically, this shark circled. I signaled to my buddy and terminated the dive. We started turning to make our way back to shore. On the third time, we saw it, curious the juvenile came head-on at my buddy and I.

As a diver, I had learned how to deal with this and I took out my spare air source and let off a bunch of bubbles. It got scared and swam off into the murky water. My brain was now focused on getting out as quickly as possible, hand over hand, crawling, and kicking our way to shore, determined to stay as low as possible. The fourth time we saw it was right behind the breakers on our way out. I remember being terrified but did not want to lose sight of it. My buddy grabbed me by the back of my BCD and hauled me over a rock when I got stuck in-between it and a set of waves. In the shallows, I sat and peeled off my fins, then hastily walked out of the water that was once my haven. I sat on some steps and hyperventilated.

My buddy was kind, and worriedly asked, "Are you okay? What kind of shark was that? It wasn't a Raggy, was it?" At that moment, I realized he didn't know it was a great white shark. So I told him. He told me I was nuts, but I had GoPro footage to prove it. The footage was shaky, but you could see it was a great white.

I also realized that my buddy being twice my height and weight, if we had descended where we should've, I would never have been strong enough to pull him down if he saw the great white and got scared first. He would have bolted to the surface and been in a lot of trouble.

To this day, I can still remember the pattern of where the grey and the white meet on that great white; it came so in proximity. That afternoon though, I went to my skipper at the time and told him I didn't want to get back in the sea. He was the one person who knew and loved the ocean in the same way that I did. I didn't know how I was going to get back in the water and was thinking of resigning. I was terrified. He told me to meet him at the pub for the rugby game and we would talk then.

When I walked into the pub, he had two drinks: double brandy with coke, ready for me. It was a strange coping mechanism. One I didn't think was appropriate, but it did loosen my tongue and got me talking. We spoke a lot that evening and he told me about his experiences and of his love for sharks. He told me juveniles are mostly inquisitive because divers look like a meal yet behave completely differently. In fact, they make way more bubbles than seals. He explained how he overcame his fears and how he wants to see every species of shark. Everyone was so jealous that we had seen a great white, and here I was thinking, *well I wish you had too and I did not!* When you are not mentally prepared to see that, it's quite humbling.

The next morning, I found myself with an open water course to teach, close to the same shore entry where I saw the shark the previous day. Setting up the gear, I couldn't tell if I was nervous or hungover. My skipper was there for support with a cigarette and a cup of coffee in his hand. When I noticed him finally, all I got in return was a quiet nod and *you can do it* motion from the boardwalk. It took me three tries to go in and under the water again. It was one of the hardest things I have ever had to do. But to this day, I am so glad I trusted my gut instinct on that dive and dropped early.

My love for the ocean won over my fear of that incident. I went on to become a Scuba Instructor and then traveled to the Bahamas where I worked my way up in a company to captain. Looking back, if I had never gone back in that ocean, or if an incident possibly occurred with that shark, I would never be where I am now. I would never have met my partner, whom I know is my person and never would have traveled as much as I have. It was a big turning point for me. I have come to love sharks with a healthy respect, and trust my intuition way more.

Years later, on one of my return trips home, I met up with that skipper for a cup of coffee on the beach. We reminisced about the old days fondly. I asked what he was thinking that day on the boardwalk after I had seen the great white. He said he had never seen anyone so terrified of a shark he really didn't think I would go back in. We laughed about it because the only reason I did go back in was that he was standing there.

Sometimes life is full of funny twists and turns"

31

HAPPINESS

Happiness is a feeling that everyone prefers to have and is dependent on the state of your mind. Each person experiences it based on the condition of their mind. Some people feel happy when they gain material objects, or a particular companion, or when they share things or ideas. Some people feel happy by causing trouble. Bringing stability to your mind is crucial.

Temporary happiness

Temporary happiness, as the name implies, is happiness only for a certain amount of time. Typically, you achieve this by chasing an object, person, place, or event.

For example, suppose you have an old phone and you desire to have the latest iPhone. For your birthday, your dad surprises you with that iPhone. As soon as you see and physically touch the iPhone, your mind feels happy. Imagine, your happiness is at 100% on your birthday. You feel happy for 10 or 20 days. As time passes, the feeling starts decreasing. One day, you lose interest in your iPhone, and your mind starts craving something new to find an equal amount of happiness similar to what you felt in the beginning.

Next time you become happy when you get a new car, friend, receive a bonus, etc. As time passes by, again your happiness drops and you become sad, looking for new external things. Your happiness reduces similar to the depreciation of a car as time continues to pass by.

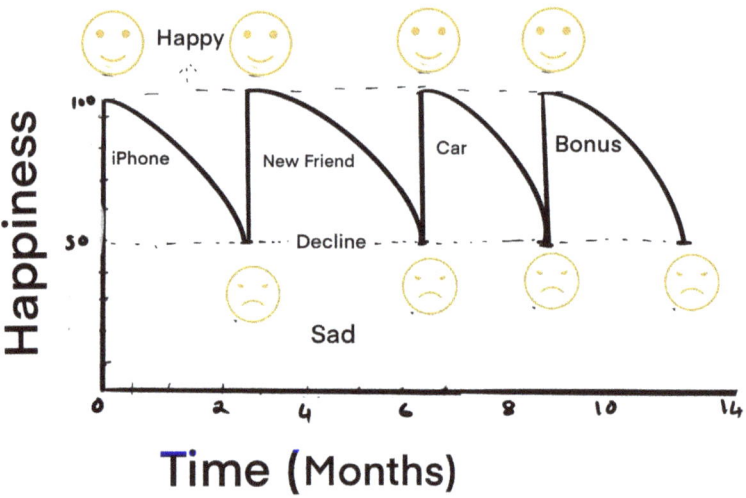

In the above scenarios, the person is looking for happiness through external objects or events with the false assumption that chasing desires brings happiness. And in essence, it's the state of your mind which controls it. For example :

1. **New Desire**: in your mind, you get a desire for a new iPhone.
2. **Expectations**: your mind relays exaggerated reports to you that if you get that new iPhone, you will be happy.
3. **Experience**: once you get the new iPhone, your mind becomes quiet for some time. However, later it jumps back again, looking for other new objects instead of the remaining happiness observed previously in that iPhone.

You realize that all the excitement was about getting the new iPhone. It was not about actually experiencing the iPhone. Therefore, you can determine that your mind is always fluctuating and chasing around your desires. It provides you with a false impression that fulfilling those desires makes you happy. Thus, it's the state of the mind that dictates your happiness.

Everlasting Happiness

- First, you need to understand who you are. You are not this body nor the mind. You are an individual consciousness (soul), and happiness is one of the qualities that make up who you already are.
- You do not have to chase external objects. Of course, we need objects in this physical world, but treat objects for comfort, not for your emotional state.
- Happiness is only achievable in the present moment. Happiness is not gained by continually postponing it to the future, so always be present at the moment.

Levels of Happiness

There are various levels of happiness. Staying at one level will always bring sadness in yourself and you should always aim to climb up the ladder to have a steady level.

- Experience happiness at the sensory level (touch, taste, see, hear, smell). It can be objects, people, or events.
- Born out of thoughts that bring enormous amounts of joy to you. For example, writing a song, solving problems, etc.
- At an intellectual level, it brings a deep level of flow in concentration and absorption, such as creativity.
- Happiness due to the joy of service to others.
- Finding happiness through deep meditation.
- Finally, it's about understanding who you are. It's one of the qualities of an individuated consciousness that make up who you are.

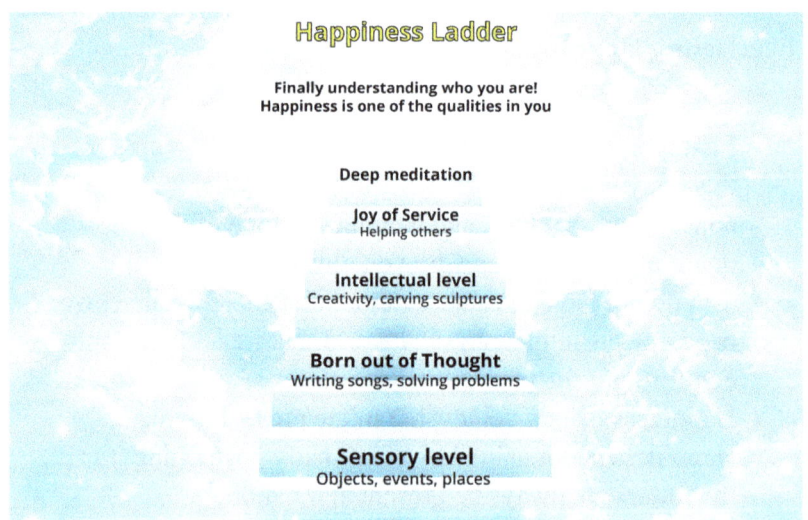

Five vital factors for happiness and well-being

According to Martin Seligman, a pioneer in the field of psychology, who has created a model for happiness and well-being called PERMA.

- **P**ositive emotions – feeling good.
- **E**ngagement – being completely absorbed in activities.
- **R**elationships – being authentically connected to others.
- **M**eaning – purposeful existence.
- **A**chievement – a sense of accomplishment and success.

By focusing on these five factors, you can flourish and bring happiness in your life.

How to bring happiness in your life:

1. Happiness is one of the qualities of YOURSELF. So, abiding in the experience of one's self brings about joyfulness.
2. Happiness is dependent on your state of mind. Therefore, you can bring calmness by doing meditation.
3. Positive emotions such as love, optimism, and greatness play a role in bringing happiness. Try to notice your emotional states. Take note of whether you are emitting positive emotions or more negative emotions. If you're in a negative mood more often, like sadness, greed, anger, and jealousy, then work on those emotions (see emotion topic for more information).
4. Try to be grateful and appreciate what you have at the moment. Often your mind tries to compare yourself with someone higher than yourself, but you should always compare yourselves to those who are lower than you and be grateful for what you have; be satisfied. It will steady your mind.
5. Try to work on and maintain interpersonal bonds with

your family, friends, and any individual people you come across in life.

6. To have a meaningful life, for instance, requires doing activities that bring deep meaning to your life, such as helping others.

7. Find your flow. Often it's defined as a deep absorption or concentration on something that interests you. You'll tend to indulge in interests that bring you happiness. It can be anything; game building, designing something, etc.

8. Your continuous thoughts create neural circuits in your brain and continuously thinking positively brings fulfillment in your life. A vital aspect of being happy is to be aware of your thoughts.

~

32

REGRET

R egret is an event that happened in the past. You try to remember that incident, which causes you to bring those emotions to the present moment in the form of regret, guilt, or shame.

Regret can be for:

- A situation or event that happened in the past.
- A particular person, such as a family member, friend, or stranger.

Regret for an event or situation:

For example, in the past, you had a job offer and you denied that offer. Now you find yourself regretting or feeling guilty about why you didn't choose that job.

In this scenario, note that

- You acted with good intentions at that time based on the situation.
- Your Higher Self knows what is right for you at that moment. Maybe the job will not provide you the happiness that you seek. There is nothing to regret about it.
- You are the creator of your reality. Instead of regret, use your creation to get a new job. There is always a job for you; you have to believe in yourself and create it without any resistance.

Regret for a particular person.

Suppose you did something wrong to someone that you regret or feel guilty. Why did you do that? In this scenario, note that:

- You are having a higher understanding now and that's why you regret or feel guilty. You take this as a positive.
- You can ask for forgiveness directly with that person and that person can choose to forgive you. However, if that

person is not ready to forgive you, then when you are alone, close your eyes, imagine asking for forgiveness with that person, bless them, release, and move on.

What do we learn from it?

1. When a regretful or guilty emotion appears, it's because some action is remembered from a new perspective or awareness. Accepting with love that you acted from the highest sense at that time is the way to go.
2. Every situation is a pre-planned interaction providing you the opportunity for spiritual growth for all who were involved.
3. Sometimes, the emotions are showing you false beliefs within you, and seek your attention to be released/ changed (refer to belief topic).

33

CHOICES AND DECISIONS

Choices and decisions we make

E veryone has free will to make their own decisions and this is one of the universal laws. There are circumstances in life where you have multiple choices or paths, and you are in that moment to decide on those choices. You make choices based on either:

1. Logical or Rational.
2. Random selection.
3. Other's opinions or they make decisions for you.
4. Following similar footsteps that others have taken etc.

The choices and decisions that you make above may either be led by your ego driving you to decide based on logic. Alternatively, through the confusion, you are scratching your chin to figure out the best choice to make. Lastly, you could have given up your power to others so that they may decide for you.

Choices – In a state of confusion

How to make a perfect choice

- When you are in complete unification with your inner being and have full clarity, then choices don't exist in regards to where you are at the present moment. You are just flowing naturally at the moment and taking the path without the option of choices. Ultimately this brings great excitement or passion within you.

No choices – Complete unification with inner being with full clarity

- Trust the feeling or internal guidance coming from your heart rather than the rational mind. Since your Higher Self is communicating through your heart with emotions, it knows what's best for you at that particular moment.

Suppose you are walking on a path in the park and you come across three diversions. One of the pathways is leading you in the right direction, the rest are not since it is blocked by bushes. In order to choose the right pathway, you need to trust the inner guidance coming from your heart through feeling (known as your gut feeling). The Higher Self knows the best way and it can see all the options on where each path leads to. So, it tries to communicate through your heart and is noticeable by feelings. In this example, your Higher Self is standing on top of the mountain. It has a complete perspective of all the views compared to your physical Self that limited view.

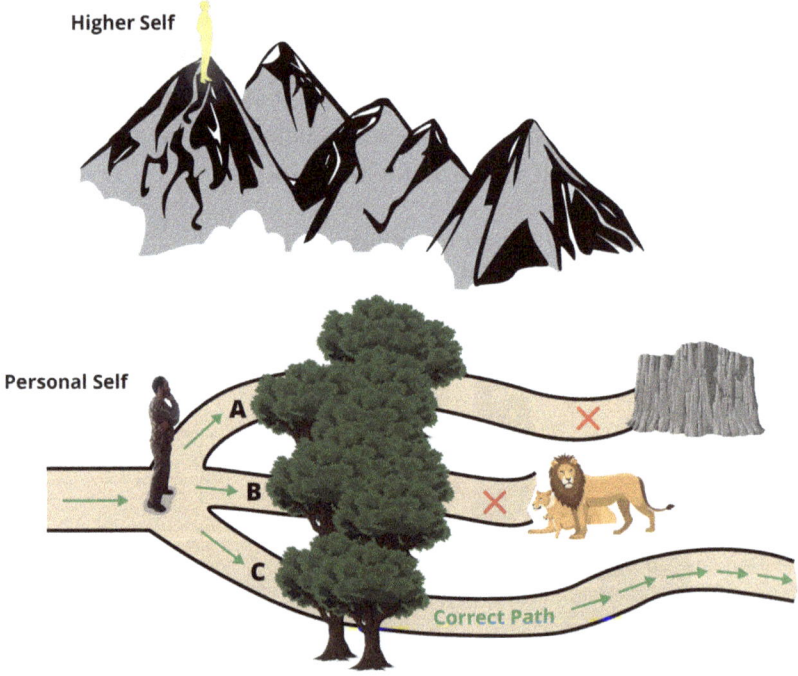

- If you are in a situation and you make a decision, then talk to your heart and check the inner guidance coming from your heart. It can concur or sometimes can direct

you in the right direction. Like, tells you to take something/go somewhere before deciding.
- Listen to your inner guidance. Trust it, make a decision, and finally apply that decision.

What do we learn from it?

- Nobody chooses you other than yourself. If someone is making choices for you, then you are giving the power to them. Take it back.
- If you are always uncertain of your choices, then you are not trusting yourself.
- Trust your inner guidance coming through your heart rather than logically figuring out the choices that your ego-mind is telling you.
- Love, trust, and kindness bring a state of confusion to rest.
- When you are deciding without choices, then you are in a natural state and completely aligned to your inner being. All you are doing is just following your Higher Self.

Real Incident

Let me give you a real example that happened to one of my friend's family. The choices and decision they made changed their life forever.

For example, fear is natural in anybody. The key is to keep your belief larger than your fear. Over the years, I have noticed that people with strong beliefs tend to fare much better in their trials.

For example, I knew of a friend who, at a young age of 10, found out her father got diagnosed with stage 4 cancer and was given ten months to live. Soon after diagnosis, her mother fell pregnant with a baby girl. At this point, you have someone who had every intention of building a family, and then they are told they're going to die with only a 5% survival rate.

There are two paths here. One, giving up and letting the doctors be right, having no control over your life. Or two, have hope. The positive belief that tomorrow will be a better day, and you should keep fighting to be there for your family and yourself. The transformation in the family was extraordinary. The mother told the father that in no uncertain terms, was he going to die. He was not allowed to give up on them and their family. They would battle cancer together, and do what they could one day at a time. He was going to win this battle for their unborn child and their family.

The father changed his lifestyle and thought process completely. It was a choice he made, a belief so strong it was life-altering in its conviction if he made these changes he would survive.

He changed his diet, he walked every day on the beach, around their small town, and greeted everyone with a smile and a polite good day no matter how much pain he was in. He spent time with his family and diligently went to his chemo sessions. Sometimes his wife, daughters, or uncle would go with him. Whenever he came out of his chemo sessions, they were there smiling and happy to see him again.

The emotional toll on the family itself exceeded the comprehension of the father. You see, it wasn't only him fighting cancer to be with his family. It was also his entire family fighting to keep him around for longer. They lived and breathed positivity.

A year or so later, his cancer progressed. Chemo did not work as well as they had hoped, so they tried radiation. Did they give up hope? No, they banded together stronger. Yes, there were tears of sadness and lots of hugs and love when the news came, but this made them all the more determined.

They made T-shirts with radiation signs on them for every family member and had a big family gathering before his first session of radiation. To the family, there was hope. He was still standing there with them, noticeably lighter in body but not in spirit.

After radiation, the family went through many more hardships, financially and emotionally. His one kidney was riddled entirely with cancer. He said it felt like he walked around with a lump of stone within him.

The doctor wanted to operate, but the father said no. Why? Because every person he had sat with going through chemo, who had gone under the knife, had not recovered. For some reason, when they were cut open, it seemed their cancer would spread. Believing that, the father did not want to be cut open but would rather weather the storm. *Note: This is an opinion of what was best for himself.*

One day the father was finally given the *recession* talk from his doctor. His cancer had finally stopped spreading. The damage report was in; a tumor around his heart that was 9cm by 13 cm had disappeared, the second spread of lymphatic cancer in his lymph nodes cleared up, and one kidney was no longer functional. He was part of that winning 5%. His belief in staying with his family, combined with his family's positivity, helped steer the course to a better day.

The father now calls the day that the doctor told him the cancer was in recession his second birthday. The extra decade with his family, that they've had so far, was viewed as a gift. They're l understanding that few others who had the same diagnoses were that lucky. Thankfully, there was hope.

The point is the cleansing, belief, and hope had to go hand in hand. Now, this doesn't mean a belief in religion or an idea in something. It is merely a conviction in something that you hold great value in a high positive vibration. He believed he would beat it with the help and support of his family and his inner unfailing conviction.

Every year, the father would go back to the Oncology center and the doctor who had helped him through that tough time. He would take flowers and chocolates for the staff that worked there and pop in for a cup of tea with them.

Years later, one of his daughters asked why he kept doing that if it was such a hard time in his life. Why did he want to go back to the place he was sick in? His response:

"Those doctors and nurses fought hard to keep positive for us in our greatest challenge. Most people who sit in those chairs in the chemo room don't make it. By going back, I say thank you for their hope in me, and their help when I was sick. I hope that I can be the positive moment they need to keep going, doing the great work they do, reminding them that some people do make it. Everyone gets down now and again. Taking a few minutes to remind them of some battles you win is important, even against all odds. Sometimes in life, you don't understand the value of a presence until it's gone."

34

JEALOUSY

Jealousy is an emotion that occurs when you see someone thrive when you are not. You try to compare yourself with someone else and feel jealous about it. It can be :

- A promotion that your friend got.
- The other team wins the game.
- Your relatives are wealthy, and you are not.
- Your friend is cruising in the Caribbean, and you are not.

This is an old paradigm, playing the game of limitation. Right from childhood, limitations have ingrained into our mind, and it emphasizes that there is only so much to go around, or the world is full of competition, or You have to work hard to win. If your relative is wealthy, it doesn't mean that you cannot be rich as well. It's just a matter of changing your perspective and understanding.

How to overcome jealousy

1. Try to take a deep breath and release it. Repeat until the mind becomes calm.
2. Decide why you have this jealousy. Are you comparing yourself to objects, happiness, people, or other's successes?
3. Never think there is a shortage; there is always enough for everyone. You are the creator of your universe.
4. If you feel jealous while comparing yourself to others, then compare yourself to someone who is lower than you in that particular aspect. For example, instead of comparing yourself to your relative or friend's richness, always compare yourself to poor people. Immediately, your mind will calm down and be content with what you have.
5. Next, at a deeper level, you need to have an understanding that everyone is connected and all are one.
6. See someone else's success as your success since we are all connected. When you are celebrating someone's success, you're vibrating at a high frequency; your desire to manifest speeds up based on the law of attraction.

Note: If someone can do it, they are opening a doorway to you, to follow in similar footsteps/path for success.

35

DOMINATION

Dominating over others

Domination is control over others while acting in the space of fear. When a person is trying to dominate others, that person is holding a negative belief that he or she has no power within them. Therefore, they are trying to control others to make themselves feel safe. They are in a complete state of denial to look within themselves and find out why they feel powerless.

For example, six team members are working on a particular project for a company. Out of those six, one of them, let's say, Angie, is trying to dominate others by informing them what to do, what not to do, demanding to provide results to her, even though she is not the manager or leader for that team. Angie is dominating others based on fear and on the assumption that she is powerless.

How to overcome domination

Identify the negative beliefs that is causing the fear. Remove the beliefs or substitute with positive ones that eliminates the fear within you.

Become powerful within. Understand who you really are and from that space; you are already powerful to create whatever you want without affecting or controlling others. In the example above, what are the negative beliefs that Angie is holding that is causing her fear and domination over others? It could be fear of losing a job and believing that only the fittest can survive in this modern age. In order for her to overcome her fear, the limited belief has to be removed.

Once Angie clearly understands who she really is and how powerful she is within, she doesn't have to be in that old belief that the fittest only survive. Instead, she can substitute it with positivity, such as, there is enough for everyone and she is the creator of her reality.

This positive belief will take the fearness out of her and become powerful inward, not projecting outside, and not controlling others.

36

ANGER

What is anger?

Anger is one of the emotions seen quite often in people
due to:-

- Conflicts.
- Frustration.
- A habit programmed from childhood.
- Built-up challenges and resentments within.

We often deal with anger by either:

- Releasing that anger on someone else or to ourself.
- Holding onto anger for a long time without releasing it, causing harm to ourself or others when sudden release.
- If you are suppressing anger without dealing with it, it can cause health issues later on in life.

How to deal with anger?

First of all, it's unnecessary to show your anger to others or yourself.

To have anger by itself is not wrong or harmful. It's one of the emotional indicators showing you that certain things within you are not in alignment.

Use this method to release anger:

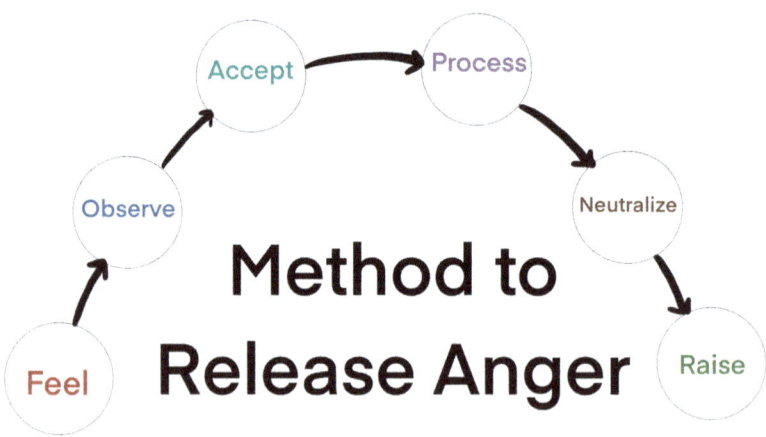

Feel: Feel the anger that is coming in you.

Observe: Observe the anger flowing in your body and mind.

Accept: Accept without any judgment and resistance.

Process: Process it by finding the root cause. What is that you are not in agreement that's causing this vibration? Beneath this anger may be a type of fear or jealousy residing in you. Is this your normal behavior from childhood? Work on it and try to change that pattern. Self-realization is the key to change.

Neutralize: Take a deep breath and release that anger during exhaling; do it quite often until you neutralize it.

Raise: Raise your vibration in order to come back to your normal state of joy and love. Your anger is on the negative side of the emotional scale, and you need to raise your vibration to a positive scale. For most of them, it's hard to raise your vibration suddenly from anger to happiness or love (check emotional scale). So, the technique should be to lift it one level at a time. As you feel comfortable in that vibration, raise it again. Use this method until you come back to your state of happiness, joy, or appreciation.

For example, suppose your anger is at 17 on the emotional scale. It would be easy to raise it one level at a time to 16. This level is discouragement compared to joy, which is at level 1. It's better than anger, and if you continue to raise your level one more level to blame, then to worry, and continue on until you come back to joy or appreciation.

Note: Refer to the emotional scale in the previous emotion chapter.

∼

37

CHALLENGES AND LIFE LESSONS

I f you ask what life is all about, some would say that life is full of challenges. Challenges are events in their life which they have no control over. Sometimes it pushes them so hard that it's unbearable. Not knowing how to overcome those challenges, they take extreme actions by attempting to end their life, or fall into depression.

A girl named Jesse

Let me tell you a story about a girl named Jesse. She was born into a low-income family. Her dad was a cab driver and her mom was a housewife. Jesse had one brother who was five years younger than her. She was a brilliant student, always happy, and had fun playing with her brother and friends. Her childhood was relatively normal. One day, her mom became sick when she was in middle school. Her mom was completely bedridden, so it became Jesses' responsibility to take care of the family.

Every morning, Jesse woke up at 4:30 am, cooked breakfast, and packed lunch for her dad. She woke her brother at 7 am, got him ready, packed his lunch, and dropped him off at school. Then got back home and cared for her mother, fed her breakfast, and gave her medication. Jesse would help her in every possible way she could before she had to go to school. After school, Jesse would go straight home and continue caring for her mom. Jesse helped her mother to freshen up, cook dinner, and then assisted her brother with his homework. It was a daily routine in her life from a young age.

At school, Jesse was a brilliant student. She was always focused, driven, and concentrated very well in class. With little time for chit chat with friends, her grades were consistently A or A+. Since Jesses' family struggled financially, she had very few dresses to wear for school. She used to wash the same one quite often and wear it repeatedly. Jesse's main goal was to study hard, get a good job, and earn money to look after her family when she grew up.

As time passed by, she got older and still kept taking care of the family. At the age of 18, she joined university, choosing English as a major. Slowly her mom started recovering from her sickness during that time. Finally, Jesse was able to breathe; her life was getting better.

While Jesse was still in college, she received a marriage proposal from one of her friend's relatives. Jesse was still 19 with a focus on getting a degree; she was not ready to get married. Her parents convinced her to settle down. They reasoned that the groom was from a well off family, and it was not polite to reject such a good offer. The groom agreed for her to continue her lessons even after they got married. He also accepted to not have any children until she finished her degree. All of these aspects made Jesse agree to the marriage.

Jesse got married. She continued her studies, and within a year, she had a baby boy, even though they had not planned for it. One day, when the baby was three months old, her husband went to another town to meet someone. On his way back, he was involved in a car accident and died. Jesse's life became devastated again. She had a three-month-old baby, her husband died, they were financially unstable, and her studies were put on hold. She thought of ending her life, but because of her baby, she decided not to. If she had died nobody would have been able to take care of her baby. Her parents were poor and far too old to help.

Jesse moved back to her parents' house with the baby. For two years, she was depressed until she started making a comeback.

Working in a manufacturing company on the morning shift and also finishing her degree part-time. If you fast forward her story ten years, she is now a university professor teaching B.A students, remarried, and finally well settled down in life.

Dissecting Jesse's Life

If you read the entire story, you come to an understanding that Jesse was born to a low-income family and went through those challenges to understand/ experience what it meant to be courageous and caring; this was her life lesson.

You may ask, why would God create such a miserable life for Jessie? It isn't God who created it. Jesse was the one who planned everything before she was born while she was still in-between lives, with the help of her guides and her soul groups. *Note: Refer to the death and reincarnation chapter.*

Why would Jessie create such challenges for herself? We always try to understand from a human perspective and think those challenges are unnecessary. However, if you attempt to understand from your Higher Soul view, the soul gains an enormous amount of understanding and knowledge through the experiences of those challenges. Ultimately gaining wisdom and leading to the expansion of Self and Source.

When you have mastered specific challenges, chances are, you may become a guide on the other side and help others who are facing a similar situation in their physical life.

If Jesse had some spiritual knowledge and understanding of who she was, then it would have helped her to see life from a different perspective She wouldn't have gone into depression or thought about ending her life.

Also, consider the karmic factor of Jesse from previous births. What goes around comes back around again. She might be paying off some of her karma to the other souls, to her husband, father, mother, or son.

How do we find out our Life lessons?

Pay close attention to the events or situations that are happening in your life. There are large and small events that provide us clues. For example:

- Financial issues; such as losing money every time and having no control over it.
- Multiple accidents happening quite often.
- A person, group, relative, or family member is bothering you all the time.
- Not able to stick to any job for more than six months.
- A bad relationship with a spouse or other family members; always fighting.

So, if you are having a bad relationship with your spouse, family member, or friend, then chances are you took this physical birth to work on a relationship, and focus on:

- Forgiveness
- Another perspective
- Humility
- Honesty
- Love

If it is related to financial issues, then the focus could be on:

- Issue related to greed
- Happiness without attachments
- Letting go of possessions

If an accident happens in your life, then the incident is giving you clue to pay close attention. Look into yourself, contemplate, and find out the underlying cause/misalignment of the accident. If it's recurring, then you haven't resolved it yet.

How do we resolve it?

- Acknowledge the events. They are showing you something; look into yourself.
- Shatter any old beliefs that you have. Build new knowledge based on who you are.
- Work on those misalignments and bring it to alignment.

For example, if you are always:

- *Angry* : try to work and bring yourself to calm.
- *Greedy* : then work on generous.
- *Egotistical* : then work on patience, humbleness, etc.
- If it is *hate* : then work on love.
- Finally, embrace the expansion, wisdom, and knowledge brought to you from this experience.

38

DESIRES

A s a human, we all have a desire for many things. There is nothing wrong with having desires, but you need to identify their origin.

Where are your desires originating?

There are two main places:

- Ego
- True Self

Ego Desire

Most of your desires that come from your ego are selfish and do not last forever. Once your desires are satisfied, the ego will still not be content and it looks for new ones again. But within your ego, you need to identify what the real intention behind the desires is.

Suppose there are two friends, Jason and Sam. They currently live in apartments next to each other with their families. One day, during a conversation, they decide that they want to buy a house next to each other in a nice neighborhood.

Finally, they purchase one next to each other, but their intentions behind the purchases differ. Sam intended to look for comfort and the safety of his family, while Jason wanted to show to his friends and relatives how successful he is and to broadcast his achievements that he accomplished in his life.

As you can see, Jason's desires were egotistic, whereas Sam's desires were not entirely egotistical. If Sam were looking for comfort and safety, it would be fine. However, if he were desiring and needing material things for happiness, then it becomes problematic. It would hinder spiritual growth, and ultimately leading to the attachment of things.

True Self Desire

Life expressed through desires born out of truth brings intense joy and a feeling of total communion with the Source.

For example, it could be your creativity, like art, music, humanitarian services, and teaching. You express it with pure intention.

How to let go of your egos' desires:

1. Any new desires that are born in you, ask yourself this

question, "Is this desire going to bring happiness and more completeness than what you are feeling right now?". If yes, then it's born from ego.

2. Now, let go of that desire born in you by quieting the mind and bring yourself to complete pure presence.
3. Allow the sense of a separate you to dissolve into the present moment.
4. Feel what you have is good enough with complete gratitude.
5. Say in your heart, "I am whole, I am complete, thank you."

39

ATTACHMENT

A ttachment is one of the major hindrances to your spiritual growth. You have seen most people get attached to many things like money, property, power, places, people, etc. You don't easily let go; you try to treat things as your property and start accumulating those items thinking that it's going to be there with you forever. Even after knowing the fact that you die empty-handed and none of the treasure goes along with you during your departure from this world. The only thing that matters is the wisdom and knowledge gained through experiences in this life; that's it.

Story of Alexander the Great

Alexander the Great was a great warrior and king of the ancient Greek kingdom of Macedon during 356 - 323 BC. At an early age of 20, he took the throne after succeeding his father. For the majority of his ruling, he spent conquering places. By the age of

30, he had created one of the largest empires during that time, stretching from Greece to India.

He had collected many treasures during those invasions. On his way back from India, he became deathly sick. He knew he would not survive. Therefore, on his deathbed, Alexander the Great had three wishes:

1. His physician alone should carry his coffin.
2. When his coffin would go to his grave, the pathway to it should be covered with gold, silver, and precious stones from his conquests.
3. Both his hands should be kept suspended out of the coffin.

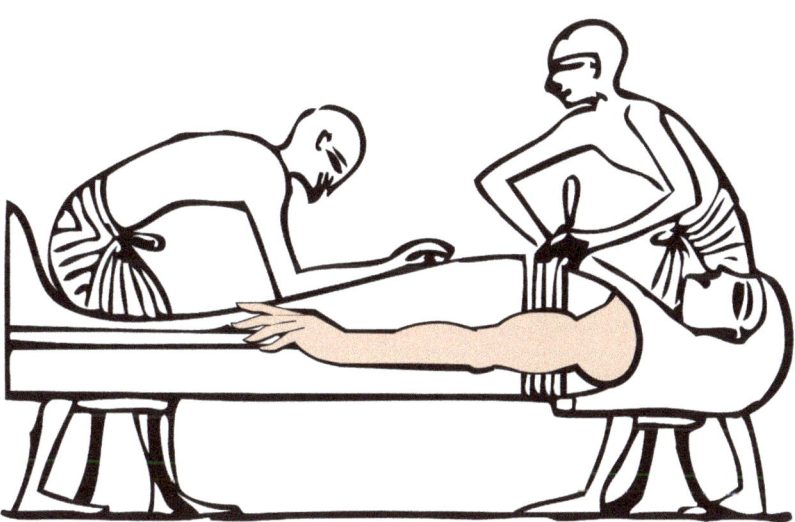

The reason for these wishes was to let the world know that:

- Not even a doctor can save a person from death.
- All his life was spent on greed. He chased wealth and conquered kingdoms for treasures and power. None of it will go with him to his death.
- Alexander the Great came empty-handed into this world, and he would go out empty-handed on his deathbed.

The life story of Alexander the Great teaches us a great lesson to be learned in our own lives.

How do we detach from attachments?

It's difficult to detach yourself. The only way you can achieve this is by practicing different kinds of attachment.

For example, a person loves tea so much that he needs to drink a cup of it every two hours. It's difficult to detach tea from this person even though he knows that he is consuming caffeine and it's unhealthy for him. The only way you can help this person is by introducing herbal tea. The person starts using herbal tea instead of regular tea, and will slowly let go of regular tea and get attached to herbal tea.

Effectively this is an attachment replaced by another external one. It solves the caffeine problem, but now the person is obsessed with herbal tea. So how does he detach completely without any attachment? The solution is to go with an internal attachment. In other words, there should be something that is pulling him from the inside; something that is powerful enough and can take away all his outside attachments, it's called meditation. By practicing meditation with the right intention, he can detach from all worldly things, objects, people, etc.

40

SITUATIONS AND VILLAINS

You live in a world where you interact with people daily. It can be your family, friends, colleagues, or strangers, and situations arise where you feel:

- Your boss or colleagues are selfish and more demanding.
- There is a misunderstanding with some of your friends.
- Unable to deal with your spouse or parents, in-laws.
- An unknown stranger is trying to control you, etc.

In these situations, you naturally tend to view yourself as being right, and they are wrong without realizing the actual reason why such situations or people come into your life.

A Group of Friends.

Let's take a group of friends. Each of them has unique characteristics, but they were able to blend easily during the early stages of their friendship. They used to have parties in each other's house, enjoy one another's company, and have fun. As time passed by, a misunderstanding started forming between them.

They started finding faults within each other. One of them began dominating the others, while some started splitting the group, making a subgroup. It became a social mess, and they eventually stopped talking to each other.

Why do these situations or villains come into your life?

No situation or person comes into your life without your consent. Whether that agreement was made before you were born or after you were born, it's free will and the choices that you have made. They tend to teach something that lacks within you and helps to bring something forward so that you can work on it and become who you are. Although, as humans, we always tend to think from a perspective that benefits or protects us. You will find that you blindfold yourself from understanding their perspective and perceive them as your villain by bearing grudges, judging, cursing, hating, or hiding from them.

How do you deal with such a situation or person in your life?

Before pointing fingers at each other, you need to have some basic understanding:

- You are the creator of your reality. You take 100% responsibility for all your actions. You manifest situations and people in your life. At a deeper level, you want to clear all your blocked energy and wounds.
- All is one, and one is all. If you understand this universal law, that we are all one, then why blame the

other person when he or she is also part of your expression?

- Everybody is playing the role you asked them to play. You wanted them to play the role of the villain before you were born. You asked them to disempower you to such an extent that you would have to go within to find the power that you have and raise from that, acquiring wisdom from that experience. It is part of the agreement that you made at the soul level in the spiritual plane. It is similar to a movie. You enjoy watching it and appreciate it. Everybody is playing their role in it. If one of the characters is a villain you are not going to hate them just because they acted as that character. When you see them in real life, you appreciate that they played their role because you know it's only a movie. Everybody is only playing their roles, and it's up to you to identify those misalignments, work on it, and raise from them.
- Reacting to a situation or person is dependent on whether you act from the truth or you are acting from your ego. The outcome will likely be unpleasant if it's from your ego. So, make sure you are acting from your truth based on who you are.

In practicality with regards to the friends' example above:

- If you are having a heated conversation with one of your friends, then first identify whether you acted from your True Self or from ego.
- If you acted from ego, then identify what is in you that you need to learn from this friend? For example, maybe you were jealous, you wanted their attention, or you wanted to lead and control the group.
- Once you have identified it, then work on it and release it. There is no point in having a grudge or judgment when you know that person is just trying to show you what you need to work on. They are there as a outer reflection of your inner world.

- If you acted from your True Self, then try to help your friend to understand who they really are and show them where the misalignment is. It's up to them to take your guidance or still act from ego. Since we live in a free-will  world, everybody has to make their own choices. You cannot interfere with their decisions. If they understand and align with their True Self, then all is well and good. If not, you did your part in helping them. Always act from your True Self with them, even though they are coming from their ego. In the worst-case scenario, release them with unconditional love, no judgment, and move on. This situation has helped you since you know that you have not misaligned and are still acting from your truth while vibrating at a higher frequency.
- If both parties are acting from ego, then the situation would be worse. Both of them can follow the steps mentioned above "If you acted from ego." [more details in Relationship chapter]

41

INFORMATION

I n this modern age, information plays a huge role in our lives. Usually, the information we hear come from:

- Newspapers, television, or radio
- Social media, books
- Families, friends, and colleagues

Often when you hear or watch any negative news, especially about things such as shootings, wars, viruses, and robberies, you tend to become emotional. You react to it by either judging, hating, harming, fearing, or sometimes adding to your belief system. It has a major impact on your vibration. You need to pay attention to the information that is shared, and it should be governed by yourself to ensure that you discern what is coming in. Carefully make sure that, it has not created any negative impact on yourself.

For example, imagine someone watches the Spartacus series. It's about how Spartacus and his fellows escaped and started an uprising against the Roman republic to achieve freedom from slave ownership. This real historic event provides some great insight into the human value and how it's right to be free. But in that process, they go through extreme agony, vengeance, and become martyrs.

After they had watched the series, the person found themselves to be emotionally triggered. They experienced sadness and realized that their vibration was low.

How do you deal with the information imparted to us?

Always discern the information that you come across, whether you hear, watch, or read it, including this book, check whether it makes sense to you based on your feelings. If it is not resonating, drop that information and take only what feels right to you.

In the Spartacus example, the knowledge and wisdom gained were on human values and their freedom. At the same time, other behaviors are portrayed that might not make any sense, such as vengeance or martyrs. None of that is necessary during this time of ascension. It's an old energy which they have already dealt with and overcome.

Pay close attention to your emotions. They tell you whether the information is uplifting, empowering, or if it is creating fear/disempowerment in you.

If information comes up and doesn't feel good to you, then don't be afraid. Don't run away from it and pretend it's not part of your experience. It's all a part of the experience in order for you to integrate all aspects of yourself to become a whole being. This is true intention you were born to achieve in this lifetime.

In practice, avoid watching, reading, or hearing negative news/information that brings fear, anger, and disempowerment within you. Instead, focus more on positive information that uplifts you to a higher vibration. Remember, whatever you focus on expands. So, if you focus more on negativity, then reality will show more of the negative things.

If you follow the information that leads you to anger or any other negative emotion, rather than indulging in that negative emotion, reach out for something that feels better. It will bring you back to a higher vibration.

Remember, the information shared is one perspective, and there are generally many other perspectives to it.

42

RELATIONSHIP

One of the biggest challenges that you face in your life is maintaining a good relationship. Whether it is with your spouse, children, siblings, parents, in-laws, friends, or colleagues. You will face issues and misunderstandings that make it hard to figure out who is correct, who is not, and what the right solution is.

How to Maintain a Good Relationship

You should bear in mind that no two people can be the same. Every person has different qualities and personality traits that make them unique. It's that very uniqueness that brings contrast to your life and many valuable learning opportunities. Imagine, if everyone had similar qualities and personalities, then the world would be robotic.

In a good relationship, there are certain things that you like and certain things you don't like. Focus on the attributes that you like or admire in a relationship instead of focusing on what you do not like about them. The world would be in a better position if everybody started focusing on things that they like in each other.

Remember, what you focus upon will expand; that's one of the universal laws.

If there is a difference in opinion or understanding between each of you, then find out what the root cause is and resolve it. It can be one or both of you acting from ego.

Never start a relationship with conditions. It will not last for long. Everyone has free will to choose and do according to their inner being. Accept changes in each other, because change is the only constant, the rest always changes.

Scenarios with solutions of your True Self and Ego

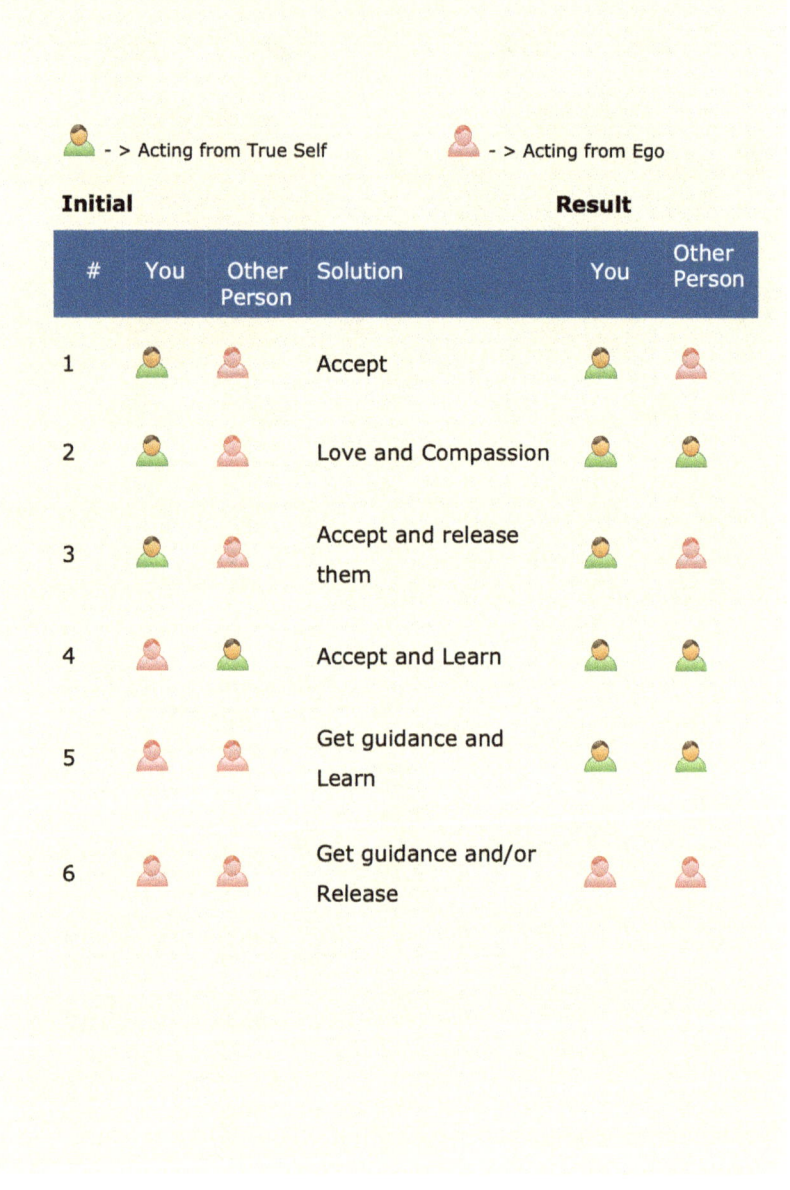

- > Acting from True Self   - > Acting from Ego

Initial   **Result**

#	You	Other Person	Solution	You	Other Person
1			Accept		
2			Love and Compassion		
3			Accept and release them		
4			Accept and Learn		
5			Get guidance and Learn		
6			Get guidance and/or Release		

1. If you are acting from your True Self and the other person is acting from ego then the solution is to accept their misalignment and focus on their positive side.

2. If you are acting from your True Self and the other person is acting from ego then the solution could come from a place of love and compassion.
3. If you are acting from your True Self and the other person is acting from ego then you could also accept and release them. This scenario happens when you are not able to bear them anymore in this life. Accept their misalignment and release them with non-judgment and unconditional love.
4. If you are acting from your ego and the other person is acting from True Self about an issue, then accept the issue. Work on it and bring yourself back to alignment.
5. If both of you are acting from a place of ego, you will need to look for guidance and learn from this experience. In this scenario, you need someone who is completely aligned with their true self to guide you. Accept the issue that both of you have to work on and bring each other back to alignment.
6. If both of you are acting from a place of an ego you will need to look for guidance and learn from this experience or release yourself from it. In this scenario, if you are still stuck to each other and acting from ego, then the situation can become even worse and create more karma. So even with or without guidance, if you are not able to work it out, then accept each other's misalignment and move on with non-judgemental and pouring unconditional love to each other.

Note: Resolving issues may be related to jealousy, attention, dependency, or anger. Check the particular emotion specified in this chapter for more details about how to resolve it.

How to deal with a negative person

Everything is energy, including our thoughts and feelings. If you come across a negative person in your life, the only way to deal with them is to maintain your higher vibration. Their behavior will bounce out from your reality when you are in a high vibrational state; nothing will affect you.

For example, say you are in a higher vibrational state which is around 70. The other person is entirely negative, so he maintains a lower vibration of 20. When you come across each other, you still meet that person, but their behavior and/or words don't affect you due to your reality being different from theirs.

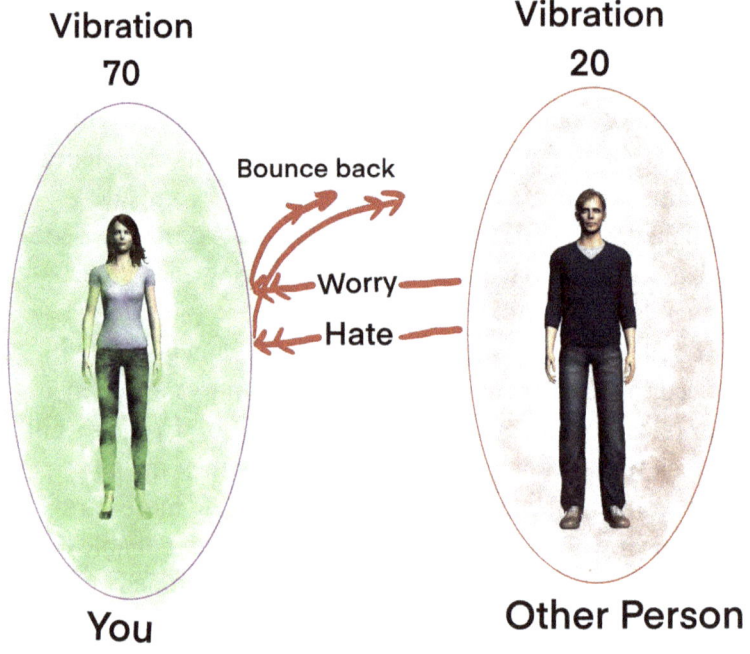

Suppose that you are more empathetic, and meeting that person brings down your vibration. Then, in that case, don't stay at that level, immediately reach for higher vibrational thoughts and move on to your original state.

43

RAISING VIBRATION

Everything in the universe is energy and vibrates at a particular frequency, including you. You are also a vibrational being; including, your thoughts, and your feelings vibrate at a specific frequency. Maintaining a high vibration is very important since that is your natural state of being. As we are so involved in worldly matters and desires that it becomes hard to maintain that high vibration.

What is your vibration at any given time?

Emotion is one of the indicators to find out your vibration. So at any moment, check how you feel. Are you feeling negative or positive emotions?

- **Negative emotions:** Unworthy, depressed, guilty, sad, angry, jealous, disempowered, shamed, doubt, worry, blame, etc.
- **Positive emotions:** Happy, bliss, empowered, passion, love, creativity, optimism, compassion, appreciation, gratitude, etc.

Negative emotion lowers your vibration, whereas positive emotion raises your vibration.

How to Raise your Vibration

There are various methods one can raise their vibration. Depending upon the circumstances and availability that suits your needs.

Breathing: Close your eyes, take a deep breath, and release it slowly. Do this, until you become more relaxed and filled with clear thoughts/feelings.

Visualization: Close your eyes, imagine a white divine light passing through from your crown chakra and rejuvenating each and every cell of your body. During this process, the chakras and aura takes all the old energy and send it back to earth through the exit point of your legs where they are grounded.

Meditate: Meditate for at least 20 minutes. You can meditate in silence or with music, mantras, or guided meditation state. Use affirmations and mantras to bring yourself back to alignment.

Nature: Go out for a walk in nature. When encompassed with the beauty and richness that mother nature offers you, it immediately brings you back to higher vibrations.

Seek out: Seek out better feeling thoughts. If you are in a situation and filled with negative emotions, then the quickest method to bring you back to your original state is to seek out thoughts that feel blissful, joyful, or happier, like imagining the happiest moment in your life.

Watch: Watch some funny or inspiring videos that make you laugh or happy.

Listen: Close your eyes and listen to light music that uplifts you.

Read: Read spiritual or inspirational books.

Gratitude: Be grateful for what you have. As you provide gratitude for each and everything in life, the universe will bring more to you.

Crystals: Crystals are like battery chargers that charge your body with high vibrations. Hold one in your hand and feel the energy of the crystal rejuvenating your entire body, bringing you back to a higher vibration.

Children or Animals: Be with your innocent children or animals. They are always at a high vibration and watching them play in full innocence will raise your vibration.

High vibes people: Avoid gossip and negativity. Stay with people who are so radiant, their energy will start resonating with you and raise your vibration as well.

Divine connection: Staying in connection with the divine all the time will maintain a high vibration in you.

NOTE: *Check my Living Librarian website under tools on how to raise your vibration through meditation with music, mantras, and more.*

44

TRAUMA

A trauma occurs to a person when a particular event, or series of events, or circumstances, have caused detrimental or have been life-threatening to them. Some of them have faced trauma since childhood. They try to suppress that energy to such an extent that the result is impacting their physical, mental, social, behavioral, and spiritual areas.

How trauma affects us

Let's take an example of Arun, a boy from a middle-class family. His father was always strict with him. For some mistakes, his father would scold and beat him. At school, he was not that intelligent. He used to fail some of his tests, especially maths and languages. It was hard for him to understand these subjects but teachers were so strict that they used to punish the students who fail by hitting their hands with a ruler or asking them to lean down outside the classroom with their mark sheet pinned to their shirt so that the entire school can watch them. It used to be an embarrassing moment full of physical abuse for Arun.

Parent scolding   **Teacher beatings**   **Punishment**

Since there was nobody that he could talk to or reveal his feelings, he buried that trauma deep within. His emotions became covered with fear, insecurity, anxiety, frustration, anger, and sadness.

Growing up as a young adult with his childhood trauma, more and more emotions were piling up, and he started attracting people, things, and events in his life that reflected those emotions, such as:

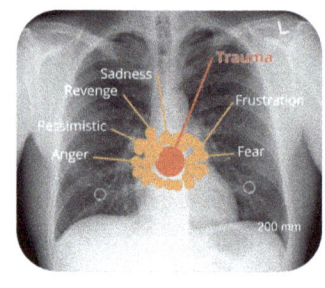

- He had enormous fear when asked to do a presentation for his boss and upper management at work.
- He always felt insecure around his friends, colleagues, or strangers, and doubted everybody.
- During his leisure time, he watched TV programs that related to sad stories.

His nature and behavior were built on those negative emotions, creating torment in his life.

How to deal with trauma

First of all, trauma needs to be dealt with and healed, not suppressed. Generally, when a traumatized person, like Arun, is triggered by others and it can bring back his past trauma. This is when people usually try to push those emotions down, numbing or repressing them. Use this opportunity to heal the blocked energy. If it isn't dealt with soon, it can show up in the physical body as an illness.

Sit in a quiet place, close your eyes, and navigate through those emotions that have covered the trauma. During this process, thoughts or feelings like anger, or revenge, may trigger you to blame others who caused it. Try to be in that high vibrational state, surrounded with love, and let go of those thoughts.

Bring all your attention to your body. Follow the movement of your breath to the place of the contraction, heaviness, or tightness.

Nurture the blocked energy with pure love, compassion, harmony, and bring peace to that trauma.

Be in that state for some time once you've finished. Then open your eyes and notice the rejuvenation and undisrupted flow of energy. It will slow your reality and change it based on the new feelings that you possess.

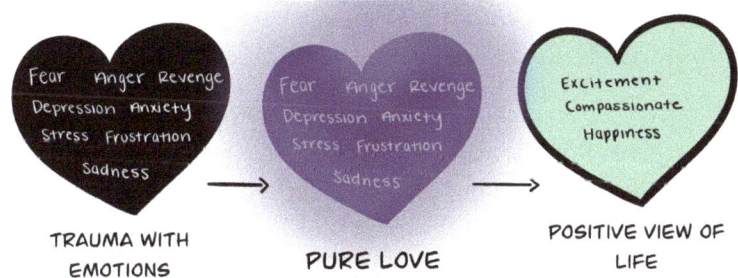

TRAUMA WITH EMOTIONS   PURE LOVE   POSITIVE VIEW OF LIFE

It's similar to a blocked pipe. All the dirt piled up to such an extent that it became blocked. Once we clean the pipe, the water starts flowing freely again.

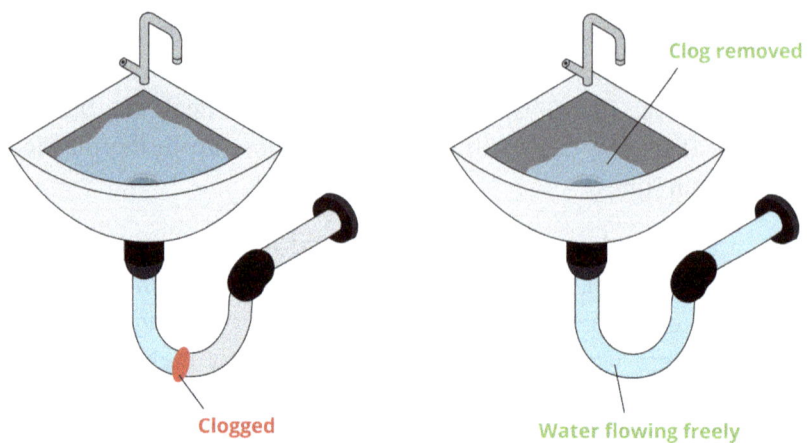

Clog removed

Clogged

Water flowing freely

The best suggestion is to be in the present moment. Following the example of children, we often see small kids argue with each other during playtime. They will be mad at each other at that particular moment but, after an adult intervention, teaching and nurturing the kids with love, they again start playing with each other as though they are buddies and as if the incident never happened. We should become more like kids in that sense.

Real Incident

Let me provide you with a real incident that happened to one of my close friends, as she stated.

"The universe does not give you the people you want. The universe gives you the people you need. To help you, to hurt you, to leave you, to love you, and to make you the person you are meant to be." Death/Life, trauma, and dealing with it: *Carolina* (Name changed for privacy purposes.)

I will never forget the day I met her. There was a grey-haired lady walking down the dock, exuding sunshine and happiness. She smiled with every bounce in her step. Carolina proudly wore a shirt with the famous pirate Blackbeard's' flag on it. Over a few days onboard, I learned that she is an incredible woman; an underwater explorer. She was first to discover a famous wreck of a pirate ship by its identifying bell, off the coast of North Carolina.

An experienced diver of over 40 years and she and her husband came on a dive trip with us. Carolina had an underwater camera setup that was her *baby* as they had never had any children of their own. It was a massive and expensive setup. Every single dive, she was first in and the last one out. The Captain at the time had said to keep an eye on her. He had an instinct you learn to listen to when you are at sea and warned us all to be wary. This Captain is a gentleman who has spent 20 years at sea. I was over three years in the company at the time and the 1st Mate on board that week. We had our full crew on board, the boats' standard Divemaster, Instructor, Engineer, and Cook, with one additional fill in Divemaster.

We were diving off an island called Eleuthera. A beautiful island, with deep walls and magnificent swim-throughs for diving, 60 plus feet of visibility in sapphire blue waters. Carolina said she was going to be skipping the next dive as she wasn't feeling well. Then the shark dive was announced as our second dive. She changed her mind and wanted to join to get some good shark footage.

During that dive, Carolina came up to the surface holding her camera in front of her out of breath. We tried to get a response out of her as it's a protocol for the diver to signal they are okay on the surface. If they don't, the procedure is to assume there is an emergency. With no response to anyone and her camera held out in front of her, she began floating down the port side to the stern. The engineer and I were on deck for surface support. The engineer grabbed his mask and fins and entered the water on snorkel gear to assist Carolina. He asked her multiple times if she was okay, and still, she gave no verbal response. I informed the Captain below deck that we needed his assistance. The engineer began towing her to the stern of the vessel. The next few minutes felt like a lifetime, and one I have relieved many times since.

Once on the stern, Carolina handed the camera to our fill in Divemaster. He passed it off to me, and I secured it. The engineer tried to get her attention to take off her fins and climb back on the boat. Her entire body became rigid, she tilted backward in her gear, flat on her back, floating on the surface, and her head started shaking. I told the fill in Divemaster to get off the ladder as he froze at the sight of her. I went down to assist the engineer. He was holding her head above the water, unable to take either of their gear off while keeping hold of the ladder. His focus was keeping her head above the water, as that was the priority. It looked like Carolina was having a seizure. I asked the group leader (also Instructor) to assist in taking off her tech gear. We quickly took off her fins and cut her out of the tec BCD as it had no buckles, and her arms were too rigid to move. At this point, we rotated her body, head towards the boat, and I positioned my shoulder right below her back to keep her head up as the engineer took her BCD away. Her face was right in front of mine, deathly pale. I couldn't process the foam starting to come out of her mouth nor the grey and white shade of her skin. All I could focus on mentally was urgently getting her onboard so that we could help her.

I remember our Divemaster pushing past the Captain, gripping one shoulder with me under the other shoulder, pushing up with an arm securing her to me. I remember the group leader holding onto the feet and pushing from the bottom. The counting of 1... 2... 3... heave, over and over and over again. I remember her face right by mine and the foam at her mouth, bubbling out and thinking *oh goodness no* as we heaved her body up step by step. Another guest had heard the commotion; she was an emergency nurse and offered to help when she heard us counting. When we reached the top of the stairs, we lay Carolina down on the floor.

The nurse looked for a pulse just as the engineer came on board with all the extra dive gear. I remember being out of breath because of the weight of hauling her up and seeing her unresponsive laying on the dive deck. I remember hearing, "No pulse, starting CPR." from the emergency nurse whose voice was suddenly serious. I remember thinking *I can not see this* and walked away, dry heaving over the side of the boat. It was a horrible loss filled sensation that overcame me, gut-wrenching.

I was determined to keep going when I realized we still had other guests onboard, I needed to set an example, so I thought *what is needed next?* The answer was oxygen. I stumbled to the bow of the boat, and the fill-in Divemaster was right behind me. We pulled out the O2 from the storage compartment. On the way to the stern, I remember asking him, "Are you O2 certified?" He swore at me and said, "Of course I am, I am an instructor." We both laughed in a weird, scared tone.

On our return, we found that the Captain was there with Carolina, he had started CPR on Carolina with the emergency nurse providing rescue breaths. The Engineer took over CPR. We set up the O2. Carolina began coughing but then became unresponsive again.

We continued with CPR, as her face turned a purple and white marble color. The nurse instructed us to cut Carolina out of her wetsuit, and we did so while the nurse slapped her face lightly and wiped the foam away, saying, "Come on back Carolina, come on, hang in there Sweetie! Don't you dare go now."

It was a horrible grating sound as the neoprene gave way to our Spyderco knives. At that moment, I had never been more grateful for a knife in my life. The engineer and divemaster rotated doing CPR still. The nurse felt for a pulse, and finally, we had a faint but steady one. We put Carolina in the recovery position, she puked out more foam, and then once her airway was clear, we attached her to O2 as the nurse instructed.

From there, the Captain instructed us to move the boat. The crew secured our boat for departure and got off the mooring, heading for the closest port. After that, it gets a bit blurry. Basically, within 30 minutes, we contacted the emergency services to meet us at the marina with an ambulance, contacted our boss (too which I cried to on the phone), and then all the crew docked the boat.

In this time, Carolina was in and out of consciousness. She would open her eyes, but no verbal response came out. Then her eyes would roll back into her head, and she would be out for a few minutes. The nurse sat with her head in her lap, stroking her hair, saying everything would be okay. I started a time log sheet and sourced her medical records on board to contact her medical aid.

Once docked, the paramedics were there and waiting. A paramedic came on board and got a full medical hand over from the emergency nurse on the prognosis. Then we tried to move her. The paramedic tried talking to Carolina. However, whenever he spoke, she would look at me. The paramedic teased her and said, "no, look at me, Carolina." The crew soon loaded her onto a stretcher, reassuring her all the way. Her husband was close by with an overnight bag, passport, and clothes.

Once we got to the ambulance, the paramedic said we would need to sit her up straight in the ambulance, and they wanted to keep her awake as long as possible. It took four of us to lift her into a sitting position and load her in. For some reason, I looked at her and said, "When you get better, you tell all the nurses about that ship you found, okay?" her eyes lit up. For the first time, I saw *her* again. She nodded, they closed the door and off she went to the hospital.

The Captain informed guests and crew that due to the emergency, there would be no more diving that day. One guest asked, "Why don't we still have the whole afternoon?" The Captain was shocked. He explained that he would not put his crew to work so soon after such a tense incident. It would not be safe, and everyone needed time to process the traumatic event. He also wanted to wait to hear if Carolina was indeed going to be okay. It was the worst diving incident any of us had seen, even the Captain of 20 years agreed. A few hours later, we got word that she was airlifted to the states and put in a decompression chamber.

According to doctors, she had suffered from an air embolism. But luckily, she would live. All the members of the crew were relieved. That night our Captain took us to the bar at the marina and bought a round of drinks. He said, in his 20 years said so. A few hours later, we got word that she was airlifted to the states and put in a decompression chamber. According to doctors, she had suffered from an air embolism. But luckily, she would live.

All the crew was relieved. That night our Captain took us to the bar at the marina and bought a round of drinks. He said, in his 20 years at sea he hadn't ever seen such a bad case, and he could not imagine a better crew to have handled it. He told us that the emergency nurse informed him that 1 out of 10 people come back from an incident like that, and wanted to say thank you to all the crew for the amazing team effort.

I called my older sister that night and cried. I could not get the image of her foaming mouth out of my head, of her skin color, or the sight of the emergency nurse slapping her and telling her lifeless body to come back. My sister has been a paramedic for 12 years, and she explained the logical side of what had happened to Carolina's body. Why the foam happened, why she was unresponsive, and that she probably wouldn't remember the traumatic event. She also explained how lucky we were to get Carolina back.

When we got back to port three days later, our boss was there waiting. The crew was tired and drained but there was a strange sense of morbid camaraderie. We spoke about our experience and felt a bit better about it. Some of us carried it better than others. The next week on a charter, I found I couldn't stand on the back deck. I kept seeing her body lying there, dead. It took me weeks to stop seeing it.

Weeks later, the Captain got a call on the boat phone. It was Carolina, and she thanked him and the crew for all their help. She had heard from the other guests about the excellent job they had done, although she admitted she couldn't remember anything about that day.

Months later, I was on a plane to Peru. We were watching a tv show, and in it, two men were in a war, caught up in battle, and hunkering down in a trench. They got hit by a bomb, and one died. The other leaned over him in the aftermath and started smacking his face saying, "Don't you dare die, don't leave. You stay here, you hear me!" Watching this scene had me panicking. I squirmed in my seat, my heart rate elevated, tearing up and immediately reached out and shut it off. I tried to get up and walk away, but I could not, I was terrified all over again. My partner held me until I stopped crying. It was a strange and unexpected trigger to a memory I thought I had processed.

It took many talks with my father to process what I had seen and done that day. His view was also that we had done the best we could, she had lived, and even though the image kept replaying in my brain, I needed to refocus my energy. I was focusing on the traumatic negative moments and needed to re-adjust.

To focus on the light in her eyes when we loaded her into the ambulance. On the fact that she was breathing again, and that the crew worked well as a team. I had lost sight of the positivity of the situation. It is the first time I have ever put that experience in writing. I still feel the sorrow and confusion of that day, although with a lot less pain and a little more peace.

To this day, the fill-in Divemaster still teases me about whether or not he is O2 certified. It is a jest, but also a sobering reminder of how quickly life can turn on its head.

∽

45

FORGIVENESS, LOVE, PEACE, AND COMPASSION

F orgiveness, love, peace, and compassion are the four ingredients to raise and maintain the high vibrational state of our being. We are aware of it, yet we find it hard to be in that state.

Most of you have come across a situation where you had poor judgment, or done horrible things in your life, and find it hard to forgive yourselves or others who have done something to you. So you still dwell in the past without making an effort to overcome it.

Scenario 1

Take the previous chapter example related to Arun. The actions taken by his teachers have caused trauma in his life. On the other side, if we look from the teachers' perspectives, they could have done those actions because of influences by their past generation doing the same thing.

Perhaps, they would have thought that the action taken would invoke a committed attitude with the students about their studies, and would hopefully improve their performance. Whatever the reason may be, they did it, with or without realizing that it is not the right way of handling students.

Once Arun realized that there is no point in maintaining judgment about those teachers. He started forgiving with full compassion and integrating all aspects of them, including their physical personality of acting out on anger. He brings peace and love to all of the past events and the people involved.

Scenario 2

Often, you have also noticed that love for another person, whether it is your spouse, parents, friends, colleagues, leaders, or even a stranger, is dependent on certain conditions. Only if that condition is met, then you will love them, otherwise you would not.

You need to change this because true love is limitless. It has no boundary, color, race, religion, or gender, nor any condition attached to it; that is unconditional love. This love emanates from within and radiates outward towards everybody and everything.

Scenario 2

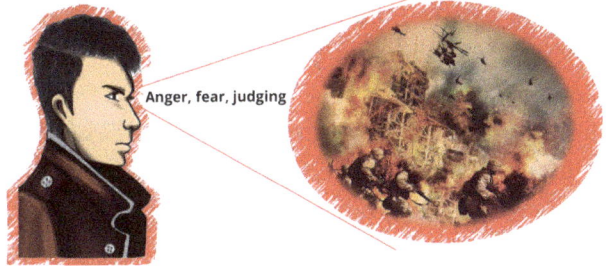

You have come across many bad and terrible things happening in this world. You watch some negative news, and you react to it through anger or fear. Now, what you don't realize is that, at an energetic level, you are adding more to that creation.

So instead, you should shift and respond with love and compassion with complete awareness that you live in duality where both the extremes exist. In other words, both positive and negative. By responding with love and compassion, you are energetically giving them the best chance to make different choices that are more aligned to love and peace, rather than fear and separation.

Practical steps to forgive and provide love, peace, and compassion

Forgiving someone who caused discomfort to you:

1. Close your eyes, and become aware of the feeling. You

may be feeling anger, fear, hate, or sadness. Accept it without judgment.

2. Know that a part of the Source lies within you, as a soul that never feels fear or anger and is always in pure love and compassion.

3. With that knowledge, expand those feelings with a deep breath in, visualize, inhale the color of the saffron hearth frequency, the whole body pervades with the color of saffron, and you exhale out to the world. Do this for a minute or so.

4. Surround and infuse the image of that person (in this case, the teachers) with the saffron hearth frequency and color.

5. As you energetically share, see them beyond their human personality as a source of energy being of love, even though they don't recognize that for themselves.

6. This exchange of love and compassion with them will open up the possibility for them to feel it. It helps them to open up their hearts for everyone and everything.

46

TECHNOLOGY

In this new age, technology plays a vital role in our lives. You use technology to such an extent that without it, you would become disadvantaged. The use of technology in the right way can help in the evolution of your soul during this awakening period. At the same time, using it in the wrong direction can cause extinction of our civilization and destruction of our planet. You can see this throughout history with Atlantis and the planet Maldek which is now an asteroid belt between Mars and Jupiter.

Observation and Suggestions

Electronics

Observation: An addiction to electronics like phones, tablets, and computers.

Suggestions: Avoid keeping phones next to your bed while sleeping. Limit yourself to these gadgets. Connect with trees, animals, and mother nature that offers high vibration all the time. Keep crystals and stones around you.

News

Observation: Avoid watching or reading negative news that brings down your vibrations.

Suggestions: Watch/read positive news that can uplift your soul.

Games

Observation:. Most of the games we see today are related to violence, such as using guns to kill for amusement. Children are increasingly getting addicted to these types of games. Imagine what the world would be if the primary source of entertainment was watching/playing games that portrayed violence.

Suggestions: Avoid playing violent games; especially for children. They learn what we teach and show them. We should start creating games that provide wisdom and knowledge for existing and future generations to come.

Social Media

Observation: Sometimes, some people use social media to get attention and for other unnecessary activities.

Suggestions: Instead, we should use social media to aid our spiritual growth. For example, we can gather people for group meditation, have discussions on awareness, etc.

Youtube

Suggestions: Youtube is a good platform if used in the right direction. There are thousands of videos posted daily related to spirituality. Subscribe to some of the channels provided by masters, channelers, or gurus that can benefit your spiritual journey.

Energy

Observation: CO_2 emissions and other bi-product waste disposals.

Suggestions: Preference should go to clean energy, which is better for our planet as well as our health.

Technology Advancement

Suggestions: Use technology advancement to improve the life of people and the planet. It shouldn't go on a destructive path.

47

CHILDREN

Some Facts, Dos and Don'ts

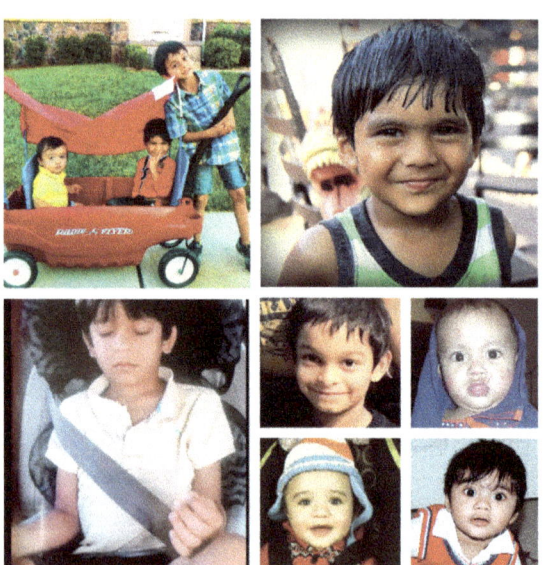

C hildren always live in the moment. They do not dwell in the past, nor do they worry about the future. As an adult, we should follow their lead. Listen to them and give them as much freedom as we can.

* Children hold much higher light than adults and are leading the way in shifting consciousness.

* They naturally know that they have to follow their passion. They help in replacing the old way of doing things with new ones that are beneficial for all.

* As parents, we should watch our beliefs, since our beliefs will be transferred to a child and held in their subconscious, waiting for discovery. The child can replace those beliefs with a new set if desired.

* Some of the children born in this era are much more psychically gifted, and the Parents/Caretakers need to nurture and encourage those skills to develop, rather than discouraging or ignoring it.

* Sometimes children talk about their previous life when they are too young since they remember everything. As an adult, listen to what they are saying instead of ignoring it.

* One of the things lacking in their education is meditation, and wisdom knowledge in their curriculums. Some schools have recently introduced it, and they have seen the benefits of it and this need to expand to more schools.

How to handle a child's negative emotions

Sometimes children get angry, upset, stressed, anxious, or come across negative emotions. As a parent, we try to help them in dissolving their feelings through various methods, and one of those creative methods is a forgiveness box, as mentioned by a famous channeler, Brad Johnson. This technique is most commonly for younger children between the ages of 2 to 12.

Forgiveness Box

1. Sit with your child and ask them: Are you upset? Are you angry? Talking to them and asking questions about why they are in that mood.
2. You and your child will create a box made out of anything, like cardboard, wood, and it has a lid on the top. Try to label it as a "Forgiveness box" and decorate the box with joyful, fun, and loving energy to it.
3. Provide a piece of paper to your child and ask them to write on this paper how they feel about their emotions. They can scribble the paper with crayon, or write, or draw something on it. They are sharing their feelings on that piece of paper.
4. Once done, you should ask them if they are finished and have put all their emotions on that piece of paper. Once they acknowledge it, you should praise them with words like *thank you*, and *you have done so well*. You are complimenting them for sharing their emotions.
5. Next, you will ask your child to fold the paper and ask them to put it in the forgiveness box. During that period, you are inspiring your child with positivity and the energy of love. Remember to tell your child as soon as they put that paper in the forgiveness box that emotion will be gone. Now watch your child get excited, and as soon as they put that paper in the forgiveness box, phrase them with compliments such as, "You did it, you are so happy now!"

All your child's negative emotions are gone, and you can use this technique quite often whenever your child gets into those negative emotions.

48

AUTHENTICITY

A uthenticity is being who you are and expressing it with an open heart without any hesitation or hidden agenda. It's the quality of being real to yourself and to others.

We lack being authentic most of the time, and in turn, causes miscommunication, distress, and sometimes ends relationships.

Sometimes when two friends are having a conversation with each other, they are sure about things that one person wants to say to another, but they might not be able to express it directly. They will often use a third person to try and tell their friend indirectly what they want to say.

Similarly, when business deals are going on between two people, you could doubt whether that opposite party is authentic to what they say and would do as agreed upon.

How to be Authentic

O Understand who you are. You are a part of the Source energy having this physical body to experience this physical reality. The characteristic of the Source is within you and others as well.

O With that understanding, be true to yourself. Meaning, what you think, say, and do is in complete alignment and according to your core principle and values. For example, when you are having a conversation with your friend and your friend requests something from you. You immediately inform your friend that you will do it, and at the same time, you will be thinking, I cannot do that, then you are not authentic to yourself or to your friend. Be truthful and express whatever you feel about that request. It doesn't matter whether you don't want to do it or you want to do it. It will help your friend decide whether to find another person who can do it instead of him believing that you will doing it.

O Always be introspective; be conscious of your thoughts and the actions that are taken. Notice how it affects or influences others. .

O Be kind and respect others. There is a saying Like attracts Like. So, when you are kind and are respectful, you will receive the same respect and kindness from others as well.

O Always be in the moment and provide unconditional love to others. For example, a friend has treated you badly in the past, and they approach you for help. Show them true unconditional love with complete acceptance of who they are by being in that present moment. Do not think about the past. Instead, do your best to provide your response openly and honestly to your friend.

O Do not be closed-minded and unwilling to take any other person's view, ideas, or their perspective. Be open-minded and willing to accept new ideas, or thoughts.

~

49

MASCULINE AND FEMININE ENERGY

Since childhood, you have been persuaded that if you are a man, you should have only male energy, and if you are a woman, you should have only female energy.

In reality, every one of us, irrespective of whether you are a man or woman, has both masculine and feminine energy.

The amount of each of these energies varies by gender. Approximately 80% of men will have more essence of masculine energy. Similarly, 80% of women will have more feminine energy.

The first three lower chakras represent the masculine energy, while the top three higher chakras represent the feminine. The center heart chakra acts as a balance in masculine and feminine energy.

Some of the traits of each of these energies are:

Masculine and Feminine Energy

Masculine Energy

- Support
- Strength
- Direction
- Goals
- Structure
- Decisive
- Materialistic
- Purpose
- Presence
- Linear & logical

Feminine Energy

- Love
- Caring
- Feelings
- Creativity
- Flow
- Expression
- Compassion
- Spirituality
- Emotions

When these energies are imbalanced in yourself, you become a wounded masculine or feminine energy. Wounded masculine energy will tend to be more dominating, angry, fearful, bragging, controlling, manipulative, overthinking, or overdoing. Whereas wounded feminine energy will be more uncaring, powerless, co-dependent, pleasing, and feeling unworthy. Well-balanced masculine and feminine energy are necessary for each of us to maintain a healthy lifestyle at a physical, emotional, and mental level.

How do you balance masculine and feminine energy?

There is not one straight answer to balance the energy. It depends upon each person to be more open and work on what is lacking in them.

If you have strong masculine or feminine energy, then work on the opposite energy that is weak or lacking. For example:

Strong or wounded Masculine : *Work on Feminine Energy*

Always providing direction and not listening : *Start listening to others*
Always focused on money or stocks : *Focus on creativity like music, painting, drawing etc..*
As a strong masculine, hides emotions : *Open up your emotions and express freely*
Think and do only certain jobs based gender : *Try to see as equal, no job is gender-based. Stop resisting and do other jobs as well.*

Strong or Wounded Feminine. : Work on Masculine

Always dependent. : *Try to become independent*
Strong emotional and always fluctuating : *Work on it, take charge and meditate*

50

ILLNESS, WELL–BEING, AND HEALING

T he human body is one of the most sophisticated biological systems that we have. It's always in a constant state of balance, unless it is tempered by our unbalanced belief, creating an imbalanced mind and body. Remember that nothing can show in your physical body unless you manifest first in your mental body.

Factors causing illness

There are three factors to occur in any illness

[*Disclaimer - The topic described in this chapter should not replace conventional medicine, but rather to complement and enhance it. Information presented here is metaphysical and should be used only with the understanding that it is not an independent therapy, but one that is a part of a holistic healing approach.*]

1. Misaligned belief, thus creating unbalanced mind and body
2. Highly empathetic to toxic thoughts and processing for others
3. Soul agreement to have experience of illness for spiritual growth.

Note: Most of them fall under category 1.

Misaligned belief, thus creating unbalance mind and body

For example, you have a belief that if you go to a particular place, you will become sick. You are making sure that you become ill when you are in that situation. In other words, you are creating a feeling of uneasiness throughout your journey, and as you reach this place, you will become sick. You are fulfilling the law of attraction; it is a vibrational match to your feelings.

Highly empathetic to toxic thoughts and processing for others

If you are highly empathetic and sensitive, you may often take toxic thoughts of others and start processing them as your own. This happens when you are interacting with others, or for example, if you are constantly watching or reading news on a daily basis. If you take all the negative things happening in the world as if they are happening to you, you are creating an unbalanced energy field in your emotional body. This ultimately shows up in your body as an illness.

Soul agreement to have experience of an illness for spiritual growth

Sometimes souls want to experience a certain illness. It's not a punishment, it provides an opportunity for tremendous spiritual growth. By overcoming those challenges that have been put purposefully in its own path, the growth would otherwise not have been possible.

Most of the illnesses can be cured irrespective of what factors have caused it when you bring balance to your mental, emotional and physical bodies.

How illness occurs

No illness can occur unless you are a vibrational match to it and it's indicated through your thoughts and feelings. Typically an illness starts appearing in your mental body and then your emotional body. This is the time to work on your mental and emotional body to bring balance before showing up in your physical body as illness. Lastly, illness will finally appear in the physical body.

Take Sam's example. Sam was a student doing his BA degree in IT. He was attractive and loved his girlfriend Kelly, who was from the same university. Sam was always happy. Enjoying time with his friends, going outdoors often, hiking, sightseeing, movies, and bowling. He was in a high vibrational state and is in complete alignment. *Figure-P3L1*

As years passed by, Sam graduated from university, got married, had three kids, and worked in a small IT company as a Database Administrator. One of the misguided beliefs he had was that in order to succeed in life was to work hard.

Sam's work started to get stressful. He was working for extended hours to support the company database administration that his job was demanding. He was always thinking about the issues at work that he had to resolve the next day. He was always unable to spend time with his kids or go out to have fun with his friends. All this uneasiness created an imbalance, and slowly started showing up in his mental fields. *Figure-P3L2*

He started showing negative emotions quite often, for example:

- When he would drive to work, he developed a hatred of traffic, and if someone cut the lane, he got angry and cursed at them.
- He used to get mad about small things at home.

Mental imbalance at this level:

The negative feelings will bring more of a similar experience to his reality, as per the law of attraction, unless he makes an effort to change his vibration. *Figure-P3L4*

- He started finding faults in everything rather than enjoying what he has.
- He stopped all his outdoor activities and became occupied by technological gadgets.

Emotional imbalance at this level:

Still has a chance to change his vibration before it gets to the physical level. *Figure-P3L5 to Figure-P3L8*

- When he browsed through the news, he was affected by the stories in his newsfeed. He gets frustrated and starts complaining about the world.
- His favorite channels would always be related to crime, drama, and war. Never realizing those emotions are passed on to the cell.
- Sam stops taking care of his body's nutritional needs. Most of the time, eating unhealthy foods and no physical exercise.

Physical illness at this level

The body responded by showing diseases, such as cancer. After the toxic emotions were allowed for such a long time. *Figure-P3L9*

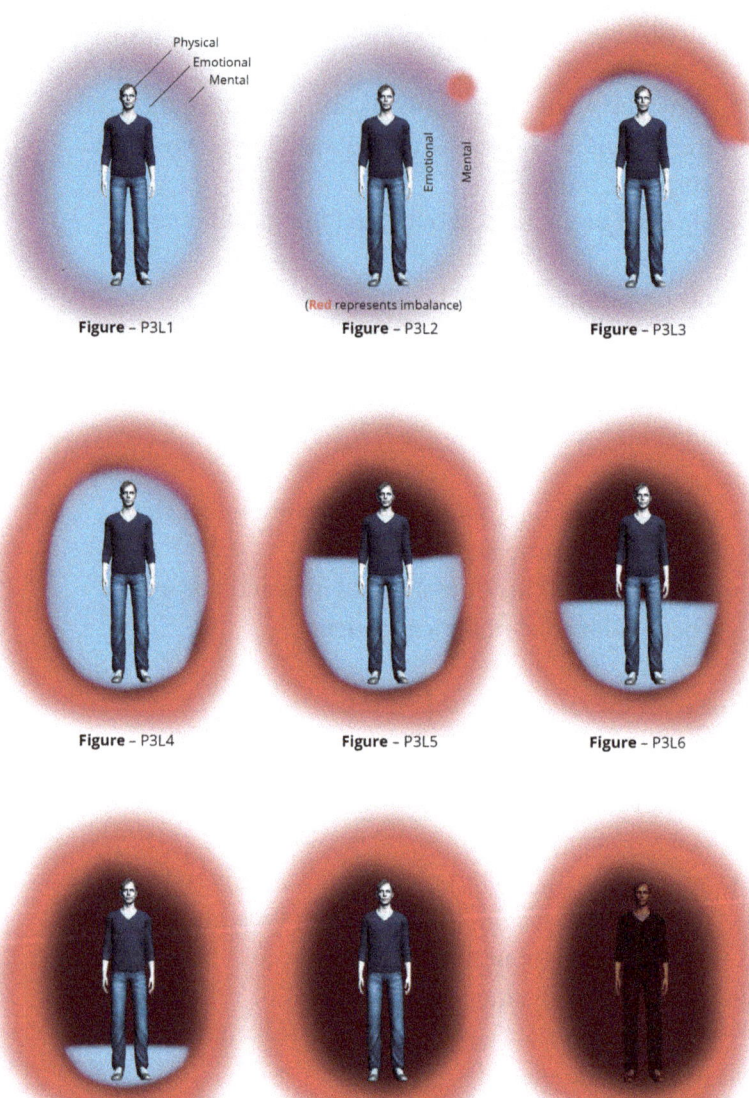

Physical
Emotional
Mental

Figure – P3L1

Emotional
Mental

(Red represents imbalance)

Figure – P3L2

Figure – P3L3

Figure – P3L4

Figure – P3L5

Figure – P3L6

Figure – P3L7

Figure – P3L8

Figure – P3L9

Though this is just one scenario for an illness to occur, there are other scenarios where sometimes you are in high vibration and other times in low vibrations. If there is a toxic thought that is dominating over a while, then eventually it may show up in your physical body as illness or pain.

How to heal your body

There are various methods to heal a body from illness or pain. Usually, you take general medicine as prescribed by the doctor, or go to the hospital. Some choose other alternatives such as Ayurvedic, acupuncture, Reiki, and other energy healing modalities. In any of these treatments, you have noticed that two different people having the same issue and same solution. One gets cured and the other doesn't, even when treated equally.

In another case, a group of researchers conducted a case study of patients with similar illnesses. They divided them into two groups. For the first group, they gave the prescribed medicine, and for the second group, they gave them pretend medication filled with water. Out of both, some were cured, even though the second group hadn't taken any real medicine. It was a placebo effect on the second group that cured some of them.

In both of these cases, why do you think some of them get cured and some not? The most common thing that we always ignore, yet is a key important factor in healing illness, is your **VIBRATION**. In other words, the emotional feeling that you project, based on your thoughts and beliefs, will dictate the restoration of your health.

High Vibes

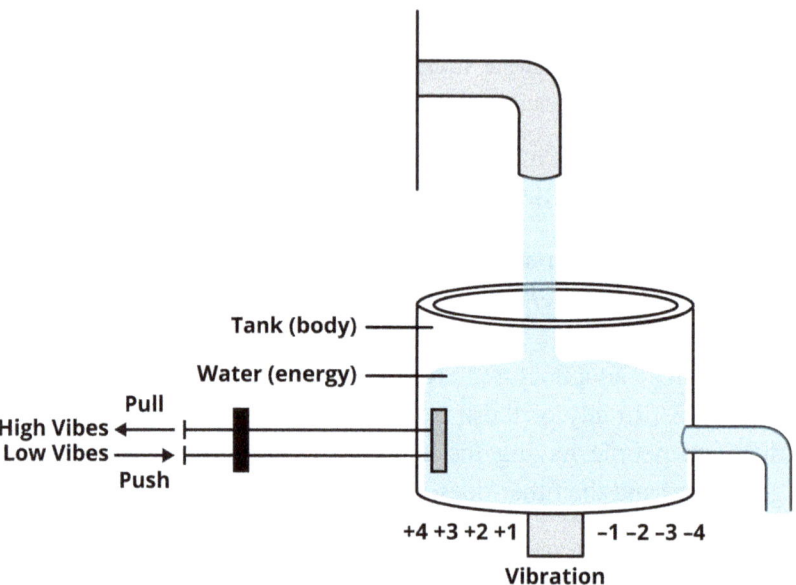

Vibration

Your vibration plays a vital role in restoring your health. Imagine your body is like a tank, and the flow of energy represents water flowing in it. When you are in high vibration, your body continues to thrive in good health, similar to water flowing without any obstruction in the tank.

If you are in low vibrations (negative emotions) most of the time, you are adding resistance to the free flow of energy, and there is still time to bring back to your natural state of vibration (positive emotions). Otherwise it shows up in your physical body.

Low Vibes

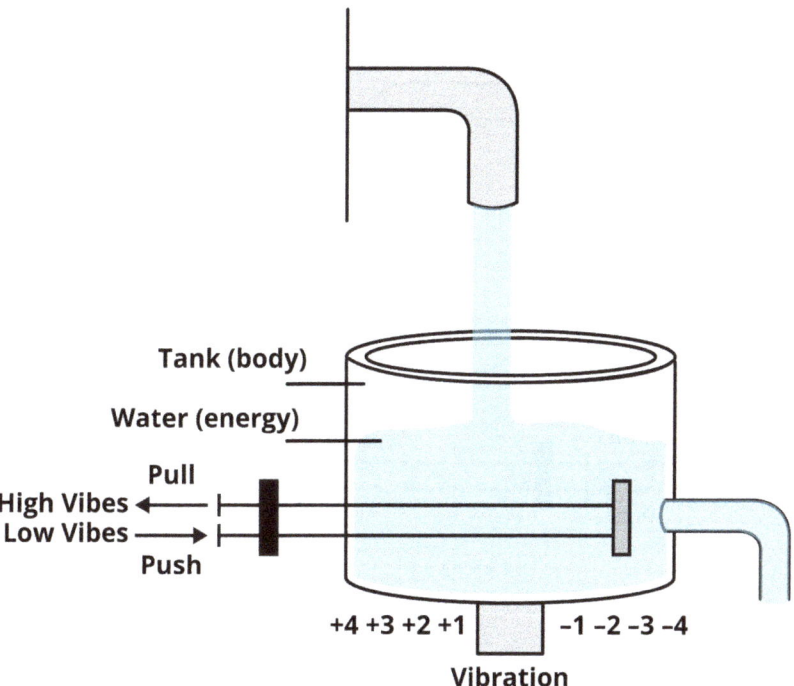

If you still continue to resist, you are blocking that energy though it's nothing but cork obstructing the water in the tank. It eventually spills from the top, which is nothing but an illness or pain, showing up in your body. Remember, sickness is just an extension of your negative emotions.

Low Vibes
(energy blocked)

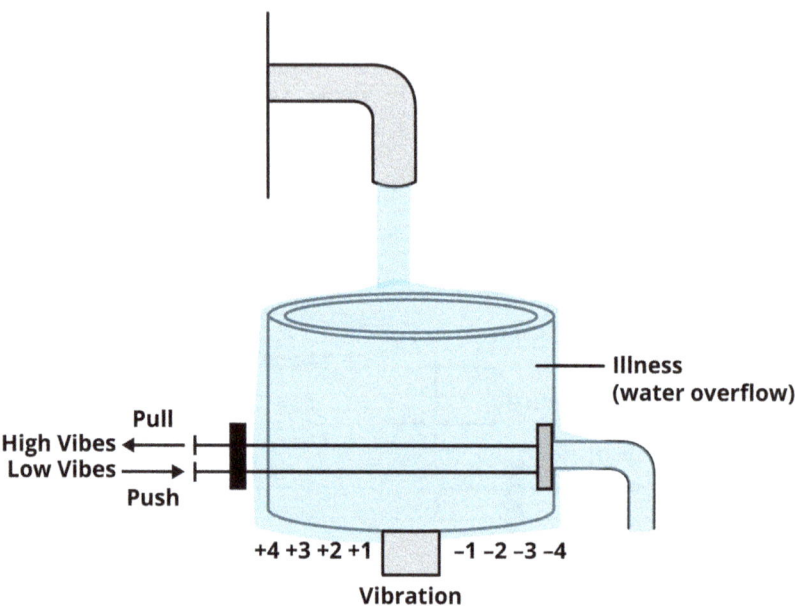

So, your vibration is the key. It is your feelings that you emit, and they form based on your beliefs and thoughts. These determine whether you are in total allowance, or resistance, to the flow of energy that you require from the source. So if you have an illness or pain, the first thing that you need to ask yourself is:

What beliefs are out of alignment that often make me think toxic thoughts, and feel those negative emotions that caused the illness in me?

Let me take my example. I had rashes on my cheeks and it appeared during a cold season. I went to a doctor, and he prescribed me a particular cream to apply to my skin. After three to four days of applying, the rashes would reduce but not completely. I could still notice it. I kept reapplying it, even though I had a burning sensation when applied.

As the days passed by, the season changed and during springtime, the rashes disappeared. I was happy, but it came back again during the following winter. Again, I went through the same issue, applying the cream, and it completely went away during springtime.

It carried on for four to five years, and one day during one winter when it appeared, I stood in front of the mirror and told myself that I'll cure it without applying any cream and that it will go away in a month. After a month, I noticed it was completely gone; it never appeared again. Let's dissect what happened here.

Issue: When rashes appeared for the third winter season, it became my belief that I would get rashes during the cold season.

Belief: I get rashes during the cold season. Every year from then on, while I am enjoying the fall colors that nature provides, at the same time, in my mind, I will be thinking.

Thoughts:

- Winter is coming, and I hate cold weather.
- Again, I have to deal with rashes. I don't like the burning sensation on my cheeks.
- I dislike the heat coming from the heater, I feel suffocated, and there is no fresh air.
- I'll use the same prescribed cream that I used last year.
- I like redness on my skin.

So, based on my belief and thoughts, I started resisting the natural flow of the Source, or well-being energy and projected these feelings.

Feelings: Worry, Hate, Blame, Angry.

As per the laws of the universe, you get what you asked for. Since we are the creator of our own realities, I got rashes during that winter season. I started repeating the same trend every year until I figured it out.

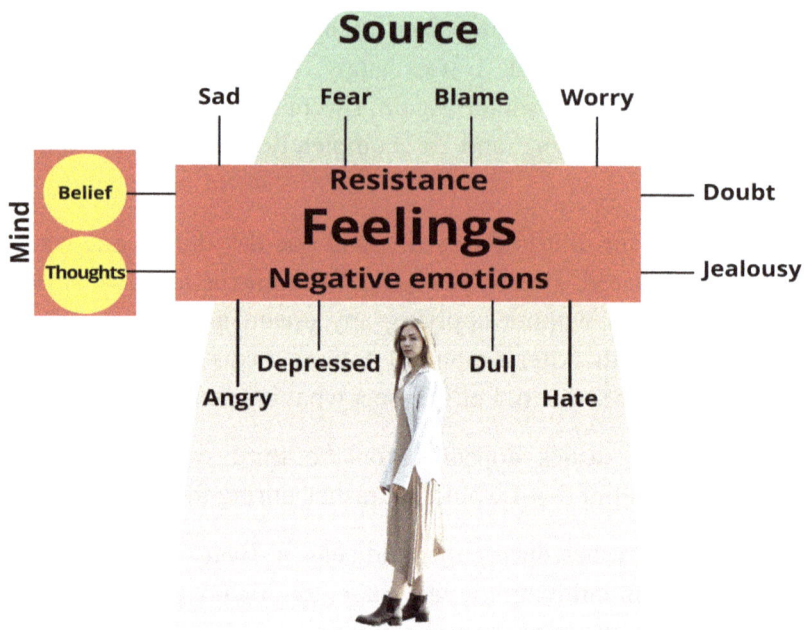

Note: *All this was happening between 2007 and 2012, and in the same period, somewhere in the year 2008, I was keen on knowing more about this reality, about spirituality, about God, who we are, where we came from, etc. I read 100's of books on spirituality. I attended a few seminars, group retreats, watched 1000s of videos on these subjects and was deeply involved in it.*

Solution

After all those years of research about metaphysical subjects and understanding who we are, I wanted to test it out with the current issue that I had about the rash on my cheek.

I remember it was in 2011 winter, I stood in front of the mirror and decided to clear the rash on my cheek for good. I was very clear about why it was happening every winter. First, I decided to take out the belief that I had about my issue.

Belief: ~~*I get rashes during the cold season and*~~ change to ***The Source energy is always flowing in me and radiating my body with high vibes.***

294

Next, my thoughts from that time onwards were utterly uplifting because of the knowledge I gained during my research, and I was sure about the issues:

Thoughts:

- I'm the creator of all things that are happening in my life.
- I love the white snow, especially when the sun is out and the snow is covering the mountain.
- Wow, kids are enjoying the snow early in the morning, they are making a snowman, sliding on snow, I wish I could do that as well.
- I like hot coffee and want to sit next to my fireplace and watch TV.
- Spring is coming, and I need to plant tulips in my front yard.

The feelings I had at that time were all on high vibrations. They positively impacted my life. Due to the law of attraction, like attracts like. I purposefully worked on my thoughts and feelings.

Feelings: Joy, Comfort, Laugh, Peace.

Imagination

Use the tool, that is your imagination to achieve the result that you want. I used this tool myself. I started with the following imagination exercise, setting aside 5 minutes every day to do it. I imagined a bright white light flowing through my crown chakra and passing through my cheek and to the entire body, radiating each cell with divine energy. Also imagining, what the result would be once the rashes were gone and how I would feel at that time. I brought that feeling into the moment when I was doing this imagination exercise.

Meditation.

I was doing meditation for at least 20 minutes every day. *You can check the meditation section in the previous chapter for more details about various types of meditation.*

Diet

Since I was a vegetarian, I en-forced myself to eat more green vegetables/leaves and fruits. Certain vegetables and fruits help in curing, or protecting, from certain illnesses. *More details in the next section.*

Treatment

In my case, I stopped using the prescribed cream. I just followed the healing modality, as specified above.

In any case, when you are in that momentum of becoming a healthy being, you will be guided by your soul through feelings to follow a certain healing modality.

End Result

After doing all these for a month, the reality changed completely, I was out of those red rashes, and it never appeared again.

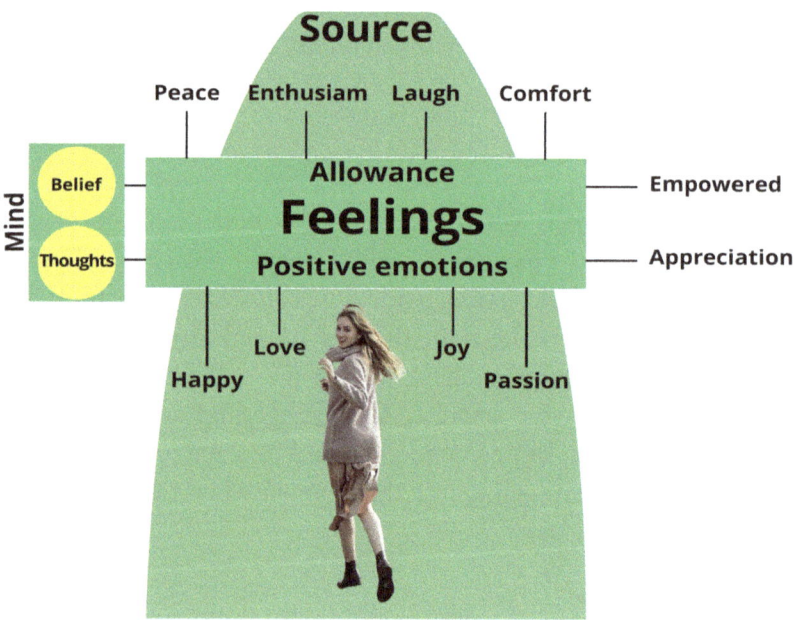

.

Understanding

With this experience, there are few things that you always need to understand.

- When you are at a very high vibration and aligned with Source energy, the illness or pain cannot exist. Since sickness and well-being are two different vibrations, they cannot co-exist.
- Illness or pain is not your enemy; it is an indicator to show you that something is misaligned, and you need to work on it. Sometimes particular illnesses translate the belief that you are holding is out of alignment with your true Higher Self. *More details in the next section*
- The Source, God, universe, or higher consciousness, whatever you name it, will always give you what you ask. So if you have been asking for something all this time, but you never get it, then you need to understand that the universe always answers your call. It will answer based on your feelings and not words.
- When you are ill or in pain, you always tend to focus on the pain and discomfort that the illness is causing. However, focus on something that makes you feel better. Why? Because as per the universal law, what you focus on will expand. In other words, if you focus on pain, it expands. If you focus on comfort, the universe responds back in kind.

- The amount of time it takes to heal your body is dependent on your dominant vibration. Any illness or pain is treatable in a matter of days when you are dominating such a high vibrational state; the illness cannot survive in that vibration. You often feel it's hard to shift your thoughts into feeling good when, in reality, you are in pain or sick. You can change this by taking small steps.

Consider that you are ill, or in pain (scale 0), you can either become completely healthy (scale +7) if you follow the path of positive feelings. Or you can become more sick (scale -7) by following the path of negative emotions such as stress and worry. It is your choice.

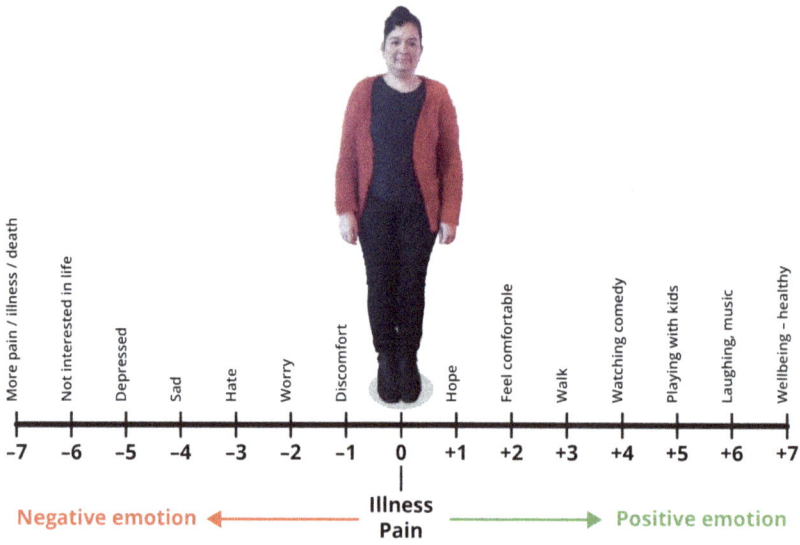

So, the most important one is to take small steps to reach the final destination of well-being by doing pleasant things. Ways to do this is by hoping for the best, relaxing in bed, listening to light music, watching something that makes you laugh, play with children or your pets. These small intentional decisions can build momentum in the right direction.

1. Your cell is as intelligent as you are. It understands and follows your command. Focusing on good feelings is an

effective way of communicating with your cell, ultimately thriving in your physical body. When your body is out of balance, your cell knows exactly how to compensate and bring it back to balance. *More details in the next section.*

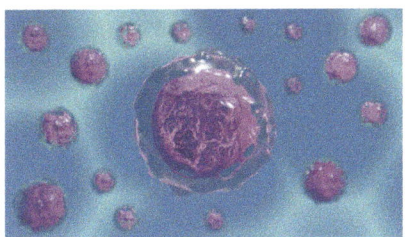

Steps

Belief: Find out the belief you are holding, which is out of alignment with your True Self, and change that belief forever.

Thought: Focus on thoughts that makes you pleasant.

Feeling: Bring that positive feeling within you, and emanate every part of your cells in the body.

Talking to your body: Our body can heal itself with just pure intent and focus alone. Talk to your energy body field and see the miracle it can bring to you.

Imagination: Imagination is a tool that can bring a positive vibration. Imagine how you feel when you reach the result of your well-being and bring that feeling in the NOW moment.

Diet: Try to follow a high vibes diet.

Activities: If possible, try to do exercise, go out in nature, play with pets, and kids. If you are watching TV or reading news, make sure it is bringing positive vibes in you by making you laugh, or smile, and not the other way around, such as worry and sadness. The goal here is to raise your vibration.

Meditate: Meditate daily to bring calmness and align your body, mind, and soul.

Treatment: Follow whatever treatment your soul guides you in the direction of becoming well-being.

Some common natural ingredients that can help you during illness

Nausea: Ginger; use ginger in food, tea or juices

Cancer: These will help in fighting cancer and boosting the immune system.

- Shiitake mushrooms
- Moringa leaf powder (drumstick leaves)
- Goji berries
- Maca powder
- Green superfood
- Water - alkaline PH 8.8 to 9.1
- Probiotics
- Capsicum

Hearth issues: Healthy fats

- Avocado
- Olive oil
- Certain nuts, walnuts, almonds, and pecans.
- Beetroot juice
- Pointed gourd
- Avoid excess dairy, soda, white bread, cheese, and microwave popcorn.
- Orange tea, helps to clear blocked arteries.

Deprived energy: Beetroot juice; Beetroot is a natural energy supply having vitamins A & C, carbs, calcium, and iron.

Illness protection: Probiotics

Broken bones: Calcium found in milk, yogurt, green vegetables, nuts, and beans

- Swiss chard leaves
- Soybeans
- Almonds
- Sesame seeds

Thyroid: Kelp; rich in calcium, magnesium, potassium, and iodine

- Green beans
- Kale
- Parsley
- Ginger tea

Haircare: Carrot; it provides beta-carotene needed for stronger hair roots.

- Spinach
- Red and green pepper
- Bean sprouts
- Walnuts
- Warm mustard oil to scalp for stress and dandruff.
- Castor oil, for hair loss

Skin care: Walnut oil; external application for wrinkles.

Insomnia: Avoid alcohol, tea, coffee, and chocolates

- Put a few drops of lavender oil on your forehead and rub it before going to bed.
- Drink warm milk with almond powder before sleeping.

Cholesterol: These help in building good cholesterol.

- Walnuts, almonds, pecans, pistachios, and hazelnuts.

- Olive oil
- Avocado
- Oatmeal, barley, and garlic.

Anemia: Eat iron rich diets such as green leafy vegetables, and dried fruits.

- Avoid coffee and tea.
- Eat two to four figs.

Constipation: Drink water regularly.

- Eat a slice of papaya in the early-morning.
- Eat overnight soaked raisins on an empty stomach.
- Eat raw green peas.

Brain: These can help you to protect the brain.

- Tomatoes
- Dark Chocolate
- Beans, lentils, nuts, and low-fat diaries.

Blood sugar: Bitter gourd juice or add bitter gourd in your recipe.

- Ivy gourd
- Coriander
- Moringa
- Green tea

Eyesight: Carrot

- Spinach
- Cauliflower

Mucus: Drink mixed carrot and lotus stem juice.

Ear: Olive oil; apply a few drops in the ear for reducing ear wax and ringing.

Reducing Fat: Green tea; twice a day to boost metabolism.

Messages from the body

Every illness, pain, or discomfort in the body is delivering a message to you that it is out of alignment and requires your attention to take care of it. There are so many books written on these subjects. I'll point out a few common messages here:

Illness and their meaning

Accidents

You have a belief in violence.

Back Pain

Your belief and action are out of alignment with your true self.

Sore Throat

Need or resistance to communication with yourself or others.

Kidney

Resistance to process your belief; Undissolved anger.

Cancer

Toxic thoughts have taken root in your mind; severe hate, resentment, anger, and frustration towards others.

Blood

Lack of interest or joy in life.

Blood Pressure

High: emotional problem not solved. Low: lack of love.

Brain

Resistance to change old patterns.

Problem with receiving messages.

Cold

Lazy in making decisions.

Delaying activities.

Cholesterol

Clogging the channels of joy.

Fear of accepting joy.

Cough

Listen to me.

Diabetics

Sorrow. Need to control. Lack of love.

Eye

Farsighted: fear of the present.

Short-sighted: fear of the future.

Feet

Fear of the future.

Not stepping forward in life.

Fever

Anger, burning up.

Gas

Firmly, holding attention, fear.

Headache

Pressure or not accepting situations.

Resistance to the flow of life.

Heart

Love, security. stress or feeling pressured.

Feeling alone and scared.

Long lasting emotional problem.

Injuries

Anger at self; guilty.

Knee

Stubborn ego. Inflexibility.

Menopause

Not feeling good enough, fear of aging, or self-rejection.

Motion sickness

Feeling of being trapped.

Neck

Refusing to see another perspective, inflexible.

Nervousness

Anxiety, not trusting the process of life.

Pain

Guilt.

Pimple

Small outbursts of anger.

Rash

Irritation over delays an immature way of getting attention.

Stomach problem

Fear of the new.

Teeth

Instability to speak the truth.

Throat

Inability to speak up for oneself.

Thyroid

Humiliation; feeling put down.

Vomiting

Fear of the new.

Weight

Fear and need protection:

Arms: Anger at being denied love.

Belly: Anger at being denied nourishment.

Hips: Lumps of stubborn anger at the parents.

Thighs: Packed childhood anger. Often rage at the father.

Note: Use your own discernment. It can also mean something else.

Diet

A proper diet is essential to maintaining good health. Whatever you consume, it becomes part of you since everything is energy. The food you eat is also an energy, and it vibrates at its frequency. So, when we eat the nutrients, the cells integrate with our being and become part of us. It has a direct effect on our vibration as well.

A few important tips on food

Food holds a much higher nutritional content when gratitude and love are shared.

Food that has impurities, preservatives, and toxins. It usually suffers from low energy levels and will provide a sluggish digestive system when compared to eating food grown organically. The body will benefit from eating purer food rather than modified, processed, or contaminated food.

If organic food is expensive, or not available, then raise the vibration with an intent of love and gratitude before consuming non-organic food.

Raw fruits and vegetables will maintain a higher vibration when consumed, compared to cooked food. Cooking and consuming food heated below 100 degrees F will have nearly double the nutrients than the food that is heated above 100 degrees F.

Suppose you eat something which is not in harmony with your body like junk food. Your cell notices the disharmony caused by ingesting junk food, and it immediately generates chemical factors to compensate. It does this to bring your body back into alignment again.

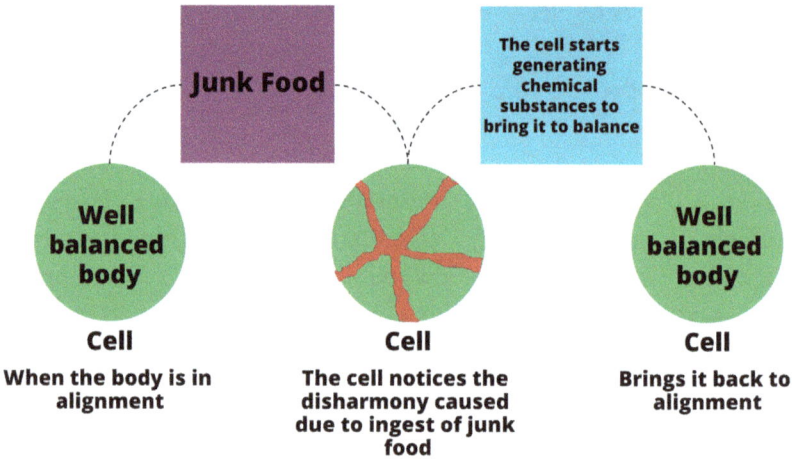

What you choose to eat is a direct reflection of the vibration match that you offer at the time of choosing. When you are in complete alignment with the Source energy, that food will all be beneficial and in harmony with your body. *Refer to the top image.*

When you are disconnected or not allowing the Source energy entirely, then the food you choose and ingest will also be less beneficial to your body. *Refer to the bottom image.*

Fresh and highly energised food

Processed food

Should you avoid eating meat?

Everyone has different opinions on this topic, and it's up to each individual to decide to make a diet they wish to follow.

I'm a vegetarian and will give my opinion based on my personal experience, studies, and research done. I came from a non-vegetarian family. During my childhood, age of 10 or 11, I saw a chicken butchered right in front of my eyes. I saw the eyes and was emphatically drawn towards it. I felt the pain of that chicken, and that was the last time I ever saw any animal killed.

Below are some of my studies, findings, and research on this topic:

- Everything has consciousness, including the rocks, plants, animals, and humans as well. However, the degree in each of them differs. Rocks have a lesser degree than plants; plants are lesser than animals; and the human level of consciousness is higher than some animals. So, it doesn't matter what you eat. You are killing both of them, whether it's a plant or animal, but eating plants have a degree of consciousness that's lesser than an animal.

309

- When an animal is on its deathbed. The emotional energy of fear and anger is transferred to all of its cells. Which is ultimately consumed by us, and becomes a part of us.
- Most of the enlightened beings I have read, heard, or seen are vegetarians.
- There are certain misconceptions that we have about proteins and that they are available only through eating meat. However, there are other ways of getting protein. Many vegetarians are living a perfect healthy life today without any issue. *Note: Check the documentary "The Game changers" related to this topic.*

Why am I not losing weight?

Reality is happening through you and not the other way around. A projector projects images outside based on the DVD it is playing inside. Similarly, you (the projector) are emitting a reality based on the vibrations you are emitting. So, weight gain is an external reflection of your internal vibrations that you're having for a long time.

Find out the root cause of those internal issues.

1.Belief

Find out the belief you are holding, which is out of alignment with your True Self and change it. Or, you can remove that belief forever. For example, you believe:

- it's in my genetics, my family has it, so I'll get it as well..
- I always remain/become fat even if I don't eat much.

2. Feelings

Subconsciously, you might have programmed yourself to have excess weight. For example:

1. You may have a fear and need protection, so being overweight resembles protection for you.
2. Suppressed anger about yourself, your family, or life itself.
3. Lack of love or expecting love from others.
4. I don't deserve it, so I won't get it.

Remove these types of negative feelings and start working on a positive side with an understanding of who you really are.

- You are the creator of your reality.
- Forgiveness and compassion are the way to move forward in life.
- Love yourself. An absence of love is fear, and it's just an illusion. There is nothing to fear. Once you know that, realize that you, the others, and the Source are the same.

3. Diet

Diet is also important to understand from a belief perspective. Whatever food you are eating, if you believe that the food you are eating is going to make you fat, it will make you fat. You are the creator of your reality, and the body is merely just obeying your command. So subconsciously, you are making your body overweight by that belief.

Suppose you are having lunch and in front of you, you have some fries and salad. What is your immediate thought and feelings towards those foods?

 *Fries*: "I am eating fries, and my body will gain weight." Even then, you are eating them because you love them.

Salad: "I am eating healthy food," and deep down, you have a feeling that salads are the food to eat to be healthy and fit. That statement above tells what vibration you are holding for that food. Some folks eat fries quite often but do not gain any  weight. There are a few who eat fries once in a while, and they gain weight. So, what is the factor that is affecting your weight? It's the resistance to the flow of Source energy i.e the belief, thoughts, and feelings that you are holding is a vibrational match to that overweight. What you resist, persist. Removing those resistances will help you to move in the direction of losing weight.

So, what diet should I follow? Eat what feels right for you without any contradiction between your thoughts, beliefs, feelings, and the food you are eating. If you think a well-balanced diet is the way to go, then go for it, with complete love, and do not fight against it.

4. Physical Exercise

Do physical exercise that makes you feel good, and you love to do regularly. Don't force yourself just because you have to do it or you won't lose weight. The motivation should come from within you and not from external sources such as your fitness instructor, friends, etc.

Imagination

Use imagination tools here. Imagine how you **feel** when you reach the result of you being slim and bring that feeling in the NOW moment. Do this quite often, and it will help you increase your vibration.

Grounding

Grounding is critical; it helps to maintain the vitality of your body and brings high-frequency energy when you connect to mother earth. So, stand on the grass with bare feet for at least 5 minutes.

Meditation

Calm your mind by meditating at least 20 minutes daily.

If you work on these four steps, you will see the result that is more aligned with what you need.

A small experiment was conducted for two and a half months with someone who I know and was desperate to lose weight. The result was astonishing after monitoring the vibration along with a well-balanced diet and exercise.

EXERCISE
DIET & EXERCISE JOURNAL

DATE	Jogging	Time (min)	Exercise	Time (min)	Relaxing in Nature	Time (min)	Grounding	Time (min)	Imagination	Time (min)	Meditation	Time (min)
4/29/201	Yes	35	Yes	7	No	-	Yes	2	Yes	2	Yes	2
4/30/201	Yes	55	Yes	7	Yes	10	Yes	2	Yes	2	Yes	2
5/1/2019	Yes	55	Yes	7	Yes	10	Yes	2	Yes	2	Yes	2
5/2/2019	Yes	60	Yes	7	Yes	10	Yes	2	Yes	2	Yes	2
5/3/2019	Yes	60	Yes	7	Yes	10	Yes	2	Yes	2	Yes	2
5/4/2019	No	-	Yes	30	Yes	10	Yes	2	Yes	2	Yes	2
5/5/2019	Yes	60	Yes	15	Yes	10	Yes	2	Yes	2	Yes	2

Results

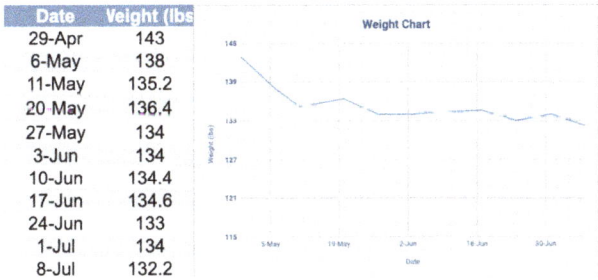

Date	Weight (lbs)
29-Apr	143
6-May	138
11-May	135.2
20-May	136.4
27-May	134
3-Jun	134
10-Jun	134.4
17-Jun	134.6
24-Jun	133
1-Jul	134
8-Jul	132.2

Aging

We believe our natural life expectancy is approximately 100 years. We wish not to become old, and yet, nature takes its course. During Atlantis and Lemuria, people used to live for 500 years.

However, as thousands of years and many civilizations passed, the belief has changed, and this is one of the main factors that determine life span.

Our body generates brand new cells every ten years. Therefore, we have a completely new physical body every ten years, but even then, we degenerate, why? Quite often, we also see that some people look older than others who look very young, even if they are in the same age group. Why? The answer lies in the belief that we're holding as an individual and as a collective.

Tips for increasing your lifespan

- Remove the belief that is holding you about life expectancy.
- Align with the source all the time and let the energy flow freely in your body without any resistance.
- Your body will always follow the rhythm of the mind, so govern yourself and maintain that high vibration.
- You should always feel good about yourself irrespective of what's shown or heard from others.
- Imagine the age that you felt alive and energetic., Bring that feeling, live to it, and the body will soon follow.
- Reprogram your energy body field that holds the key to rejuvenate every cell in your body.
- Lastly, have a well-balanced diet and regular exercise.

Water

Water plays a crucial role in our daily lives. Without water, you cannot survive. Your body is about 70 - 92% water. From a scientific perspective, after the big bang, the entire universe was formed using these three elements: hydrogen, helium, and lithium, as a hot gas. Other elements, including oxygen, were created from star fusion.

Pure water contains two molecules of hydrogen and one molecule of oxygen (H2o), but it does not exist in nature. There are few natural dissolved substances like calcium, magnesium, sodium, potassium, chloride, and fluoride. The human body is quite flexible and accepts a wide variety of water compositions. So to be healthy, water must contain some of these minerals.

What's happening in today's environment?

Unfortunately, apart from natural minerals, water contains synthesized contaminants. Some of them increase the concentration of ordinary minerals like chloride and sodium. However, some produced by industry or agriculture are toxic, such as pesticides, insecticides, waste residuals from industries, heavy metals, fluorine, and hydrocarbons. The main ones include petroleum and engine oil (to name a few). If you drink such type of water without filtration, then you know what's going to happen to your health.

How do we avoid drinking unhealthy water?

You can use various precautions to prevent drinking unhealthy water.

1. Stop contaminating the water.
2. Drinking filtered water and especially reverse osmosis, which is one of the most effective methods to filter tap

water. This technology is designed to remove a large percentage of contaminants by filtering the water through semipermeable membranes.

Have you ever thought water has memory and consciousness?

By praying to water, you can improve the overall quality of the water. It's scientifically proven by Dr. Masaru Emoto, one of the leading researchers and pioneers in conducting experiments on water. He showed that by praying to water or playing the right frequency of music, it creates beautiful crystals in water molecules. He demonstrates that human vibrational energy, words, thoughts, and music can affect the molecule structure of water.

Note : More information and detail images can be found in Masaru-emoto.net

He conducted a simple procedure in his lab by exposing glass of water with different words, music, or pictures and then freezing and examining the aesthetic properties of the resulting crystals with microscopic photography.

He found out that water exposed to positive speech and thoughts would result in beautifully formed crystals when that water was frozen. But when exposed to a negative intention would yield "ugly" frozen crystal formations.

Similarly, when you add flowers inside the water or add a picture next to the water, the molecule structure then contains some flower or picture characteristics.

Restructured water

A few other scientists have also researched this topic. When a particular subject (person) drinks restructured water, their blood cells show a healthy response. This provides some proof of healing modality.

Also, a group of people prayed to a small amount of water and poured that blessed water to a large amount of polluted water. The dirty water transforms and is blessed, showing that the power of focused positive intention can change it into structured water.

Does water have consciousness?

A few scientists have also conducted experiments with water consciousness. They took water from a single container and divided it into two portions and separated them at a great distance. When they exposed one of them to outside influence, it changed the structure and properties of that water. Whereas the second container acquired an identical property/structure which was similar to the first container after some time. Even though, It was at a great distance thousand miles away and had no influence from the outside. This shows that the water can imprint subtle energy

Based on these studies, we come to an understanding of how effective it is by praying or blessing water by thoughts, words, or pictures that can change the molecular structure of water and provide vital life force energy to your body.

Incorporating changes at home

I made a few changes in my home.

Problem

We use city water that is recycled, and possibly may contain:

1. Hard water.
2. Bacteria or other contamination while delivering through pipes.
3. Fluoride in the water can cause calcification. This is one of the problems for the pineal gland. Fluoride suppresses the psychic ability.
4. It doesn't contain structured water molecules

Solution

I installed a water softener and reverse osmosis system underneath the sink. After installation, I tried checking the water quality between my fridge (had a built-in filter) and reverse osmosis, the quality of water in reverse osmosis was far better than any other filters. This technology is designed to remove large percentages of contaminants, including fluoride, by filtering the water through semi-permeable membranes.

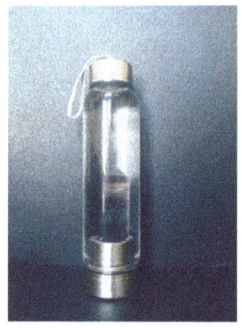

For structured water, I'm using a water bottle that has a crystal attached to it until I transition to a bigger commercial one that is available in the market.

I also made sticker labels and stuck them to some products.

Reverse Osmosis Water Tank: This has many positive labels such as Love, Peace, Divinity, Thank you, Eternal.

Refrigerator: I have a digital display refrigerator. So, I added the same notes on the fridge: Love, Thank you, etc.

On some of the milk bottles and food, I wrote Love.

So, with few minor changes in our daily habits, the water quality can be drastically improved and can provide vital life force energy to our body.

Benefits of Music

Music is hugely impactful on your vibrations. The rhythms of music passing through the air and reaching through the ear of the listeners, bringing peace, calm, and soothing experience. Irrespective of

what level the state of mind each listener is in, music raises the vibration instantly.

Certain illnesses can be cured by listening to specific sounds or music of particular frequency. The frequency enhances their neurological functions, and these are vital functions of patients. It has been well documented and talked about in the new age community. Sound frequencies such as 432hz bring healing energy to the body and influence a patient's spiritual development.

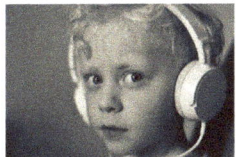

Children who were having problems with short term memory loss were introduced to music, and the results were astonishing. They completely recovered

It's worthwhile noting that in schools, students who study music score higher in terms of grades than students who study without music.

Grounding

Grounding is a technique that has been used for many millennia by our ancestors to reconnect to mother earth and bring our body, mind, and soul into alignment.

Earth is slightly negatively charged, and when you stand on it with bare feet, the natural energy of the negatively charged free electrons balances your positively charged body, bringing you into complete alignment.

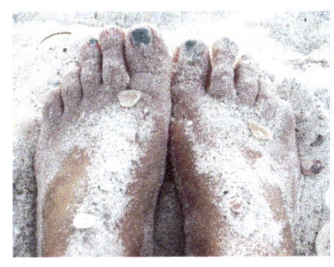

Benefits of Grounding

- Raises your vibration and helps to bring you back to the present moment.
- Aligns your body, mind, and soul.
- Heals depression, stress, anxiety, and balances your hormones.
- Improvements in sleep, digestion, blood circulation, and immune function.
- Grounding and exercising will affect the metabolism, bringing a positive nitrogen balance.
- Improves facial blood flow circulation and reduces blood viscosity.

How to Ground

Usually, shoes or slippers that you wear, act as an insulator. Thus, disconnecting yourself from the earth's electron flows. Take off your shoes and you can stand barefoot on grass, soil, or water on a beach for at least 15 minutes daily to see the benefits. You can also sit with hands and legs touching the ground as well.

Scientific experiment conducted

A scientific study conducted by researchers from the University of Arizona was able to show a tangible result and study the benefit of grounding by measuring cortisol levels, inflammation, and proteins in the body. They took two sunflowers and put them in two separate glasses of water. One they grounded with a piece of wire and the other not. Over time, it showed that the PH of water changed to a more alkaline. The sunflower which was grounded was healthier than the other flower. This shows the importance of grounding and reconnecting to the earth.

Crystals

Crystals are one of the natural abundances found on earth that hold high-frequency energy, healing modalities, and information about earth's history. Each one has an energy signature and when placed on a particular part of your body, they interact with your energy field center (chakras) of the body.

Thus, bringing transformation and noticeable subtle shifts in your vibration and healing ability. Similar to tuning a guitar from a tuning fork, the guitar being you, and tuning fork represent a crystal.

Every crystal has healing properties, and the right one can rebalance your energy. You should be able to identify them based on their name, characteristic and healing modalities they hold.

Benefits of Crystals

- It helps in healing certain illnesses.
- Getting good sleep when you place it underneath your pillow or next to you.
- It helps in balancing certain emotions and blockages.
- Increases focus during meditation.
- Increase your brainpower.
- Helps in creativity flow.
- Strengthen your intuition.
- Brings prosperity, abundance, and success in life.
- Assists in connecting to higher dimensional beings.

Selecting Crystals or Stones

There are so many crystals available in the market.

- Go with the feeling, trust your intuition, and choose the crystal that draws your attention or gravitates to you.
- Crystals have healing abilities. Choose based on the healing you require. (mentioned in the next section).
- Beware of any artificial or colored one; choose natural one. For example, natural quartz crystals can only be white or dark. Various other shades may be artificial.

Cleaning and reprogramming the crystals

Crystals should be cleansed and recharged after every use. It absorbs low vibration with great ease, and it's better to reboot for the next use.

1. Take a bowl of pure water and add a pinch of salt to it. (Salt neutralizes the energy).
2. Soak the crystal in that bowl of water for a few hours.
3. Take them out of the water, wipe them dry, and place in direct sunlight for a few hours.
4. Hold and set your pure intention on the crystals. You do this by sending your thoughts to it, visualization, or speaking out. If you prefer another method, you can write mantras, positive affirmation, and healing affirmation on a piece of paper, and place it under the crystal so that it'll program for the next use.

Where and how can I use the crystals?

Crystals have various uses.

- During meditation, you can hold the crystal in your hand or place it in front of you (if it's a big crystal or stone) and meditate.
- During energy healing, such as Reiki, you can place each particular crystal on seven chakras and work on it.

- You can also wear it as a pendant on your neck, a particular crystal that you feel to have it at that moment.
- Place a few charged crystals near your bed at various locations of your home. They help in cleansing and keeping the energy balanced in your home.
- Place it with your bike, car or suitcase when you travel.
- Place it on your workplace near a computer or other electronic equipment.

Information from Crystals

We are beginning to discover that the crystals that are buried deep underneath the surface of the earth hold certain information about our past lives on earth with regards to ancient civilizations like Lemuria, Atlantis, Mayans, and Egypt. Crystals also help our ascension process to awaken the truth of who we are, as we're guided intuitively to particular places and spots that ground to mother earth.

You can access the energy and information that was put there underneath the surface by you or other dimensional beings.

A few types of crystals / stones and their purposes.

Some higher vibration crystals and stones.

Moldavite, elestial quartz, herkimer diamonds, datolite, stellar beam calcite, pink danburite, and phenacite.

Protection.

Sugilite, purpurite, smokey quartz, charoite, and malachite.

Grounding.

Lodestone, obsidian, and black tourmaline.

Awareness, deeper connection to spiritual realms.

Petalite, lavender fluorite, nirvana quartz, libyan gold tektite, white cryolite, brookite, orange creedite, blue celestite, labradorite, muscovite.

Good sleep and calming.

Scolecite.

Stress and anxiety.

Selenite crystals, datolite, blue lace agate, lapis lazuli, and clear quartz.

Fear and grief.

Datolite, aquamarine, selenite, and obsidian.

Brain.

Golden herderite, and peachy white heulandite.

Joy and happiness.

Aurora quartz, amber, and citrine.

Psychic abilities.

Clear apophyllite, tiffany stone, and amethyst.

Manifestation.

Golden topaz, amber, green prehnite, and hiddenite.

Negative energy absorption.

Tourmaline, sulfur, and smoky quartz.

Amplifiers.

Lolite, and herkimer diamond.

Love and Relationship.

Dioptase, quartz, lapis lazuli, and yellow tiger eye.

Peace.

Blue lace, and blue aventurine.

Depression.

Amber, clear quartz, and smoky quartz.

Creativity.

Iolite, and ametrine.

Confidence.

Moonstone, and hematite.

Addictions.

Labradorite, and amethyst.

Crystals related to the seven chakras

Crown - Clear quartz, labradorite, selenite, moonstone, herkimer, and sugilite, ametrine.

Third eye - Amethyst, sugilite, fluorite, tanzanite, lepidolite, and charoite.

Throat - *Sodalite*, celestite, blue kyanite, lapis, and blue lace agate.

Heart - Rose quartz, morganite, green kyanite, emerald, peridot, and green calcite.

Solar Plexus - Citrine, amber, yellow tiger eye, topaz, and yellow zircon.

Sacral - Orange calcite, carnelian, amber, peach moonstone, and sunstone.

Root - Red calcite, black tourmaline, hematite, obsidian garnet, and red jasper

Crystals related to various illnesses

Aches - Sunstone, charoite, and magnetite.

Aging - Green selenite.

Allergies - Zircon, and carnelian.

Asthma - Malachite, amber, and tiger's eye.

Blood - Amethyst.

BP - *for low:* Calcite, ruby, and sodalite.

BP - *for high:* Chrysoprase, dioptase, and emerald.

Bladder - Topaz, and amber.

Cancer - Emerald, rhodonite, bloodstone, and sugilite.

Cold - Amber jet, sulfur, and blue lace agate.

Coma - Lapis lazuli, moldavite, and tanzanite.

Cough - Amber, topaz, and aquamarine.

Constipation - Ruby, and amber.

Diabetes - Serpentine, jade, citrine, and muscovite.

Digestion - Pearl, rhodochrosite, and citrine.

Dental - Fluorite, and blue lace agate.

Ear - Celestie, orange calcite, and aquamarine.

Eyesight - Emerald, opal, tiger's eye, topaz, agate, and cat's eye.

Fever - Rock crystal, ruby, hematite, and opal.

Forgetfulness - Emerald.

Hair problem - Agate, lapis lazuli, and onyx.

Heart - Cuprite, garnet, rose quartz, and charoite.

Heartburn - Dioptase, peridot, and clear quartz.

Headache - Sugilite, turquoise, amethyst, and amber.

Kidneys - Rose quartz, amber, citrine, and hematite.

Knees - Azurite, and jadeite.

Menopause - Lapis lazuli, lithium, ruby, epidote, and diamond.

Motion Sickness - Sapphire.

Neck - Aquamarine, and clear quartz.

Nightmare - Ruby, jasper, hematite, amethyst, and topaz.

Nutrition - Fluorite, lazulite, and buddstone.

Radiation - Calcite.

Skin - Obsidian, and corundum.

Teeth - Amber.

Thyroid - Amber, aquamarine, citrine, and blue tourmaline.

Tumor - Bloodstone, sapphire, smoky quartz, and amethyst.

Urinary - Relieve: amber, ruby, calcite red. Prevent: blue lace agate, and carnelian.

Weakness - Emerald, hematite, and carnelian.

Wrinkles - Ulexite, and fluorite

Crystal Grid Formation

The arrangement of crystal in particular sacred geometrical shapes along with pure intention will amplify the manifestation of desires. Using a combination of stones and crystals with sacred geometry structure will create a unique energy signature that you can use to manifest a desire that you are seeking. Use your intuition to guide you to create your own crystal grid formation.

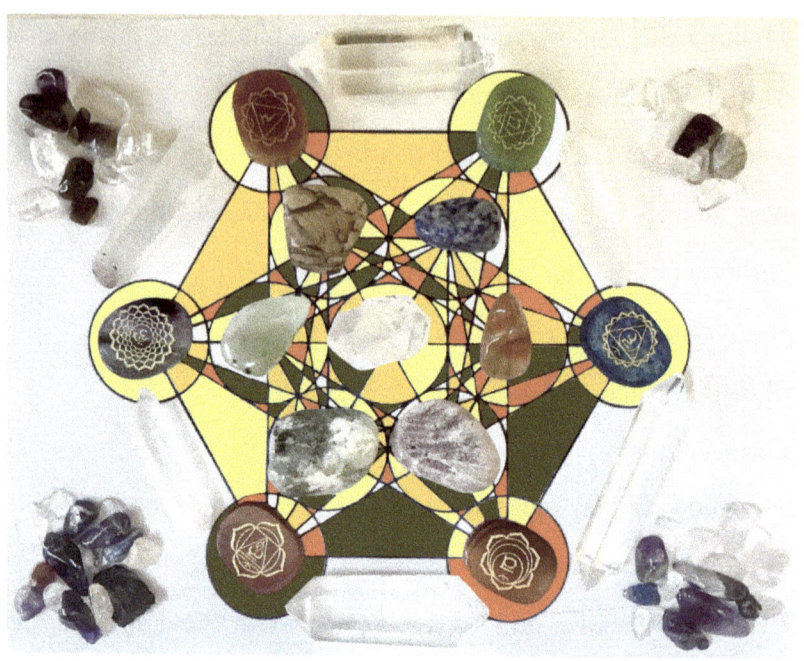

Nature

Nature is one of the natural pharmacists. You have to heal your physical, emotional, and mental bodies, and bring yourself into complete alignment with your soul. As soon as you hear, see, or imagine natural images such as the ocean, mountain, glaciers, forest, or animals, you immediately notice a change in your vibration. It brings calmness to your mind, excitement, joy, or even a smile on your face.

Remember that it's such a high vibrational tool that you have at your disposal.

Go out into nature for walking, hiking, or just sitting under the tree and enjoying the serenity it brings to you. As soon as you connect to the earth, you ground yourselves into physicality and contribute to the collective human consciousness. Thus, leading others to follow the same footsteps and helping them to raise their vibration as well.

PART IV

RADIATE

After you have finished enquiring, gaining knowledge, and cleansing your body and mind, then it is time to go much deeper within and radiate the qualities of the Source, such as unconditional love, compassion, bliss, peace, perfection, and purity in every part of your core being. Thus, ultimately transcending you beyond this physical reality.

Analogy: The polluted water is using very refined filters to clean further until it becomes pure water again.

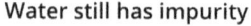

Water still has impurity

Part 4 of the book indulges you in the feeling of Sources qualities. As you start doing this daily (along with deep meditation for long periods), your body, mind, and soul will come into complete balance and the Source qualities will start reflecting within you.

Note*:* Seeking a master's initiation and guidance on your spiritual progress will help you progress faster.

51

ABSORB AND FEEL

S it in silence and perceive each of those Source qualities mentioned in this chapter within you. As you begin doing this daily, it starts reflecting on every part of you. As mentioned in previous chapters, Feeling is the language of the soul and a key to the manifestation of your longing. In this case, your desire is coming from your True Self, the desire from knowing to becoming the Source.

The more you start doing it, the more you'll feel comfortable in pushing the boundaries of your understanding; ultimately growing as a seeker.

For example, the LOVE discussed here is Pure Unconditional Love. So irrespective of what your external reality is showing you in the present, or if you have gone through bumpy past issues, you try to neutralize and project pure love to everyone and everything unconditionally.

Go through each of these words and let the feelings flow through your perception for 5 minutes at the minimum.

How do you feel when you see this puppy? Do you have a conditional love? Probably not. Check your feelings, and you see, you have pure love coming from your heart. This is the unconditional love you need to have for everyone and everything.

Compassion

Peace

Bliss

Perfection

Purity

~

52

GO WITHIN

The next stage is to remove your focus from the outside world, and go deeper within, into a meditative state, and immerse yourself in universal consciousness. When you start doing this on a regular basis, during the process, the true reality will start unfolding itself.

Below are some of those details mentioned in:

- Samadhi by Patanjali
- Sant Mat tradition

Samadhi

Samadhi is the state of oneness through meditative absorption and is considered one of the highest states of mental concentration that a person can achieve while still bound to the body. This is the state where the meditator, the act of meditation, and the object of meditation (God) are ultimately united and merged into one. It is similar to a river merging into the ocean; the soul merges with the Absolute.

According to Patanjali, Samadhi has several Levels.

1. Level 1 called Savikalpa Samadhi
2. Level 2 called Nirvikalpa Samadhi
3. Level 3 called Sahaja Samadhi
4. Level 4 called Dharma Megha Samadhi
5. Level 5 called Kaivalya Samadhi

Level 1 called Savikalpa Samadhi

The first level is where you transcend all mental activities, including your human consciousness, for a short period of time while you are in a meditative state. You return from the undisturbed silence state to the disturbed state; waking, dreaming, and sleeping.

You cannot preserve that experience outside of meditation; the samsara (a past impression which conditioned your life and desires) has not dissolved and is still in seed form. Four stages are possible as per Patanjali.

Stage 1 Savitarka Samadhi

A stage of gaining knowledge. It gives a sense of distinguishing the real from unreal. The mind focuses solely on the gross aspect of a physical object and gains full knowledge of it.

Stage 2 Savichara Samadhi

It's a silent state where thinking is available, but the mind is quiet. In this stage, the mind contemplates beyond gross aspect to subtle aspects of objects such as its shape, texture, sound, attraction, etc.

Stage 3 Sa-Ananda Samadhi

It's known as blissful samadhi. In this stage, the mind is free from the objective world and you move beyond intellect. It will be in the tranquility of the settled mind, focusing on the inner power of perception.

Stage 4 Sa-Asmita Samadhi

The final stage of level 1 samadhi where the consciousness of wholeness and the mind becomes purified while penetrating deeper. The gross and subtle elements, the object-like thoughts, disappear. Only the pure ego and the oneness remains. There is an awareness of individuality, no fear, or desire known as the cosmic consciousness in Shankara Tradition. The mind becomes fully awake.

Level 2 called Nirvikalpa Samadhi

This is a level 2 state where there is only infinite peace and bliss. In fact, not only do you feel bliss, but you become it. The ego and Samskaras are then utterly dissolved, and only pure consciousness remains. The yogi attains some of the omniscient and omnipotent qualities of the cosmic.

Level 3 called Sahaja Samadhi

Some yogis have added this level of Sahaja Samadhi. They say this is the Samadhi that arises naturally and spontaneously, bringing expanded awareness, peace, increased energy levels, and clear thinking. It's where you find your inner silence along with the daily activity.

Level 4 called Dharma Megha Samadhi

A high stage that cannot be gained by effort alone that reveals itself when all other efforts have dissolved, including the desire to know God or to be enlightened. It's the transition state to the next level and where the yogi's liberation is secured.

Level 5 called Kaivalya Samadhi

At this final stage, the yogi has gained independence from all bondages and has achieved the ultimate liberation, or moksha, while still in the physical body.

Sant Mat tradition

In Sant Mat tradition, there is a spiritual practice called Surat Shabd Yoga. (Surat: soul, Shabd: sound current, Yoga: union). You practice by going within to discover your True Self and attain enlightenment, which ultimately reunites you with the Absolute Supreme Being. One of the prerequisites for this type of practice is to have an initiation by a perfect living master, or Sat Guru.

Since your mind always wanders and requires a great effort to bring it to stillness, the master emphasizes this three-fold method during meditation practice or sadhanas:

1. Simran (mantras).
2. Dhyan (concentration).
3. Dhuni Adhyas (sound, current).

Your body has nine openings: ears, eyes, mouth, etc. these are called Gates. These nine gates reflect the outer experience, but there is a tenth gate, the third eye, that opens up for inner experience.

During meditation, you should practice using this three-fold method daily to reach higher planes of existence and ultimately become one with the Absolute Divine; thus, reaching enlightenment.

Simran is the silent repetition of a mantra given by the master during initiation, though you can use any mantra if not initiated. It helps in withdrawing your attention from the outside world, setting your focus on the inside world. The mantra assists your mind from being scattered outside.

Dhyan is concentrating your attention on the third-eye center. In the beginning, while focusing on the eye center, you may be glazing darkness, or you can imagine the master's face.

Eventually, you will see lights of various shapes, and out of that light appears the radiant form of the master who will guide you. From then on, the master will guide you through the inner voyage of higher planes of existence, until you reach the totality of consciousness, Sachkhand, or the Source.

Dhuni Adyas is listening to your inner sound current, which is the vehicle for your journey within. The sound that is coming from your consciousness is connected to Source (Sachkand, or The Totality of Consciousness).

As a meditator, when you put your attention to your inner sound, you will hear various sounds at first. Soon as you fine-tune your concentration, you will start hearing melodious bell sounds, and the sounds will become louder and louder and you need to keep a hold of it.

From there, the inner journey begins where you experience the out of body sensation for the first time. You realize that you are not this physical body; you are energetic bodies. You will also start to experience higher planes of existence, as described in the previous chapter.

As you focus your attention inward, further and further, you start peeling the covers (physical, astral, and mental) that you have been wearing this entire time, one by one, to have an experience in the physical world.

You discover you are the soul, or unit of consciousness, and exist beyond the mental realm. As an individuated soul, you still need to go further in your spiritual journey until you reach Totality of Consciousness. It is only possible through love and devotion, with the help of a perfect living master, who is with you all the time in the radiant form and for the entire length of your inner journey.

Once you reach the journey from Par Brahm to Sachkhand, with the help of a perfect living master, you will finally discover that you are not one unit of consciousness. You are the totality of it, experiencing it in a single reality.

Note: Refer to the Grand scheme of creation in chapter 9 Creation.

PART V

LIBERATION

There are two kinds of liberation that can happen in this life:

Permanent liberation
Temporary liberation

Permanent liberation occurs when you are naturally enlightened and leave the body through death or Mahasamadhi. You will be liberated from the cycle of birth and death and ultimately merge with the Absolute; becoming one. *Analogy: Enlightened State -* The water realizes the purity of itself.

Pure water

Liberation - When pure water is heated, it starts evaporating and ultimately turns into steam. The jar then becomes empty. Similar to steam, we turn into pure awareness and become liberated from the body forever.

Water evaporated, jar empty

Temporary liberation: If a death occurs in between your spiritual progress, you will temporarily leave your body in this life, reincarnate again with a new life, continue where you left off on your spiritual growth. This cycle continues until you become enlightened and permanently liberated from the cycle of birth and death. *Analogy*: The polluted water still needs to be cleaned further to become pure water again.

Water still has impurity

Part five of the book, discusses about liberation and the process of death and reincarnation.

53

PERMANENT LIBERATION

Enlightenment and Liberation

Enlightenment, or self-realization, naturally occurs when you are ready and have done enough internal work. This is the stage where you come to a full understanding of everything and become one with Source.

You realize you are that pure awareness where the entire reality is appearing within this awareness which includes your body, mind, time, space, higher dimensions, etc. And you also realize that you are eternally enlightened and that ignorance is gone.

After enlightenment, you still have the body and perform your daily routine as long as you live in this material world. However, you distinguish yourself from the body and operate from that pure awareness. You negate the reality that is appearing to you. You are now entirely liberated from the cycle of birth and death, and all your karmas nullified.

Ultimately, once you are liberated with the body through the process of death or Mahasamadhi, you merge with Source and become a universal being of pure existence, consciousness, and bliss.

Notes:

1. *Usually, an enlightened person, while still holding the body, will try to teach others about the ultimate reality, (Source) and Self (Soul), to provide insight about the path to get liberated.*
2. *Mahasamadhi is when an enlightened person chooses to leave the body intentionally. It is often through a deep conscious meditative state.*

54

TEMPORARY LIBERATION

As a human, you will go through the normal death process, may reincarnate again with a new life, and continue where you left off on your spiritual growth. This cycle continues until you become enlightened and permanently liberated from the cycle of birth and death.

Note*: Depending upon the spiritual progress that one has achieved in this life, the location of the next rebirth can vary due to ascension taking place at this time on Earth. So those who do not want to let go of their 3D reality and are happy in playing the same old game of duality, power, fame, fear, limiting beliefs, controls, attachments, etc. will have an opportunity to move on to the other 3D reality planets and continue their lives. Since Earth will be a 5D planet and only inhabitants with higher frequency who resonate with her can live in the new environment.*

The next chapter will discuss the Death and Reincarnation process.

55

DEATH AND REINCARNATION

Everything in nature follows a process. The plants sprout and start to grow in the spring, bloom in summer, the leaves start falling in autumn, and die in winter. That is the life cycle of a plant. Similarly, you are born as a baby, grow as a child, become a young adult, and finally die when you reach old age.

You might notice that in the next season, the plant sprouts and repeats the cycle. Similarly, you reincarnate again as a baby and follow the reincarnation cycle. Death occurs only for the physical body and not the soul, which is eternal. So in general, you are that timeless soul living temporarily in a human body, having a physical experience.

Once the physical body dies, you go back to your original spirit form in the spiritual realm.

Before Death

The last thought must be an uplifting and elevating one because a pleasant one will multiply a hundredfold. Similarly, an unpleasant thought will also multiply a hundredfold. The mind cannot discriminate between pleasant and unpleasant. Even with uplifting thoughts, the person's reflections will naturally jump to the primary concerns that a person has during his life. So it is recommended to lead a joyful life with peace, love, and harmony.

Some people may notice a change in reality. They might see their guides, spiritual masters, or even their dead relatives. They would have come to help the dying person by giving them the comfort and accompanying the soul to the other side of the veil.

During Death

You are a Being of 4 parts composed of the soul, physical body, astral body, and mental body. According to the Indian scriptures, during the time of death, the astral cord which connects the physical and energetic bodies is disconnected. The soul will then push out of the body through one of the orifices; this exit point is purely dependent on the type of life that the person has led while on earth and will be decided entirely according to cosmic energies. Some may exit through the eyes, and the enlightened souls may exit through the crown chakra at the top of the head.

There are also five vital force energies which govern various parts of the body. These energies are:

- **Samana Vayu**: the laterally moving energy which helps in digestive functions.

356

- **Prana Vayu**: responsible for respiration; the upward moving force of the chest region.
- **Udana Vayu**: the energy that compresses and separates the physical body from astral.
- **Apana Vayu**: is responsible for excretion and reproduction; the downward moving energy of the sacral region.
- **Vyana Vayu**: responsible for the circulatory system; the energy moving in circles in the entire body.

Notes: Vayu is also called air or ether.

As soon as the spirit leaves the body, the Vayu's' will slowly exit the body as well.

1. Within 21 minutes, the Samana Vayu (which is also responsible for maintaining the body temperature) will exit. You will notice the body is cooling down.
2. Within 48 to 64 minutes, the Prana Vayu will exit. There are small chances of reviving the person back before the next Vayu exit takes place.
3. Between 6 to 12 hours, the Udana Vayu (which is responsible for buoyancy) will exit. The body becomes heavy when compared to that person being alive.
4. After Udana exits, somewhere between 8 to 18 hours, Apana exits, and then the sensory aspect is gone.
5. Ultimately, Vyana Vayu will exit between 11 to 14 days (if the cause of death is old age), or 48 to 90 days (if it is accidental).

Once the person's soul is out of the body, he/she can hear thoughts from their families and friends who are mourning and may try to communicate with them to console their loved ones, but no one will perceive their attempts. Some souls hover around their bodies until cremation or burial.

A Real Incident

A friend describing her story to me.

"This story is about a father and son with a close spiritual relationship. The son lived on the coast and the father stayed in the city. The son was saddened to hear one day that his father was admitted to a hospital after suffering a stroke. A few weeks later, he had not recovered yet and passed away in the hospital. The father was a very fit and busy man. It was an unexpected death since he was an honorary member of a hockey club and boxing club at the age of 65. He played a lot of golf and was a very successful businessman.

Years later, the son explained to his now grown-up daughter that the night his father passed away, he had woken up suddenly in the early hours of the morning. The son said he saw his father right above his bed, not fully formed, but his essence that he intuitively recognized. The son explained that he had a feeling that his father had come to say goodbye. Afterward, the son woke up his wife and cried for an hour before they got the phone call from the family in the city. They were calling him to let him know that his father had passed away.

The son and father had a deep relationship. They would intuitively know when one or the other was in trouble, or when one was lonely/happy; no matter the physical distance. As a young kid, the son would travel out of his body and across vast distances to visit his father. He could always return to his body with ease after his journey. The son never understood how or why he did it, nor did anyone else. He just knew that he could and would do anything to be closer to his father when he was in boarding school.

Years later, I found that I have the same relationship with a dear friend. Call it intuition perhaps, but whenever she or I am upset, happy, or have a heightened emotion, we instinctively reach out to each other even though we are continents apart now. Ever since I met my friend, I knew she was special to me but I never understood until reading this".

After Death

Note: The soul is always pure, eternal, and full of love. The soul is to be taken as a human imprint of emotion and mind in the next few sections.

Depending on the level of awareness and spiritual growth, each human's experience may differ based on their belief and the choices they make. Eventually, they all reach the spiritual world and the soul group they belong to based on their vibrational resonance.

Dr. Michael Newton, a clinical psychologist, and one of the pioneers in hypnotherapy has regressed many patients for more than 40 yrs of his practice.

He was able to gather information about the afterlife during their hypnotherapy session of their patients and soon discovered that there were similar commonalities of what they were saying.

In the deaths of most of his patient's previous lives, there was a specific process and steps for each transition which is summarized below.

The Process

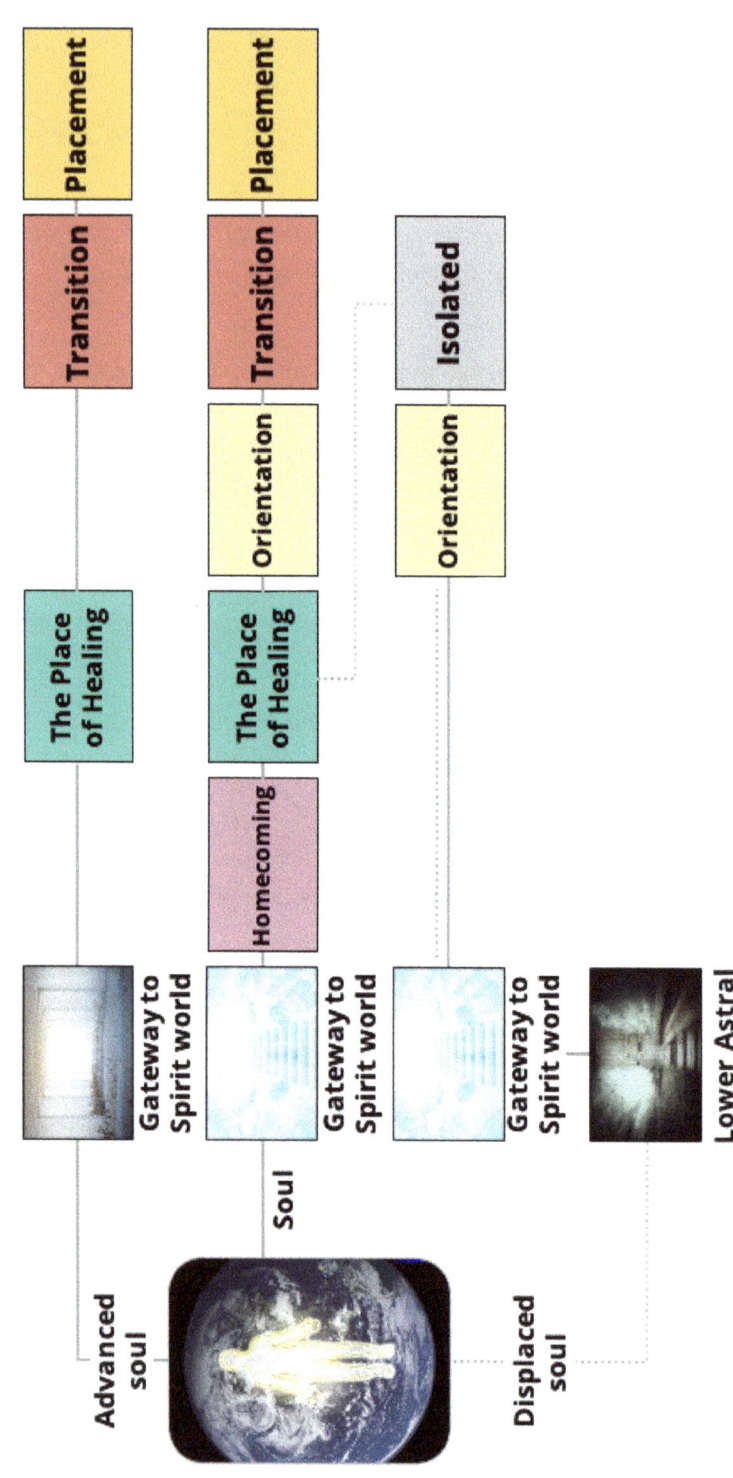

Advanced soul

Placement — Transition — The Place of Healing — Gateway to Spirit world

Soul

Placement — Transition — Orientation — The Place of Healing — Homecoming — Gateway to Spirit world

Isolated — Orientation — Gateway to Spirit world

Displaced soul

Lower Astral

Gateway to Spirit world

Most of them report a light tunnel portal opening up right next to them, or they need to rise above earth before they enter the tunnel. When they are inside, they see a bright light emitting a sense of love, compassion, and peace that appears at a distance. As if there is some magnetic force, they are pulled gently towards it. As they move closer to the light, the circle of light slowly grows and then they are within the light floating around in a cloud-like substance.

After crossing tunnels, few others reported coming across a layer of light. Others hear music such as bells, humming, or buzzing sounds. Some even see crystal stones and palaces.

Homecoming

Once crossed over through the tunnel and inside the light, you will be greeted and comforted by your guides or soul family members. It always varies and depends on each individual. It can be your soulmate, a member of your family, or friends who were there with you in your recent or past life.

It is vital to keep in mind:

- The soul is formless and can take any shape, feature, or
  form. Your family members take the necessary Image
  Form for you to recognize a familiar face. A Soul's form
  can change when you meet them again, depending upon
  the situation and feeling at that time.
- The welcoming souls may not have to be the same
  spiritual group that you belong to since everyone is in a
  different development level of their spiritual growth.
- Souls who are highly evolved or advanced souls may
  skip this process of meetings. Since they are aware of
  who they are and know where they are going in the spirit
  world.

The place of healing

The departed soul will have an imprint of their most recent life.
So in the stopover zone place of healing, the soul is cleansed and
healed by a stream of pure loving energy before going to the next
orientation stage.

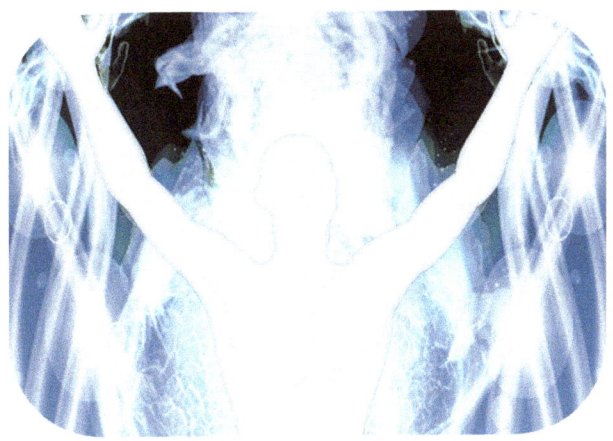

Orientation

In this stage, you sit with your guides to get an orientation to a spiritual environment. You will go through your life review with the guide. Some have reported being shown their entire life history like a movie projection, without any judgment, whether they have done good or bad deeds.

REPORTS by some say that during life review sessions, they not only felt their own emotions but the emotions of others as well and how they felt in those scenarios.

The orientation can vary depending upon the soul and their state of mind after life ends. The less experienced and abruptly transitioned, the soul may require extra attention by the guides compared to more advanced souls.

The orientation allows us to do our self-evaluation without any judgment. To know ourselves and determine how much progress we have made in our spiritual evolution during recent life transitions. It also allows us to reflect on what we can improve upon as a soul.

The orientation feedback given by our guides, or elders, is provided without any condemnation and done with complete love and forgiveness.

Transition

After orientation, all souls arrive at a staging area by either an accompanying guide or independently directed by an unseen force pulling them to the staging area. They prepare them for their final placement to the soul group they belong to. It's similar to any major airport hub, where passengers arrive and fly to their destination based on their ticket.

Placement

Each soul is in a different stage of their evolution and placed into a particular group in the spirit world based on their soul awareness level. The soul who is entering their final destination in the "Soul cluster group" feels like they have come back to their home. The soul recognizes the group of friends it has been bonded with and rejoices.

The soul cluster group is like a learning and support group for souls to evolve with for a while. There are primary groups that have a close inner circle. They have common objectives which they continually work out with each other. The inner-circle group is around 3 to 25 souls. The secondary group is similar to the form of a community group.

After they arrive at their soul group, they are requested to appear before a council of elders who engage them in direct examination of a souls' activities before returning them to soul groups.

Advanced Soul

Some advanced souls may skip some of the processes above as homecoming, orientation since they are familiar with the spirit world. Even though they skip orientation with their guide, they may be interviewed at a later stage by their master guides.

Displaced Soul

There are a few displaced souls who are severely damaged and don't want to go back to the spiritual world after death.

There are two types of displaced souls.

   1. Souls who do not want to accept they are dead, fight to

return to the spiritual world for many reasons such as vengeance, personal anguish, etc.

2. Souls who have been subverted by or with criminal abnormalities during their human life.

They are usually called ghosts or demonic spirits. A few are known for invading the minds of people with harmful intent. The subverted spirits by criminal abnormalities will undergo seclusion upon entering the spiritual world and are isolated. They will not mix with the other souls for a while. Ultimately, they are placed together in groups of their own to intensify learning under close supervision.

Spirit Realm

The spirit realm's atmosphere is full of love and caring for each other. As a soul, you will always be in utter bliss and you will tend to do activities that you love to do. You will also enjoy the beauty and exploration of the multi-layered structure that this realm has to offer. Even here, you continuously learn and grow with wisdom and knowledge. At the same time, you pay-off some of the karmic debt at a slower rate when compared to paying off a sizable debt during the physical incarnation.

Here are some of the activities that you can do:

If you are an advanced soul, you can be a guide, mentor, and spiritual teacher to some of the souls who have taken physical incarnations.

If you are a young soul, you usually go to school to learn from an advanced or wiser soul. Similar to how kids learn by going to school in the physical world.

Some of them will be nursery souls watching over the newborn souls tendering them with love, caring, and encouragement. Similar to a nurse looking after the newborn baby in the hospital.

Few skilled souls have more control and fitness with the energy they may choose to work within the creation process. Initially, when they are learning the skill, they practice shaping energy as an individual or as a group. As they become more skilled, they begin with rocks, minerals, crystals, air, fire, water, etc. on a younger planet in the physical universe.

Sometimes, you can relax and enjoy the beauty of the spirit realm. Nature is so vibrant with colors and perfection that you have never seen those vibrant colors on earth.

You can go to the healing place the "Temple of the dome" to have your soul bathed with pure divine light and bask in that bliss.

You can go to the library and gain knowledge and wisdom. When you open any book, it provides you a holographic sequence of the event taking place right in front of you on the subject you are reading. It is similar to sci-fi movies where they show the holographic events happening when you open a book.

You can go to the Akashic realm and access records sometimes referred to as a tapestry place. It's a multidimensional library that has records of all the souls about their past, present, and future of every thought, word, action, belief, and experience that they ever had or will have. Keep in mind that time is an illusion. Everything is happening in the PRESENT moment.

There are other limitless activities.

Note: Refer to chapter nine, for more details about other dimensions.

Reincarnation

Once the soul has spent enough time in the spiritual world by taking rest, they go through some learning and training sessions with their spiritual guides and/or their soul groups. The soul can make a decision to reincarnate based on these factors.

1. Am I ready?

2. What physical lessons do I need to undertake?
3. Where and who shall I be in my next life?

The soul doesn't need to be born in the physical world to grow and evolve. It evolves in the spiritual world if it wants to, but it will be a slow growth when compared to birth and experiencing physical life. Moreover, the spiritual world would provide the soul a theoretical knowledge. It is through life in the physical world that a soul can grow and evolve at a faster rate.

Selecting a new life

In this process, the soul considers when and where to be born on earth or another planet. The soul thinks about things such as what body they need to have and who would be their parents etc. The selection of these choices is critical for the lessons the soul needs to learn. The soul enters a life selection arena where they have the opportunity to view their new life they are going to take and how they fit into that environment and the challenges it faces. The soul also reviews the risk and critical life-changing choices it can make at certain times in its life. These are all shown in a simulation.

It's an environment where they can see themselves in the future in different roles and various scenarios. By the time the soul leaves the arena, it will have chosen the location, body, function, and one storyline they'll take into a new life. Think of it as similar to selecting options in a particular video game before playing.

Nowadays, you'll have noticed there are many options in games to choose before playing a video game. You can choose the avatar, tools, and scenes. As a player, you would select an avatar, tools, and a scenario you want to play. Play in the preview mode, see if you like it, or can change the selection before beginning the actual game.

Preparation

Once the soul has decided the body and the location to be born, it enters the preparation stage. Preparation is necessary for the soul to know and identify its soulmates, and other partners who will be with that soul playing their roles.

It's a place of recognition where the soul meets all other souls with whom it will come in contact with at a particular stage in life while on earth. It could also be a turning point and life-changing situation for that soul.

Recognizing others is shown through signs and is given by prompters, who are similar to guides but specialized in this preparation area. The sign can be anything such as a particular laugh of that person, a ring, or chain, etc. The signs are infused in the souls' memory so that at a stage later on when they come across that particular partner, they know it is them. And they have come to teach us, or it's time to work on the next phase in life.

Most of the soul partners in your current life can be your spouse, children, parents, and friends. Once done with identifying the signs, the soul next meets with their guides and the council of elders before embarking on plans and assess the souls' motivation of taking a physical life.

Reborn

The soul is now ready to be born in the new life and say a final goodbye to their soul group in the spirit world. It's escorted by the guide initially and ultimately goes alone in a sort of tunnel at a faster rate and joins the baby in the mother's womb. It's the time where the soul and the body of the baby integrate and bond together.

.

Few additional points of information during rebirth.

The soul can enter any time inside the womb and the body of the baby. There is no specific time for it to happen. It can be in two months or right at the moment that the baby is delivered.

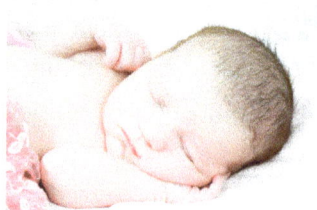

When in the womb, the soul quite often travels to other places. This can be from meeting other soul friends to visiting a place in it's previous life, etc. Even when the baby is born, the soul travels until the child is 5 to 6 years old.

The amnesia of not remembering everything happens after the baby is born and in the early few years of life.

Near-Death Experience (NDE)

You have often heard many cases about near-death experiences where they are dead only for a few minutes and then come back to life. It happens quite often when they have a sudden life-threatening accident in their life and temporarily the soul leaves the body for a few minutes. During that short period, the person has an indescribable experience even though they were declared medically dead or they have a limited mind and sense awareness.

Most of the NDE cases either have:

1. Positive experience
2. Negative experience

Positive experience

Some of the positive experience reported are:

- Watching the operation from the ceiling and seeing their body being operated on by doctors.
- Being in another world.
- Going in a tunnel and encountering beings.
- Going through a life review.
- Experiencing divine white light.
- Experiencing no pain and peace while outside the body.
- After experience will have psychic gifts such as precognition.
- They hear voices or sounds.

Negative experience

- They felt they were dead and worried about it.
- Horrifying experiences in other places where they met negative beings.
- They are in a void all alone.

All those different NDE experiences people have, whether positive or negative, are based on the state of mind and how they have been living their life. Most of them will have a transformational change in their life after the NDE experience.

CONCLUSION

What have you learned from reading this book? A lot of questions arise in one's mind with regards to what you're experiencing in your life and what the book is trying to teach. There is a gap between these two. This gap is nothing but the current and future state of YOU. Your future state depends upon what action you take at this moment when you are reading this particular sentence. Are you ready for a change within yourself? Or do you think you have finished reading another book and it's time to move on with the same old routine?

If your answer is the latter, then you need to understand that we are on this earth for a short period and during this short period, we make all sorts of unnecessary fuss, fights, arguments, greediness, power, comparison with each other, whether it's with your family, friends, stranger or even a country. Is that really necessary?

Let's suppose for the sake of argument you come to know that you might pass away within a year. What would your reaction be? Do you still behave the same way? Or do you transform into being a better person and try to forgive, make peace, and have more compassion/love for everyone and everything? If it's the latter, then why can't you make that change without the fear of death being added.

You know that we all belong to one Source Consciousness and are individuated to experience different realities. After experiencing everything, we merge back to Source. If this is our true nature, then why are we identifying ourselves as separate from each other in this physical world? The pain or happiness that others experience is nothing but an aspect of you experiencing it in another body. If everyone completely understands this, then we will immediately see the world in a far better place.

So if you are ready to transform, then start making changes within yourself. The book provides you with the basic wisdom, knowledge, and a process in order for you to kick start with a new understanding/approach that you can take to overcome the old behavioral pattern that you have been taking all these years and come out as a new YOU.

In General, there are few basic understandings you should be aware of.

1. There is only one Source. The rest is the individuation of that same Source energy.
2. We are all one and connected to each other through the fabric of Consciousness or Source energy.
3. We are eternally pure consciousness (soul) and are neither this body, senses, or mind.
4. We create our own reality based on the dominant vibration that we are holding at any given time.
5. We need to govern our own thoughts and feelings all the time. Our ego-mind should always be in alignment and balanced with our True Self.
6. Remember, change is the only constant; the rest is always changing.
7. We need to see everything from a neutral perspective irrespective of whether that event you are experiencing is positive or negative.

8. The ultimate goal is to radiate that Source energy within you to the fullest extent and see everything/ everyone as an aspect of you in another form.
9. The ultimate path is to go within and find out your true Self.
10. Always be an observer without any judgment.
11. Unconditional love, peace, compassion, and bliss are your true nature.

Practically, what action can I take? There are so many ways that you can make changes in yourself and for a better community. For example:

- Use those basic principles as a guideline while interacting with others.
- Start meditating every day. Go within to experience & expand the real You.
- Do what you really love to do.
- You can take care of the planet and all its inhabitants by making certain changes such as: recycling the used products, avoid destroying trees, don't harm animals, use clean technology, avoid contaminating water, soil, and plants, etc.
- Form a group (Satsang), and have a group meditation, spiritual discussion, etc..
- Do self-evaluation on a regular basis and check the status of your spiritual progress you are making.
- Observe your own thoughts and emotions (feelings). Check your existing reality and make changes if necessary. This is done by changing your thoughts and emotions. Note that there is always a time delay for physical changes to show up in your reality since we live in a physical world and things take time to manifest in your reality.

If you have any other great ideas, stories, and/or comments that you want to share, contact me through my LivingLibrarian.com website. The site also contains various tools and information that you can use for your spiritual growth.

The ultimate goal of this book is to uplift the souls to their full potential and help them with a clear understanding of who they really are. If I'm able to uplift at least one soul through this book, then the book has done its job.

POEM - WHAT DOES IT MEAN TO BE INVINCIBLE?

Every time I get up after facing a roadblock,
I feel I am invincible.
Every time I think about opportunities
rather than problems, I feel I am invincible.

Every time I look for another approach
a different door to knock, I feel I am invincible.
Every time I get up to help someone else despite of what I am
feeling,
I feel I am invincible.
Every time I believe my faith is stronger than whatever I am
facing,
I feel I am invincible.
Every time I see the sun shining after a long dark night,
I feel I am invincible.
Every time the divine sends me someone my way to help and
lighten my load, I feel I am invincible.
Every time I spring back to my normal joyous self after missing a
few beats of life, I feel I am invincible.
Every time I feel I have the power to create something that will
stay beyond me, I feel I am invincible.
Every time I don't accept someone's judgement of me,
I feel I am invincible.
Every time I don't let other people's opinions, expectations and
unfair demands take over my sense of self, I feel I am invincible.
Every time I believe there is a solution that is waiting to be
discovered,
I feel I am invincible.
Every time I believe the law is working in favour of us as a
collective,
I feel I am invincible.
Every time I believe whatever is best for me will manifest,
I feel I am invincible.

~ Shivani Yadav ~

~

POEM - WHAT IS LIFE?

Life is love.
You can fly so high,
but fall so hard.
It will leave you breathless,
Wondering what went wrong.
Wondering if it was meant to be.

But it was worth the pain.
You never realize how rare it is,
to feel that experience.
Like the breeze against you,
as you stand on the edge of a cliff.
Or the chills you have,
as you look down scared,
you will fall down.
But you won't fall again.
You will stay strong.
You will find a way.

~ Diya Dev ~

BIBLIOGRAPHY

The following books, articles, conferences, website, and videos have been consulted to write this book

LivingLibrarian.com

Brad, Johnson The Reality Whisperer, 2017 edition

Dr Sant Kumar Bhatnagar, The Teachings of Buddha, 2008 Edition

Lilli Bendriss and Camillo Loken, The Shift in Consciousness

Dr Michael Newton, Journey of Souls, Fifth Revised Edition 2010

Sheldan Nidle, You Are Becoming a Galactic Human

Daniel Scranton Wisdom Teaching

https://youtu.be/zQUDAWSlKs4

https://youtu.be/swpSy6smh9o

https://youtu.be/GiGXfEcugHc

https://livinglibrarian.com/new/the-transformation-within-by-lord-melchizedek-by-natalie-glasson/

https://www.youtube.com/watch?v=Vqs6X9rVfFY&list=PLl7okrylH_G6TksHCweTMsV7pDM-RTZTDj&index=84&t=0s

https://www.youtube.com/watch?v=Ab0prJD81Gk&list=PLl7okrylH_G6TksHCweTMsV7pDM-RTZTDj&index=83&t=0s

Somayaji, Awareness [2007], pg 22 Manasa Foundation

J.M Mehta, Divine Message of God to Mankind vedas [2011 Edition]

Defining God by Sarvapriyananda in one of his sathsang message https://youtu.be/CoF0pOcKOCc

Conscious Awareness, Dimensions: https://www.consciousawareness.info/dimensions

Satsang by Eshwar ji https://youtu.be/ZYBcqpcpcG4:

Guy Steven Needle, The history of God

Randolph Winter, The Pleiadian Mission

Rob Gauthier, Densities and Dimensions master class

Exploring astral world by Brad Johnson : https://youtu.be/IlDKfM2osE8

Ways of Mystics : https://wayofmystics.webs.com/thepath.htm

Causal Plane : http://www.outofbodytravelguide.com/the-causal-plane.html

http://www.salrachele.com/webarticles/thetrapofthefourthdimension.htm

https://www.mountainrunnerdoc.com/sant_mat_part_one.html

https://medium.com/sant-mat-meditation-and-spirituality/the-ascension-of-the-soul-into-interior-regions-of-light-and-sound-part-2-introduction-to-the-8e0acab4e224

Spiritual Gems by Huzur Maharaj Sawan Singh. sound current

pg 54.

Ask and it is Given - by Esther and Jerry Hicks (The Teachings of Abraham) 2006

https://youtu.be/0gz1TppHX9g

https://youtu.be/-KGcmkggtHI

https://happyscience-na.org/about/teachings/spiritual-truth/the-truth-of-the-spirit-world/

https://ramakrishna.org/fouryogas.html

https://www.speakingtree.in/blog/m20-moksha

https://wayofmystics.webs.com/thepath.htm

https://www.hinduwebsite.com/hinduism/h_soul.asp

https://en.wikipedia.org/wiki/Vishishtadvaita

https://tricycle.org/magazine/noble-eightfold-path/

https://www.zenlightenment.net/the-eightfold-path/

https://exemplore.com/new-age-metaphysics/Life-in-the-Spiritual-Worlds

https://livinglibrarian.com/new/astral-body-is-a-capacity-of-sense-perception-by-iswar-puri-living-librarian/

https://livinglibrarian.com/new/consciousness-is-the-creator-of-everything-puri-living-librarian/

https://livinglibrarian.com/new/discover-your-true-self-you-are-not-a-body-but-a-soul-pulkit-mathur/

http://www.meherbabadnyana.net/life_eternal/Book_One/Astral_World.htm

https://livinglibrarian.com/new/soul-journeying-part-1-kryon-channeled-by-lee-carroll/

https://upliftconnect.com/what-is-enlightenment-really/

https://livinglibrarian.com/new/a-process-for-receiving-higher-dimensional-energies-%e2%88%9e-daniel-scranton/

https://youtu.be/eFhvfI55zEo?t=3454

https://youtu.be/xyPeMnl26Ss

http://www.thelawofattraction.com/12-spiritual-laws-universe/

Randall Monk - Timely guidance https://www.timelyguidance.com/category/universal-laws

https://www.youtube.com/watch?v=IzEoshQsuq8&t=222s

https://www.getcenteredcounseling.org/single-post/2017/06/06/Hang-on-It-only-gets-better-4th-Density-is-a-lot-more-fun

https://lovehaswon.org/precession-of-the-equinoxa-birthing-of-higher-consciousness/

https://archive.org/details/Holy-Science/page/n15/mode/2up/search/yugas

https://aarondoughty.com/why-you-must-shift-from-3rd-density-to-4th-density-now/

https://en.wikipedia.org/wiki/The_Holy_Science

https://www.getcenteredcounseling.org/single-post/2017/06/06/Hang-on-It-only-gets-better-4th-Density-is-a-lot-more-fun

https://livinglibrarian.com/new/chakra-detoxification-%e2%88%9e-daniel-scranton/

https://livinglibrarian.com/new/releasing-the-habit-of-time-sue-lie/

https://livinglibrarian.com/new/the-process-of-ascension/

http://www.vanamaliashram.org/Time_Space_Death.html

https://www.mike-picone.com/consciousness-shift-3-states-of-consciousness/

https://www.thesoulmatrix.com/2017/07/31/what-on-earth/

https://youtu.be/Eph64zCeKb0?t=2280

https://www.kryon.com/k_chanelgrandR03.html

https://livinglibrarian.com/new/understanding-timeline-split-jenny-schiltz/

https://2empowerthyself.com/the-trinity-of-mind-the-conscious-subconscious-and-unconscious-mind/

https://www.ananda.org/ask/levels-of-consciousness-and-what-they-represent/

https://livinglibrarian.com/new/what-the-coming-energies-will-bring-%e2%88%9e-daniel-scranton/

https://livinglibrarian.com/new/transcending-the-mind-louise-kay/

https://livinglibrarian.com/new/states-of-consciousness-sue-lie/

https://livinglibrarian.com/new/time-malleable-create-time/

https://www.noraherold.com/nora-s-blog/timeline-splits-the-pleiadians

https://www.noraherold.com/nora-s-blog/timeline-jump-imminent-the-pleiadians-calliandra

https://youtu.be/n6iLwYenwJUhttps://youtu.be/KuNZGuT40Ic

https://livinglibrarian.com/new/choosing-creating-timelines-%e2%88%9echanneled-daniel-scranton/

https://youtu.be/m6iBLa8aZNA

https://www.historydisclosure.com/collective-consciousness/

https://tmhome.com/benefits/study-maharishi-effect-group-meditation-crime-rate/

https://www.youtube.com/watch?v=DZZuQxRvjXU

https://www.youtube.com/watch?v=yLFXEtMiVwk&t=471s

http://thegreaterpicture.com/collective-consciousness.html

https://livinglibrarian.com/new/3-steps-change-world-love/

https://youtu.be/eszy3R19G-M?t=1470

https://www.chakras.info/7-chakras/

https://blog.mindvalley.com/7-chakras/?utm_source=blog

https://livinglibrarian.com/new/clairvoyant-clairsentient-clairaudient-one/

https://livinglibrarian.com/new/your-sixth-sense-%e2%88%9e-daniel-scranton/

https://www.michaelteachings.com/what_is_channeling.html

https://www.amandalinettemeder.com/blog/what-is-clairvoyance-clairaudience-claircognizance-and-clairsentience

Linda Howe, How to read the Akashic Record

Taryn Crimi, https://www.angelic-guides.com/

https://livinglibrarian.com/new/different-perspectives-serve-%e2%88%9ethe-9th-dimensional-arcturian-council-daniel-scranton/

https://livinglibrarian.com/new/massive-changes-on-earth-%e2%88%9e-daniel-scranton/

https://youtu.be/d9gwm4wOBkM

https://livinglibrarian.com/new/the-impact-of-co-vid-19-by-saint-germain-natalie-glasson/

https://cafeausoul.com/dreams/inspired-by-dreams/dream-expert-kari-hohne/types-dreams

https://livinglibrarian.com/new/5-steps-to-getting-what-you-want-%e2%88%9e-daniel-scranton/

https://blog.mindvalley.com/vibrational-energy/

https://ourreturnhome.com/how-we-create-our-reality

https://livinglibrarian.com/new/how-to-create-your-reality-by-master-el-morya-by-natalie-glasson/

https://livinglibrarian.com/new/the-evolution-of-manifestation-the-pleiadians-through-nora-herold-living-librarian-2/

https://youtu.be/6aWFYtFc5T4

https://youtu.be/LZnLZHfw2ko?t=2483

https://livinglibrarian.com/new/death-human-body-karma-mind-soul-attachments-puri-living-librarian-2/

https://livinglibrarian.com/new/karma-seeks-serve-not-punish/

Spiritual Gems by Huzur Maharaj Sawan Singh..

https://youtu.be/0gz1TppHX9g?t=963

https://youtu.be/jJYPsQasP-Y?t=2581 Kryon (also check contract in the same video next)

https://livinglibrarian.com/new/beliefs-the-pleiadians-enorah%e2%80%8a-through-nora-herold/

https://livinglibrarian.com/new/yourbeliefandyou/

https://livinglibrarian.com/new/beliefs-parents-transferred-children/

https://livinglibrarian.com/new/how-to-change-a-belief-system-%e2%88%9e-daniel-scranton/

https://livinglibrarian.com/new/the-basic-principles-of-how-one-can-remove-a-belief-by-dr-taryn-crimi/

https://livinglibrarian.com/new/emotions-by-taryn-crimi/

https://youtu.be/A_uDAkb_6RI

https://youtu.be/HDJr3MCfMFI

https://livinglibrarian.com/new/leaving-the-old-paradigm-behind-%e2%88%9e-daniel-scranton/

https://www.youtube.com/watch?v=p72enmYGO84&list=PLl7okrylH_G6TksHCweTMsV7pDM-RTZTDj&index=62&t=0s

https://www.youtube.com/watch?v=fwtkmSL7ECw

https://livinglibrarian.com/new/transformation-of-fear-and-the-function-of-anger-the-pleiadians%e2%80%8a-through-nora-herold/

https://youtu.be/zk2Hs3m848Y

https://livinglibrarian.com/new/the-practice-of-conscious-change-randall-monk/

https://livinglibrarian.com/new/take-the-spiritual-growth-from-your-challenges-%e2%88%9e-daniel-scranton/

https://livinglibrarian.com/new/challenges-that-span-lifetimes%e2%88%9e-daniel-scranton/

https://livinglibrarian.com/new/challenge-louise-kay-living-librarian

https://livinglibrarian.com/new/desires-are-not-unspiritual-bad-or-wrong-louise-kay/

https://en.wikipedia.org/wiki/Alexander_the_Great

https://livinglibrarian.com/new/consciousness-creates-different-bodies-by-ishwar-puri/

https://livinglibrarian.com/new/the-secret-human-history-%e2%88%9e-daniel-scranton/

https://livinglibrarian.com/new/acting-from-truth-louise-kay/

https://livinglibrarian.com/new/how-information-affects-you-%e2%88%9ethe-9d-arcturian-council-daniel-scranton-living-librarian/

https://livinglibrarian.com/new/shadow-work-the-pursuit-of-joy-%e2%88%9e-daniel-scranton/

https://livinglibrarian.com/new/how-to-improve-any-relationship-by-dr-taryn-crimi/

https://livinglibrarian.com/new/romantic-relationships-are-changing-%e2%88%9e-daniel-scranton/

https://youtu.be/YpFbpjhqM_k

https://livinglibrarian.com/new/how-to-release-trauma-%e2%88%9e-daniel-scranton/

https://livinglibrarian.com/new/integratingchildhoodtrauma/

https://youtu.be/KuNZGuT40Ic

https://youtu.be/m2dJG926m4Y

https://youtu.be/uraDbhfFvsk

https://livinglibrarian.com/new/forgiving-being-the-love-%e2%88%9e-daniel-scranton/

https://livinglibrarian.com/new/3-steps-change-world-love/

https://livinglibrarian.com/new/love-knows-no-boundaries-love-love

https://livinglibrarian.com/new/the-love-that-binds-daniel-scranton/

https://livinglibrarian.com/new/love-yourselves-unconditionally-%e2%88%9e-daniel-scranton/

https://livinglibrarian.com/new/awakening-in-the-information-age-%e2%88%9e-daniel-scranton/

https://livinglibrarian.com/new/artificial-intelligence-nanotechnology-and-enlightenment-maria-chambers/

https://livinglibrarian.com/new/be-like-the-star-children-%e2%88%9e-daniel-scranton/

https://livinglibrarian.com/new/indigo-children-guides-to-the-future-by-cherokee-living-librarian/

https://livinglibrarian.com/new/beliefs-parents-transferred-children/

https://livinglibrarian.com/new/new-breed-humans-expect-children-incarnating-now/

https://www.kryon.com/CHAN2016/k_channel16_columbus.html

https://youtu.be/Tx3VRRvt_uw (Brad)

https://livinglibrarian.com/new/conditional-unconditional-love-%e2%88%9e-daniel-scranton/

https://medium.com/personal-growth/the-5-key-ingredients-of-an-authentic-person-259914abf6d5

https://livinglibrarian.com/new/power-created-body-power-can-heal-body-channeled-taryn-crimi/

https://youtu.be/8yqDK7HJKHQ

https://youtu.be/5KjIxIXOLD8

https://youtu.be/PrnP8ILWsq0

"Heal Your Body" by Louise Hay

"Soul Speak" by Julia Cannon

https://youtu.be/yllX6xY1484 (aging)

https://livinglibrarian.com/new/aging-process-not-necessary/ (aging)

https://www.healthline.com/health/foods-that-help-you-heal#mushrooms

A complete handbook of Nature's care -

https://youtu.be/Ja6yYPZT36A

https://www.soulventure.com/what-is-grounding/

https://youtu.be/bSk2faYUGRQ

https://livinglibrarian.com/new/energy-of-stones-and-crystals-meline-lafont/

Books - Crystals for healings - Karen Frazier

http://www.healing-journeys-energy.com/Crystals-for-Physical-Issues.html

https://anandaindia.org/blog/a-test-of-titiksha-yoganandas-nine-day-diet/?utm_source=ONTRAPORT-email-broadcast&utm_medium=ONTRAPORT-email-broadcast&utm_term=COM%3AContacts&utm_content=Om%E2%80%93Spirit%E2%80%93Bliss&utm_campaign=01282020

https://livinglibrarian.com/new/new-energy-delivery-systems-on-earth-%e2%88%9e-daniel-scranton/

https://mail.google.com/mail/u/0/?tab=rm&ogbl#label/Spirituality%2FKnowledge/FMfcgxwHMGCPMqdtkzgWkLtkrgPjhjvg

http://www.vanamaliashram.org/Time_Space_Death.html

https://ijcp.in/Admin/CMS/PDF/21.%20SpiritualUpdate_I-JCP_April2019.pdf

https://isha.sadhguru.org/us/en/wisdom/article/stages-of-death-shraddh

https://youtu.be/KuNZGuT40Ic

https://youtu.be/RG6GV0GbjKk

https://thehappyastra.home.blog/2018/12/13/what-happens-to-the-body-after-death/

https://www.near-death.com/reincarnation/research/michael-newton.html

https://livinglibrarian.com/new/align-with-source-create-universes-%e2%88%9e-daniel-scranton/

https://livinglibrarian.com/new/consciously-guiding-your-thoughts-by-dianne-robbins/

https://livinglibrarian.com/new/how-to-raise-your-vibration-by-dr-taryn-crimi/

https://livinglibrarian.com/new/love-knows-no-boundaries-love-love

https://chopra.com/articles/the-3-levels-of-samadhi

https://isha.sadhguru.org/ca/en/wisdom/article/samadhi-to-go-beyond-existence?gclid=Cj0KCQjwhtT1BRCiARIsAGl-Y51JJXlgccYI-g5zbq5BCfL6pUdXte5seVKOD7YQNkagnUce-q9X20JD4aAs3aEALw_wcB

https://youtu.be/JN1vwZHFyE8

https://en.wikipedia.org/wiki/Mahasam%C4%81dhi

https://en.wikipedia.org/wiki/Jivanmukta

https://chopra.com/articles/the-3-levels-of-samadhi

https://www.ananda.org/yogapedia/samadhi/

https://vedicfeed.com/stages-of-samadhi/

https://savy-international.com/meditation/samadhi/

JohnKMill profile for video : https://www.fiverr.com/share/8xQYEr

AUTHOR WEBSITE

www.livinglibrarian.com

Toola Available.

Wisdom and Knowledge articles
Spiritual masters videos and their websites
Meditation music / guided
Spiritual songs / mantras
Recommended books
Downloadable few book images

Lightning Source UK Ltd.
Milton Keynes UK
UKHW051130240820
368731UK00001B/5